FORCE
OF NATURE

JOE SAKIC, A STAR-STUDDED TEAM, AND HOW THE
COLORADO AVALANCHE BUILT A STANLEY CUP WINNER

PETER BAUGH

TRIUMPH
BOOKS

Library of Congress Cataloging-in-Publication Data available upon request.

This book is available in quantity at special discounts for your group or organization. For further information, contact:

Triumph Books LLC
814 North Franklin Street
Chicago, Illinois 60610
(312) 337-0747
www.triumphbooks.com

Printed in U.S.A.
ISBN: 978-1-63727-298-5
Design and editorial production by Alex Lubertozzi
Photos courtesy of AP Images unless otherwise indicated

For Mom, Dad, Maggie, Riley, and Dante

CONTENTS

FOREWORD

THERE'S NO PLACE to watch an NHL game quite like the space between the benches, and there's no space between the benches in the NHL as tight as the setup at Ball Arena in Denver. It's nearly impossible to climb into without bruising a body part, but once you're there, you're thrust into the middle of the action—providing a full appreciation for the speed, skill, and physicality of the modern NHL. It's also an ideal spot to eavesdrop on the communication— the coaching, elation, hockey chirps, and frustration, of course—that unfolds throughout the course of a game.

I'll never forget October 26, 2021, as I was assigned to report between the benches for an early-season ESPN broadcast of the Avalanche and Golden Knights in Ball Arena. Things were escalating between the rivals, who were playoff opponents the previous spring, when a player on Vegas shouted right over me to the Avs bench: "Hey! Get out of the second round, why don't ya?"

For Colorado, there was likely no insult as piercing as this. At that point, the Avalanche were a damn good regular season team. They had all the right ingredients to win a Stanley Cup, and maybe the best collection of star players in the league. But they just couldn't get over the playoff hump, losing in the second round for three consecutive years—most recently to the four-year-old Golden Knights in 2021, culminating with Nathan MacKinnon's epic postgame presser in which he vented, "I'm going into my ninth year...and haven't won shit."

When the Avs finished with an NHL-low 48 points in 2016–17, GM Joe Sakic didn't panic. He viewed it as a necessary low for the larger plan. Instead of blowing up the team, as many managers would have been tempted to do, he showed patience with rookie coach

Jared Bednar. Sakic relied on his staff to draft well—and did they ever, highlighted by selecting Cale Makar at No. 4 the following summer. The GM made the necessary tweaks and gained a reputation for fleecing his peers in trades, like acquiring Devon Toews in 2020 for a pair of second-round picks.

Sakic had reason to believe. The recent trend in the NHL? Cup winners had been great regular season teams for a while, but all battled through playoff heartbreak before getting over the hump. That was Washington in 2018. That was St. Louis in 2019. That was Tampa Bay before the Lightning won back-to-back titles in 2020 and 2021.

And in 2022, that was finally Colorado too. The Avs lost that game to Vegas in October, and who knows how many times they heard a version of that "second round" chirp throughout the season. But the outside noise couldn't have been louder than the inside pressure they felt to win—and that's what fueled them to etch their name in hockey history.

The story of how they finally did it is a compelling one, and I can't think of anyone better suited to tell it than Peter Baugh, who was around the team more than any journalist was in the season that they won. When I met Peter, I was instantly struck by his curiosity. There's a humility about him that's so pure, and quite honestly rare in this business. He never assumes he knows the story but approaches every topic with earnest fascination. He wants to understand the inner workings of a hockey team, and because of his pleasant demeanor, people are compelled to give him honest answers.

As a national reporter, you swoop in from city to city and try to capture the scene as best you can in that given moment. But Peter has been in the trenches with the Avs, providing proper boots-on-the-ground reporting that the fans deserve. I followed Peter's reporting the entire season, and when I found out he was writing this book, I couldn't wait to delve into more of it. Because the Avs did get out of the second round—but there's a lot more to the story than that.

—Emily Kaplan
National NHL reporter, ESPN

INTRODUCTION

JOE SAKIC SURVEYS his city, the one he's helped build into a hockey hub nestled between mountains and plains. He stands on a makeshift platform in front of the City and County Building, round sunglasses over his eyes and a championship hat on his head. Throngs of fans stretch before him, crowding into Denver's Civic Center Park, excited to bask in a shared, joyful experience.

More than two decades earlier, wearing the captain's C on a white Avalanche sweater, Sakic walked onto the same stage in front of the same building, the Stanley Cup lifted above his head. Now he's back, not as a Hall of Fame player but as one of the NHL's most highly regarded general managers. He's the enduring face of the organization—the connective tissue between its days in Quebec City and Denver. A link between Hall of Famer Michel Goulet and future Hall of Famer Cale Makar. The executive returning his team to the heights he helped it reach as a player.

Scanning the family and staff seats directly in front of the stage, Sakic catches sight of Chris MacFarland, his assistant general manager and fellow architect of the championship team. He beckons his friend forward, throwing him an all-access credential so he can join the team brass and players on stage. When Sakic tries stepping to the microphone, his three longest-tenured players block his path. Drunk on victory and beer, Erik Johnson, captain Gabriel Landeskog, and Nathan MacKinnon throw their arms around their boss for a group hug. What good is a peak if not shared with those who helped you reach it?

"Twenty-one long damn years," Sakic says when he finally reaches the lectern, his players watching from behind. "It's been a long time, but we're back. We're back."

In this moment, with midday sun fighting to hold off oncoming rain clouds, Sakic and the Avalanche are more than back. They're the team that knocked off a dynastic Tampa Bay Lightning squad. They're the team whose .800 winning percentage in the postseason was the best since Wayne Gretzky's Oilers in the 1980s. And with 72 combined regular season and playoff victories, they're the winningest team since the introduction of the salary cap in 2005–06 and tied for the winningest ever.

Eight days later, Sakic will be in Montreal for the NHL Draft, working to build another team capable of reaching this point. He will trade away draft picks for a new goalie rather than bring back Darcy Kuemper, the man between the pipes when Colorado finished off Tampa Bay. It will be a cool, calculated move—one representing the fleeting nature of championship teams, one made with a steady head, not an impulsive heart. And later that night, midway through the first round of the draft, Sakic will stand on stage to accept the Jim Gregory General Manager of the Year Award, receiving applause from Canadiens fans who used to view him as a rival.

All of that happens on the day he turns 53. But these days he doesn't give much thought to his own birthday. It's as if it's just another day, something that means less than it did when he was younger.

Winning, though, never loses its charm to Sakic. Player or executive, Nordique or Avalanche, age 26 or 53. It doesn't matter. The quest for victory still drives Sakic, no matter how mild-mannered he comes off. And that drive permeates the team he's built. The team standing on stage in front of thousands of Denver fans. The team with the silver Stanley Cup on a table by their sides.

PROGRESS AND STAGNATION

A SHARP CHEER erupted from the box at the Golden Knights' T-Mobile Arena, where Sakic and MacFarland watched their team try to stave off elimination. André Burakovsky had wristed a shot past Marc-André Fleury to tie the game late in the second period. For a moment, there was hope.

The optimism was short-lived. Golden Knights defenseman Alex Pietrangelo scored less than three minutes later, and Vegas ran away with the game in the third period, eliminating the Avalanche from the 2021 playoffs. For the third consecutive year, Colorado had lost in the second round, this time in the most egregious fashion yet. Coach Jared Bednar's team had built a 2–0 series lead, only to collapse and lose four in a row. The Avalanche didn't even make it to Game 7, as they had the two previous years.

But despite the third straight disappointment, Colorado was firmly in its championship window. This wasn't the plucky young team of 2019 or the banged-up club that nearly made the conference finals in 2020. This group was a force—or at least it was supposed to be. Sakic had acquired standouts Devon Toews and Brandon Saad going into the season, and at the trade deadline he said the team was as deep as the Avalanche would have. He didn't assemble that roster envisioning a second-round exit.

Colorado had mowed through its competition most of the year, winning the Presidents' Trophy for the best record in the regular season and then dominating St. Louis in the first round. Now, after the collapse, they were done. Vegas's core had shined brighter than the Nathan MacKinnon–led group of Avalanche stars. The Golden

Knights' depth wore down Bednar's club, and Fleury outplayed Colorado's Philipp Grubauer.

There were lessons to be learned, but they would have to wait for the hurt to dull. As Cale Makar rested his head on the toe of his stick, watching Vegas celebrate, pain reverberated through him and his teammates. MacKinnon described his feelings succinctly with words he'd be asked about over and over again the next season.

"I'm going into my ninth year next year," the dejected center said, "and I haven't won shit."

Other Avalanche players felt the same way. The locker room was quiet as players changed, some pulling off a Colorado jersey for the final time. They were shocked and devastated. How had this team, with the talent to win a championship, come so dramatically short? On the plane ride home that night, all captain Gabriel Landeskog could think was that they blew the series.

The loss was a fork in the road for the Avalanche. When the pain faded, would it prove fruitful? Heartbreak in sports, after all, can work as motivation if channeled properly. Or was Colorado simply a talented bunch missing some element that championship teams possess? Did something with the coaching staff or cast of players need to change?

That was for Sakic to decide.

• • •

The legend of Sakic is bigger than Denver, the place where he won two Stanley Cups as a captain, as well as the 2000–01 Hart Trophy for league MVP. His excellence resonated, too, in Quebec City, where his NHL career started for the Quebec Nordiques before they moved to Colorado. He's still beloved there, as he is on the other side of the country as well. In his hometown of Burnaby, British Columbia, a street is named Joe Sakic Way.

Joe Sakic's way took unexpected turns after his playing days.

Some players seem destined for front-office roles. Longtime hockey journalist Pierre LeBrun, who writes for The Athletic and is a TV reporter for Canadian TV station TSN, always believed Hall of

Famer Steve Yzerman, for example, would become a general manager. Sure enough, he now holds that position with the Red Wings. But LeBrun never sensed that Sakic envisioned a day-to-day, front-office life. That probably wouldn't have been his path, at least not until he got a nudge.

In 2011, less than three years removed from his retirement, Sakic took a position as executive adviser and alternate governor for the Avalanche. This was the type of job LeBrun thought matched Sakic's interests. He could stay involved without the burden of an overwhelming amount of day-to-day responsibility.

But before long the team's ownership group, led by Stan and Josh Kroenke, wanted the former captain to take on a bigger role. The Avalanche franchise looked lost at the time, having failed to make the playoffs three years in a row. The highly regarded, coolheaded Sakic could serve as a stabilizer. Josh Kroenke, Stan's son, approached him and asked if he'd become executive vice president.

Sakic wasn't sure about the offer. He deliberated with his wife, Deb, wondering if he'd regret not giving the position a shot. He could learn about hockey from a new perspective, and the Avalanche meant the world to him. Sakic wanted to stay with the only professional franchise he'd known, to be part of the team's rebuild. "Why not go for it?" he thought to himself. Deb felt the same way. He accepted.

So Sakic began making decisions on a daily basis, and the organization quickly felt his presence. Within a month of taking the position, he and Josh Kroenke flew to Florida to meet with Hall of Fame goalie Patrick Roy, who helped the Avalanche to Stanley Cups in 1996 and 2001, in hopes of luring him back to Denver as head coach. The trio played golf at a Jack Nicklaus–founded club in Jupiter, Florida, and shortly after, Roy agreed to join the team.

In the summer of 2013, Colorado picked MacKinnon first overall, and the young center was an immediate force, winning the Calder Trophy as the league's top rookie. MacKinnon, Landeskog, Matt Duchene, and Ryan O'Reilly gave the Avalanche one of the brightest young forward groups in the league. They captured the 2013–14 Central Division title with 52 wins.

The fiery Roy seemed to be working out behind the bench. The Avalanche added general manager to Sakic's title. The duo of Hall of Famers, heroes of a previous championship generation, appeared to be on their way to ushering in a new one in Denver.

After a step back during the 2014–15 season, which saw the Avalanche miss the playoffs, Sakic made another important addition, not to the roster, but to the front office. He wanted to hire an assistant and consulted people he knew around the league. Two of his former Colorado teammates, Dan Hinote and Brad Larsen, both of whom were working in the Blue Jackets organization, spoke highly of Columbus assistant general manager Chris MacFarland. Sakic trusted their judgment, and he clicked with MacFarland when they talked. He brought him on to be his right-hand man as assistant general manager.

Though he'd have the same title with the Avalanche that he did in Columbus, MacFarland didn't see the transition as a lateral move. He believed Colorado would give him more opportunity to work on the player personnel side at the NHL level than he had with the Blue Jackets. He insisted on bolstering the Avalanche's analytics staff, and his new general manager was receptive. Sakic views analytics as a useful tool—not the end-all, be-all, but something that, combined with scouting, can be helpful when making decisions.

So Colorado hired Arik Parnass, who had degrees from Georgetown and Stanford, as a full-time analyst in 2016. He had experience interning with and consulting for NHL clubs and had created a data-driven project, breaking down power play units league-wide. Over time, the Avalanche brought on more analytics staffers and gained a reputation as one of the smartest front offices in the league.

MacFarland has a far different background than Sakic. While his boss was establishing himself as an NHL great, MacFarland was getting a law degree from Pace University, then moving up the ranks in the Blue Jackets organization. But the two clicked quickly. MacFarland appreciated how Sakic listened to opinions from his whole staff, and he quickly earned the GM's trust with his knowledge of the salary cap and the other business sides of the game.

Before long, when players, agents, or executives talked about Sakic, they usually mentioned MacFarland in quick succession.

It wasn't just Joe. It was Joe and Chris.

As the Avalanche emerged as an elite team, MacFarland's name occasionally was linked to open general manager jobs. But Colorado didn't allow him to interview with San Jose or Anaheim during the 2021–22 season, making one thing clear: the organization had a succession plan in order. "[MacFarland] allowed [Sakic] to peek over the other side of the mountain and say, 'This could be the smooth exit I was looking for,'" LeBrun said.

But back in 2015, when MacFarland first joined the team, the buck still stopped with Sakic. And life was about to get much more difficult.

• • •

The 2016–17 season got off poorly before games even started. In an unexpected turn, one that left the Avalanche front office scrambling, Roy resigned in August, just weeks before training camp began. He released a statement saying he didn't feel his vision aligned with the organization's. He wanted more weight in the team's decision-making.

Neither Sakic nor Roy has gone into detail about the decision, but reading between the lines—and judging by what came next—it appeared Sakic wanted to take a patient approach and rebuild the roster, whereas Roy wanted to be more all-in on the present.

The team hired Bednar, who was coaching Columbus's AHL team but had never coached at the NHL level, shortly before training camp. The Avalanche got off to a 9–9–0 start. They weren't great, but they weren't terrible either.

Then everything went wrong. Erik Johnson, one of the team's top defensemen at the time, broke his fibula blocking a shot in early December, and All-Star goalie Semyon Varlamov—who, at his best, was capable of stealing games and keeping Colorado afloat—underwent season-ending hip surgery in January. Duchene, whose favorite player growing up was Sakic, requested a trade in December, wanting to move to a team with postseason hopes.

Joe Sakic looks on with Josh Kroenke (center) during a press conference to introduce Colorado's new coach, Jared Bednar (front), in August 2016.

On top of that, all of the team's best players were having down years. MacKinnon had the second-lowest point-per-game rate of his career. Landeskog had his lowest. Tyson Barrie's scoring numbers dipped. Only promising youngster Mikko Rantanen, the team's 2015 first-round pick, reached the 20-goal mark, scoring exactly 20. The Avalanche had four players with 20 or more goals the year before, a season in which they still missed the playoffs.

Beyond the injuries, Duchene's trade request, and the under-performing players, Colorado lacked the depth needed to plug holes. Of the team's 13 players to appear in at least 75 percent of its games that season, four never played another NHL contest.

By year's end, the Avalanche had 48 points in the standings—more than 20 fewer than any other team and the lowest full-season total since the introduction of the salary cap. MacFarland hadn't expected the Avalanche to be great—he thought they could compete for the last playoff spot for a bit, then fade at the end of the season—but he didn't expect them to have an abysmal season, let alone a historically bad one.

"That was rough," he said.

There were mornings Sakic woke up wondering why he was still the general manager. Sometimes he thought ownership might make the decision for him. He wouldn't have blamed them, considering how poorly the team had performed. Popular analyst and author Steve Glynn, known in the hockey community as Steve Dangle, had the same thought, posting a now-infamous tweet in June 2017: "Joe Sakic really ought to be fired."

But MacFarland knew the Kroenkes wouldn't move on from Sakic. "Joe is a Hall of Famer and an icon," he said. "He wasn't going anywhere." MacFarland, however, had worries about his own job security. It was a stressful time for everyone. LeBrun remembers other executives wondering why Sakic was putting himself through the struggle. He didn't need the money, and he was already one of the sport's legends from his playing days.

In the end, the ownership group accepted its front office's patient approach, which paid off long-term. With the worst record in the league, Colorado had the best odds to land the No. 1 pick in the 2017 Draft Lottery. But the Avalanche didn't win the lottery or even get the second or third pick. They ended up with the fourth selection—a blow after an already brutal season.

LeBrun ran into Sakic in the hours after the lottery, which took place in Toronto two months before the draft. He could see the dejection in the general manager's face. After a year of terrible play and terrible luck, the Avalanche still couldn't catch a break.

"I think he felt like the Avalanche were kicked in the teeth a bunch of times that year, and losing the lottery was like the punctuation of it," LeBrun said.

Sakic got a call that night from director of pro scouting Brad Smith. "It doesn't matter," Smith told the general manager. "We're going to get a great player." Sakic repeated a similar message when talking to LeBrun, and that summer in Chicago, the Avalanche selected a strong-skating, raw defenseman named Cale Makar.

Before long, Smith's words would seem more prophetic than anyone could have imagined.

• • •

The 2017–18 season marked a shift for Colorado. Things started going right. MacKinnon emerged as a superstar, finishing second in MVP voting, and the front office made a series of unsexy but effective moves to bolster the team's depth. Sakic signed Alexander Kerfoot, an NHL-ready forward, as a college free agent out of Harvard. Additionally, the team selected veteran defenseman Patrik Nemeth off waivers from the Stars. Those players, plus 2016–17 waiver additions Mark Barberio and Matt Nieto, helped give Colorado a more respectable lineup top to bottom.

Then came the Duchene trade, one of Sakic's big wins as general manager. He didn't buckle after the center's trade request the previous year, instead waiting until he got an offer he deemed fair. MacFarland's take was that the front office knew the Avalanche had a player who was still young, talented, and under contract. They were in no rush to sell low. Finally, in November 2017, a three-team deal got done. The Avalanche obtained a haul of pieces, including young defenseman Samuel Girard and the draft pick that became Bowen Byram.

As the season went on, Sakic could see the players starting to believe. It was a tight, fun group, one that gave fans faith in the future. There was reason to be excited in the present, too. Heading into the 82nd and final game of the season with the Blues in town, Colorado was still in playoff contention. If the Avalanche could pull out a regulation win, they would make the playoffs—a feat, given the lows of the previous year. With three minutes left in the game and the Avalanche up a pair of goals, Landeskog seized the puck and flung it on the empty net. MacKinnon, Nemeth, Barberio, and Rantanen mobbed their captain, bringing him to the ice. Making the playoffs wasn't the ultimate objective—and many of the team's players wouldn't be there when the Avalanche ultimately reached that pinnacle—but it sure felt good.

"I don't think I have ever been part of a group with such team chemistry," Landeskog said after the game. "This is a big accomplishment."

The team was young, plucky, and fun. There were roster holes, no doubt, but the group gave everyone, from fans to management to the players in the dressing room, reason for hope. And though Colorado lost to Nashville in the first round of the playoffs, it had taken an important step. The front office continued to add over the next off-season, trading for Nazem Kadri, signing Joonas Donskoi, and taking a free agency flier on Valeri Nichushkin, a former top-10 pick.

Sakic had something going.

• • •

When does gradual progress become stagnation? With the three consecutive second-round losses, had the Avalanche stalled out? What did the Vegas series say about this group?

Sakic is a patient man. He showed it when he stuck with Bednar after the brutal 2016–17 season, and he showed it when he waited to trade Duchene until a team met his asking price. But the off-season after the Golden Knights loss was perhaps the greatest test yet of his patience.

And for better or worse, Sakic trusted the core he'd built and the coach he had in place. The Tampa Bay Lightning served as a blueprint. After a disastrous first-round exit in 2019, the front office hadn't broken up its group of star players or fired coach Jon Cooper. That foundation remained as they brought in new complementary players, and they won the Stanley Cup in both 2020 and 2021. Sakic took the same approach.

Still, with the team up against the salary cap, the Colorado general manager had tough choices to make. Most importantly, Landeskog, the Avalanche's unquestioned leader, was a pending free agent.

C

DEADLINES SPUR ACTION, but Gabriel Landeskog was experiencing nothing but inertia. The Avalanche captain was at his off-season home in Toronto, reaching out to his agent what felt like every five minutes.

It was the evening of July 27, 2021, and Landeskog was set to hit free agency the next day. NHL teams can re-sign their own free agents for up to eight years, but if they don't get a deal worked out by the midnight before the market opens, the maximum term a contract can carry is seven years.

That deadline mattered to Landeskog, who wanted an eight-year contract. He'd built a life in Colorado, going from an 18-year-old, first-round pick to the unquestioned leader of a Stanley Cup contender. Denver was home. It was where he and his wife welcomed two children. He felt a connection to both the city and its hockey fans. He didn't want to leave.

But if his camp and the Avalanche didn't reach a deal by 11:59 PM Eastern Time, the chances he'd be staying would drop. Landeskog kept checking the time, counting down the hours.

Free agency hadn't gone the way Landeskog expected. He figured a deal would come together quickly, one that would make both sides happy. But that hadn't happened. The process dragged out. The Sakic-led front office wanted to keep Landeskog, but it also didn't want to do anything rash. Sakic had to assess the situation with an even-keeled mind. The captain was 28 and played a hard-nosed style. How would his body hold up into his thirties? Would an expensive, long-term contract age poorly? Under the salary cap, would a big deal preclude the team from bolstering its roster in other areas?

That led to an impasse. The gap between what the Avalanche were offering and what Landeskog's camp wanted was notable. Landeskog told The Athletic that he was disappointed the sides hadn't worked something out. For the first time in his career, he lacked the one thing he'd had through every other off-season: certainty.

"Were we nervous?" Sakic said. "Yeah, we were a little nervous he would go somewhere else."

Landeskog had hoped to work out an extension with Colorado the previous year. He never wanted negotiations to get to this point. He hadn't wanted rumors swirling about signing with the Blues or the Oilers or the Islanders. He wanted to be with the Avalanche.

And surely he would, right? Surely Colorado wouldn't lose its captain, not with the organization on the cusp of breaking through. Not with the ups and downs Landeskog had gone through to help get it there. This was a guy who, as a kid, had a picture of Peter Forsberg (his childhood hero) and the Cup-winning Avalanche on the wall of his room in Stockholm. Surely the sides would work something out. They had to. Right?

But as an anxious Landeskog waited in Toronto, his agent, Peter Wallen, still didn't have the answer he wanted. The captain kept checking his iPhone. The questions kept swirling. The minutes kept passing. Midnight drew nearer.

Finally, his phone rang.

• • •

Milan Hejduk knew he was at the tail end of his career. It was 2011–12, his first year as captain, and he was already in his mid-thirties, coming off a season in which he had failed to score 20-plus goals for the first time since he was a rookie. And though the forward was the last remaining link between the 2001 Stanley Cup team and the current roster, he didn't think it was right to keep the C on his jersey. He knew he was no longer the player who received MVP votes and led the league in goals, like he had in 2003. He believed one of the team's main contributors should have the captaincy.

Hejduk was a free agent after the season, and he told then general manager Greg Sherman he would be willing to play another year. He was only nine games shy of the 1,000-game milestone and was looking forward to helping the team's young players grow.

But it was time to give up the captaincy, he told Sherman.

Hejduk, whose No. 23 is now retired, hadn't thought about Landeskog as his successor. The young Swede, who had won the Calder Trophy in 2011–12 as rookie of the year, was mature beyond his years, but he was still only 19, not even allowed to legally grab a drink while at dinner with teammates.

But Sherman and then coach Joe Sacco mentioned Landeskog to Hejduk when they were talking through their decision. The more the veteran thought about it, the more it made sense. "What can you say negative about Gabe?" Hejduk said. He knew Landeskog had a good head on his shoulders. He knew he'd be a face of the team for years to come.

Landeskog also had experience as a young captain, just not at the NHL level. While playing major junior hockey in the Ontario league, the Kitchener Rangers chose him to lead their team as a 17-year-old. He was with players more than two years older than him, and no European had ever been captain in Kitchener's history.

So Hejduk called Landeskog, who that off-season was in the Toronto area, where his now wife is from. He didn't mention the captaincy, but he told his young teammate to let him know when he was back in Denver. He wanted to talk.

With a potential lockout on the horizon, Landeskog assumed Hejduk wanted to touch base with players about the upcoming season. But when he returned to Denver and went to the practice rink for a meeting with Hejduk, none of his other teammates were there. It was just Landeskog, Hejduk, and Sacco.

Hejduk spoke.

"I feel like it's time for me to pass it on to someone else," he said. "And I think that person is you."

Landeskog didn't see this coming. He didn't know how the rest of the players, some more than a decade older, would take the decision. He was excited, of course, but nervous, too. He called his father, Tony, who told him to keep being himself. That's what got him to this point, after all.

Not long after the meeting, Landeskog went to the Avalanche's arena for a passing of the torch ceremony. Hejduk presented him with a burgundy jersey, a C stitched into its chest. Landeskog pulled it over a white button-up shirt and smiled for pictures with Hejduk. His face was full of youth, lacking the beard he sports now. He was officially, at that point, the youngest full-time captain in NHL history.

Looking at pictures years later, Landeskog can't believe how young he appeared as he stood next to Hejduk. He was a kid, suddenly tasked with leading both the team's rising young talent and its veterans. When, on the advice of an older teammate, he held his first players-only meeting, his voice quavered. It was laughable how nervous he was, he said years later.

The Avalanche players were aware of his situation. The team took a leadership-by-committee approach as he adjusted, and he remembers teammates having his back. He talked to older players, inquiring about everything from travel logistics to planning off-ice team events. Leaders learn by asking questions, and Landeskog asked a lot.

"I think he was born for the job," teammate Greg Zannon said.

With the arrival of Nathan MacKinnon in 2013–14, the Avalanche took a jump, finishing with the second-best record in the conference. But the growth stagnated over the next few years, and the team cratered with its 48-point season in 2016–17. As captain, Landeskog had to field questions from reporters loss after loss. That was hard when no one knew how to explain what was going wrong. Answers are hard to come by when you're spiraling.

Landeskog tried to leave hockey at the rink and stay level-headed at home, but it wasn't easy while the team was in free-fall. "Are we really this bad?" he would think to himself. And what did that say about him as a player? As a teammate? As a captain and leader? In the darkest moments, he struggled to see the Avalanche climbing out of this hole and becoming a championship contender. That season, he said later, was as close to rock bottom as you can get in the NHL.

At points during the year, Landeskog heard his name in trade rumors. The Avalanche were terrible; they could recoup a haul if they chose to move a young, talented player such as their captain. It wasn't what Landeskog wanted, but he's sharp. He knows how the business side of the sport works. If Sakic thought it was in the organization's best interest to trade him, he knew he'd be out the door.

Landeskog wanted to be part of the solution and told Sakic as much. To the captain's relief, the deadline passed without a deal. Matt Duchene, who had made his trade request by this point, also stayed put. During that stretch, Sakic called Landeskog. He told the forward he had no interest in trading him. Just as Landeskog wanted to stay, Sakic wanted him around. He was their captain. That wasn't changing.

The disastrous season left Colorado at a crossroads. The roster still featured promising players such as Mackinnon and Landeskog and Mikko Rantanen. But something needed to change. Ahead of training camp the next year, Erik Johnson—one of Landeskog's closest friends on the team—remembers reaching out to some of the core players and leaders. He wanted to meet. To talk through what went wrong. To grow.

Landeskog recalls the meeting vividly. Defenseman Tyson Barrie hosted it at his house near Washington Park, a picturesque area in an affluent part of Denver. The group included the captain, as well as Johnson, MacKinnon, and respected veteran Blake Comeau.

Things will go wrong over the course of a season, Johnson stressed to his teammates. The Avalanche needed to avoid dragging each other down when that happened. "Let's eliminate any of the excuses or bitching," Johnson emphasized. "Let's do it the right way and see what happens."

Comeau believed the team had taken on the wrong mindset during the season—the opposite of how he's seen clubs with championship aspirations operate. If the Avalanche outshot an opponent, players would view it as a step in the right direction, even if they lost. In Comeau's mind, a culture of mediocrity had crept in, leading to results that were worse than mediocre. The Avalanche needed to nip it in the bud in the coming year.

"We never wanted to go through that again," Landeskog said. "We had to start laying the foundation for what was to come and how to be better and how to really take charge."

The meeting was a step. The players took ownership. Each knew they had to be better. And everyone entering the team's dressing room would have to know the team's standards. It wasn't the only reason they eventually turned things around, Johnson said. But it probably helped.

Every year, when a team wins the Stanley Cup, the captain starts a handoff in which the trophy is passed from teammate to teammate. Each player gets a moment to celebrate, to skate around the ice, Cup over his head, as a champion in a moment kids envision growing up. As the Avalanche turned the corner, Landeskog made a promise to Johnson he would repeat later. When *this* team did the damn thing, when they reached the heights of Sakic and Forsberg and Patrick Roy and won the Stanley Cup, Landeskog would hand Johnson the trophy first.

That couldn't happen if they were on different teams. But here Landeskog was, on the eve of free agency, still without a deal to stay in Colorado. He had been the team's constant, growing from a youngster whose voice faltered at a players-only meeting to a man in his late twenties and 100 percent comfortable as a charismatic leader. He took it on himself to welcome younger players to the team, whether that meant giving them rides to the rink or chatting with them after practice. He fought opponents if he took issue with how they treated a teammate. Coach Jared Bednar trusted him. And early in the 2020–21 season, MacKinnon called him the perfect captain.

Was all that about to end?

Colorado forward Gabriel Landeskog, during a game in February 2022 vs. the Detroit Red Wings, has been the Avalanche's captain since he was 19.

"I've always known that come September, October, I'm going to pull on that Avs jersey," he said.

But now, he didn't.

• • •

The call wasn't from Wallen. It was from Joe Sakic.

"Joe, listen," Landeskog told his general manager. "I don't want to go anywhere."

"Well, we want you here," Sakic replied. "So let's get something done."

That—plus a little bit of compromise—was all it took. Landeskog wanted an eight-year deal, perhaps longer than the Avalanche felt was wise for a physical forward in his late twenties.

But they conceded, and Landeskog accepted the $7 million annual salary cap hit the team wanted.

"I probably should have picked up the phone and called [Sakic] earlier, and I'm sure he feels the same way, so we didn't have to deal with the stress of going all the way to the wire," Landeskog said. "But now it makes for a good story."

As soon as they hung up the phone, Sakic and Wallen got to work, ironing out the finer details of the deal. They were in a time crunch to beat the midnight deadline but got it done. The Avalanche announced the agreement at 11:43 PM. Seventeen minutes to spare.

Wallen said his client was "happy like a baby" at the deal's completion. He wasn't alone. Nathan MacKinnon had been hopeful the sides would find common ground but had gone to bed as the night dragged on. Landeskog called to tell him the news. MacKinnon was thrilled. In his eyes, it was vital that the team got something worked out.

"We're super lucky that we did," MacKinnon said. "There'd be no Cup without Gabe."

3

OFF-SEASON CHOICES

THREE DAYS BEFORE working a deal out with Landeskog, Colorado signed its top defenseman, Cale Makar, a restricted free agent, to a six-year contract. Between those two moves, Joe Sakic solidified both his captain and burgeoning star as part of Colorado's Nathan MacKinnon–led core going forward.

But pay bumps for Landeskog and Makar, along with the flat salary cap and the Seattle Kraken expansion draft, made it impossible to keep every contributor from the 2020–21 team that won the Presidents' Trophy for best regular season record in the league.

Ryan Graves, one of Sakic's savvier trade acquisitions, was the first domino to fall. In 2018, he came to Colorado from the Rangers in exchange for Chris Bigras. Graves proved capable of playing on a defensive pairing with Makar and led the league in plus-minus rating in 2019–20. It was one of Sakic's great subtle moves; he received a legitimate NHLer, one who played in 149 games for the club, in exchange for a player who hasn't appeared in an NHL contest since.

The Avalanche could only protect three defensemen, seven forwards, and one goalie in the expansion draft. Then the Kraken would get to pick one unprotected player from every team. Sakic knew he was going to protect defensemen Makar, Devon Toews, and Samuel Girard, all of whom were better skaters with more offensive ability than Graves.

But Graves was a useful player, and the Avalanche front office knew Seattle would likely take him if he was left exposed. So, instead of losing him to expansion for nothing, Colorado traded him to New Jersey, getting back a second-round pick and Mikhail Maltsev, a young forward on an entry-level deal, meaning he was exempt from the expansion draft.

Shortly before making the trade public, Sakic called Graves, who was at his off-season home on Prince Edward Island. He told him the news and the Avalanche's reasoning behind it. The defenseman understood. He knew a move was possible, but there's no way to fully brace yourself for a trade. He was sad to leave the first team to give him an NHL shot.

The move was a cruel reminder: when a club makes a run at a championship, some players who both grew with the team and helped it grow don't get to reach the summit.

Trading Graves left forwards Joonas Donskoi and J.T. Compher as the most attractive unprotected options for Seattle. Longtime Avalanche defenseman Erik Johnson, the No. 1 pick in the 2006 NHL Draft by St. Louis, was available, too. Earlier in the year, Sakic had called Johnson, who had a no-movement clause in his contract, meaning he had the right to both be on the protected list or veto any trades. Wanting to protect other players, Sakic asked if he would waive the clause. Johnson agreed instantly. He was coming off a brutal 2020–21 season in which a concussion limited him to just four games. At points, the injury made him question if he would play again. He assumed the Kraken wouldn't take him and wanted Sakic to be able to protect all three of the roster's most valuable defensemen.

"With the team we have here, it would not have been a team-first move to not waive it," he said.

The decision paid off, both for the Avalanche and Johnson, who went unselected. Seattle took Donskoi, a winger coming off a career-high 17-goal season. That proved to be a blessing in disguise for Colorado. Compher, who had struggled offensively the year before and averaged the fewest minutes per game of his career, didn't have to leave. As a 26-year-old center with strong underlying defensive numbers, he still had value. Donskoi, meanwhile, recorded only two goals in 75 games for Seattle in 2021–22.

The salary cap, which hadn't gone up since before the COVID-19 pandemic because of lost league revenue, limited Colorado's flexibility in free agency. Brandon Saad, who scored the second-most Avalanche playoff goals in 2021, signed a five-year deal with the Blues, and effective fourth-liner Pierre-Edouard Bellemare went to the Lightning.

But the departure causing the most ramifications was goaltender Philipp Grubauer. The season before, he had put together a career year, posting a .922 save percentage, leading the NHL in shutouts and finishing as a finalist for the Vezina Trophy given annually to the league's top performing goaltender. The Kraken, flush with cap space as an expansion team, offered him a six-year deal worth nearly $6 million a year, and he jumped at the opportunity to be one of the faces of the league's newest team.

That left a void for Sakic to fill at a position he couldn't afford to mess up. Unlike at forward, there weren't cheap replacement options on the free agent market or players in the organization ready to step up. Pavel Francouz was under contract and had been a solid option in net two seasons before, but he was coming off double hip surgeries that prevented him from playing at all in 2020–21. The Avalanche would be taking a massive risk going into the season with him as their No. 1.

So Colorado needed someone. Former Toronto goalie Frederik Andersen could have been an option had free agency started a little differently. Sakic was still trying to work out a deal with Grubauer, according to The Athletic's Pierre LeBrun, and talks didn't fizzle quickly enough for the Avalanche to make a splash in the free agent goalie pool. Andersen signed with Carolina. He had a good offer from the Hurricanes and couldn't afford to wait for Colorado.

When the free-agent goalie carousel stopped spinning, the Avalanche still had no one in net. Sakic needed to make a trade. He had prepared for this situation, though. Ahead of free agency, he reached out to Arizona general manager Bill Armstrong to let him know he might be interested in Coyotes goalie Darcy Kuemper. With Grubauer gone, Sakic called Armstrong again. Trade talks began.

Kuemper had a reputation around the league as a good goalie who had never played on teams with much of a chance in the play-offs. Over his first nine seasons, he finished in the top 10 in Vezina voting twice and had a .917 save percentage, but he had only been in 18 playoff games. Nine of those came early in his career with Minnesota. The other nine were with Arizona. Four of his postseason appearances with the Coyotes were in the play-in round of the 2020 Edmonton bubble playoffs, which featured added teams because COVID-19 ended the regular season early. Kuemper had a dominant .933 save percentage during that series to beat the Predators.

Though Arizona lost to the Avalanche the next round, he had some massive moments, including a 49-save outing in Game 3. The Avalanche players remembered that series well, and they were excited to have him in the fold.

"We were a way better team, but Kuemper was the one key part of their team that kept them in the series," Mikko Rantanen said.

Sakic paid a hefty price to get the goalie, beating out Edmonton to make a deal happen. He gave up the team's 2022 first-round pick, young defenseman Conor Timmins and, if the Avalanche were to win the Stanley Cup, a 2024 third-round pick. Kuemper had only one year left on his contract. At least Arizona retained $1 million of his $4.5 million salary cap hit, giving the Avalanche a bit of extra flexibility.

The move was a departure from Sakic's norm. He had never traded a first-round pick, let alone for a player with only one year left on his deal. But this season with this core carried high expectations. The Avalanche couldn't afford not to have a goalie ready for the play-offs. If acquiring one meant he had to overpay, so be it.

It had been a tough off-season for Colorado, given the amount it had lost at forward, but acquiring Kuemper made assistant GM Chris MacFarland feel like he could breathe. The team had a strong defense, plus a forward group that—even if it had lost some depth— had close to as much top-end talent as any team in the league. Now goaltending was figured out, too.

Aside from the Kuemper trade, Sakic didn't make splashy off-season moves. Instead, he picked up cheap veterans he felt he could trust. In came Darren Helm, a longtime Red Wings forward who won the Stanley Cup in 2008. The general manager signed defenseman Ryan Murray to a one-year deal as well, and he traded for Kurtis MacDermid, a physical defenseman whose presence is felt as much for his willingness to stick up for his teammates as for his skill. Then, as preseason neared, the Avalanche signed Jack Johnson and Artem Anisimov to professional tryout contracts, meaning they would have the chance to make the team in training camp but could be released at any time.

Johnson, who had 950 games of NHL experience, mostly with Columbus, had what he called "the definition of a cup of coffee" with the Rangers in 2020–21, playing 13 games before core muscle repair surgery ended his season. The 34-year-old defenseman talked to coach Jared Bednar and MacFarland before agreeing to the deal, wanting assurance that he had a real chance to stick with the club. And there was. Colorado believed his sturdiness and penalty-killing ability made the chance worth taking.

"You've got to try," his wife, Kelly, said when he was considering taking the offer.

So he did. Johnson, who had considered retirement after his surgery, left his Columbus-area home for training camp in Denver, feeling good physically and not too nervous mentally.

"Worst-case scenario," he told his wife and kids, "Dad's home in a week."

The Avalanche entered training camp as the betting favorites to win the Stanley Cup, even after losing Saad, Donskoi, and Grubauer. The core Sakic had in place was more than capable of winning a bevy of regular season games, and he had until the trade deadline to continue building his team for the playoffs.

When players returned to Denver from their off-season homes, MacKinnon hosted a preseason party at his house. Erik Johnson and a few other teammates gathered in the backyard that night, trying to pick out a song the team should play in the locker room after wins.

Johnson brought up King Harvest's "Dancing in the Moonlight," which he'd heard at a wedding that summer, but the group decided it was too slow to be the first song in the victory playlist.

Then "Heat Waves," a song from the English indie band Glass Animals, started playing at the party. With its catchy beat, the song had been gradually climbing the pop charts. Johnson liked it, and one lyric in particular made it feel like the right choice:

> *Sometimes, all I think about is you*
> *Late nights in the middle of June…*

The song would serve as a reminder. Even when enjoying a win, the team wouldn't lose sight of its goal: playing in and winning the Stanley Cup Final. Taking advantage of late nights in the middle of June.

4

PREP FOR THE CHASE

THE STING OF THE Golden Knights series lingered. One of Jared Bednar's friends told him the pain was just the hockey gods testing him, seeing how badly he wanted to win. When approached properly, losing breeds both hunger and experience.

Avalanche training camp started in late September 2021. The night before it began, players drove to the suburbs and trickled into the Inverness Hotel for a team meeting and meal. Everyone was there, from the team's stars to players who would be reassigned to the minors or cut within weeks. They wore slacks and polos, eating steak, chicken, salmon, salad, and pasta for dinner. The beginning of seasons lend themselves to optimism, but not every team realistically comes to training camp thinking it has a chance to win a Stanley Cup. With the level of players sitting at this dinner, though, a championship was already on Colorado's mind.

Standout defenseman Devon Toews didn't necessarily view 2021–22 as a make-or-break season, but he knew there was an urgency within the team. Colorado's roster had been good enough to win it all the season before, and keeping a team like that together is somewhere between difficult and impossible.

Windows are fickle. They don't always stay open as long as expected, especially in a league with a salary cap. Sakic wouldn't be able to pair this much depth with this kind of high-end talent forever. For anyone at that first team meeting, the coming season could be the best chance they ever would get to finish on top. You never know which kick at the can will be your last.

Sakic and Bednar both spoke to the players that night. They reiterated that the team had only one purpose, and that was to win a Stanley Cup. Bednar believed it important not to hide from the disappointment of the Vegas series. The Avalanche would have to learn from it if they were going to come close to reaching their goals. Sakic's message was simple: the Avalanche had unfinished business.

Jack Johnson, who had agreed to his tryout deal three weeks earlier, was a complete stranger to the club, but he instantly sensed the expectation and desire among his new teammates. External questions from analysts and TV personalities might have revolved around Colorado's three consecutive losses in Round 2 of the playoffs, but that wasn't the focus among players, coaches, or management. They had higher ambitions.

After listening to Sakic and Bednar talk, the message from the team's decision-makers was clear to Toews—"If the pieces aren't right, then we'll find the pieces and make the moves that are needed to win it."

• • •

Day 1 of training camp took place at Family Sports Center, a two-rink public facility about 25 minutes from downtown Denver. The building isn't hockey-specific, nor is it used only by the Avalanche. Kids attend figure-skating lessons and have birthday parties there, and the complex features indoor bumper cars and a laser tag area in addition to the rinks. It's an older facility, a far cry from the new state-of-the-art practice rinks in Boston and Detroit. Near the Zamboni entrance, there's a dip in the ice. Players have to be careful skating into the boards in that area. "It fucking sucks," one former Colorado player said.

None of that impacted the team's energy for camp. On one of the first days, as Mikko Rantanen and Cale Makar walked toward the ice together, Rantanen put his arm around the defenseman and kissed his helmet. Intensity and focus didn't preclude a little goofiness or warmth.

Before cuts, the Avalanche had more than 50 players at camp, so Bednar split them into two groups. MacKinnon was in the first group, and his session got off to a less-than-ideal beginning when one of the reserve goalies allowed a rebound after a shot. The puck bounced off the goalie and struck MacKinnon's face. He left the ice bleeding.

Fifteen minutes later MacKinnon was back, his face decorated with a few stitches. He's not one to miss time on the ice. Tough way to start camp, he said afterward, but he was all good.

"Goalie is cut, though," he quipped.

The last time MacKinnon had spoken at a press conference was after Game 6 against Vegas, when he had lamented his lack of playoff success entering his ninth season. The pain was still raw in that moment. Losses like that never fully lose their sting, but more than three months had passed since then. MacKinnon could talk about it with a broader perspective now. The team was growing, he said. It was learning how to play postseason hockey.

He believed he and his teammates had come a long way. When new challenges would emerge in the coming season, they would be ready.

• • •

Every returning Avalanche player had to answer questions—from reporters as well as themselves—about the team's loss to Vegas. But no one was under more scrutiny than a man who didn't even appear in the series: Nazem Kadri.

Kadri missed every Golden Knights contest after the NHL Department of Player Safety suspended him eight games for an illegal check to Justin Faulk's head in Round 1 of the playoffs against St. Louis. Kadri had cut across the ice on the play and hit the defenseman's head with his shoulder. Faulk fell to the ice and didn't move. He wouldn't play again in the series. His furious teammates charged toward Kadri, and officials ejected the Avalanche forward.

Colorado's second-line center already had two playoff and three regular season suspensions on his record before the Faulk hit, all from his 10-year tenure with Toronto. That history played a role in the Leafs trading him to Colorado—they didn't feel they could trust him—and it influenced the league's thinking when it came down hard on him after the Faulk hit, according to the Department of Player Safety's statement.

Kadri said he was trying to make a responsible defensive play and break up the scoring chance, that he had no intent to injure. But, by the time he got home that night, he assumed a suspension was coming. With Kadri's disciplinary history, he didn't get the benefit of the doubt. Not from the league, certainly not from the Blues, and not even from everyone in Colorado. *Denver Post* columnist Mark Kiszla called him "a cheap-shot artist," saying the Avalanche should cut ties with him. His behavior was stupid and goonish, Kiszla wrote. The team shouldn't tolerate it.

Kadri barely slept in the days after the hit. He tried to appeal the suspension but had no luck. In a decision with which he strongly disagreed, an independent arbitrator upheld the Department of Player Safety's initial ruling.

A team's second-line center is critical in the playoffs, especially against a club like Vegas, which found ways to limit MacKinnon and Colorado's top line. When the Avalanche needed Kadri, all he could do was watch. He wasn't eligible to return until Game 7 of the Golden Knights series.

The Avalanche, of course, didn't make it that far.

Despite questions about Kadri's future in Colorado, Sakic didn't trade him. The Avalanche wouldn't have listened even if teams had seriously inquired. Good No. 2 centers are hard to find, and he didn't want to risk losing his. Bednar supported his player, too, saying he saw a difference between the Faulk play and ones for which he'd been suspended in the past. The Toronto hits were retaliatory—instances of Kadri getting frustrated. That wasn't what happened against the Blues, in Bednar's eyes. The coach believed Kadri's explanation of the play.

"I've seen Naz grow up and try and be real intentional about what he does," Bednar said. "Everyone loses their cool here and there, but to me, he didn't just go do something dumb. He just missed his check by a couple of inches."

That distinction didn't matter to the league when it handed down the eight-game suspension, but it mattered to the coach's faith in his second-line center. That trust was meaningful to Kadri. His wife, Ashley, said he wanted to play his heart out for the team because it gave him another chance.

In his first press conference of training camp, Kadri told reporters he was happy that Faulk had recovered but reiterated he meant only to prevent him from getting to the net. His teammates trusted and supported him, he insisted. They understood who he was as a person.

Kadri's words reflected what he was thinking and offered a look at his perspective. But any redemption would have to come on the ice, not in front of a microphone.

· · ·

The Avalanche weren't fully healthy coming into camp. Cale Makar had injured his wrist during summer training. He was on track to play in the season opener, but he was limited at practices, wearing a red non-contact jersey. He didn't play in any of Colorado's six preseason contests. His father, Gary, later said he wasn't sure Cale was ever 100 percent healthy during the regular season.

Toews, who underwent off-season shoulder surgery, wasn't going to be ready at the start of the regular season, leaving the Avalanche thinner than anticipated on defense. And though it looked like the team would enter the year with a healthy goalie tandem of Darcy Kuemper and Pavel Francouz, Francouz sprained his ankle in a preseason game. It was another bad break for the No. 2 goalie, who had missed the previous season after undergoing double hip surgery. As Francouz would go on to show, backup goalies can be vital to a team's success. But the Avalanche would have to wait a while to see him in action. Fortunately for Colorado, neither Francouz nor Toews were going to miss significant time.

Camp brought more than just injuries. There were promising developments, too. The Avalanche agreed to a three-year extension with Logan O'Connor, a fourth-line player who had originally signed with the team as a college free agent out of the University of Denver. Not blessed with the natural ability of MacKinnon or Makar or Rantanen, the 25-year-old had to work for everything he got in the sport. You can see it in the way he plays. He's a tenacious forechecker who brings energy to every shift, using his plus-skating to capitalize on opponent's mistakes. The extension solidified his role as a dependable contributor for the next several years.

Some of the prospects showed flashes, too. Oskar Olausson, picked out of Sweden in the first round of the 2021 draft, scored a pair of goals in preseason games, displaying his promising wrist shot. He showed off his teeth, too; he couldn't hide a grin after either goal.

Nonetheless, the Avalanche sent him back to junior hockey for more development after his third preseason game. He wasn't ready for NHL hockey as an 18-year-old, but he had displayed the promise that made him a first-round pick. So too had Justin Barron, the team's selection at 25th overall in 2020. André Burakovsky, who was 26 at the start of camp, was surprised to learn his new teammate was only 19. It made the Swedish winger feel old.

Barron played in four of the team's preseason games and was much closer to NHL-ready than Olausson. His goal going into camp was to make the team, and he came close. The Avalanche didn't cut him until two days before the season opener. Erik Johnson called him as close to an NHL player as the Avalanche had among their group of prospects. Other NHL teams would see that soon, too. Barron had potential—either as a future Avalanche player or as a chip in a deadline trade.

Artem Anisimov, the Avalanche front office deemed, did not. Once a player capable of scoring more than 20 goals, the 33-year-old struggled to keep up with Colorado's speed during preseason action and didn't look like someone who could contribute much to a club with championship aspirations. The Avalanche released him from his professional tryout contract five days before the season. He signed with a KHL team in his native Russia.

Jack Johnson, meanwhile, hung around, his camp trending in a different, more positive direction. In the years leading up to 2021–22, the 34-year-old had become a punching bag in hockey's analytics community for his poor underlying numbers. The Athletic's Dom Luszczyszyn wrote that he got a "ludicrous contract he doesn't deserve" after he signed a five-year deal with the Penguins in 2018, and JFreshHockey's Projected Wins above Replacement model rated him in the third percentile of the league heading into 2021–22.

At his peak, though, Johnson had been a top-pair defenseman on Columbus teams in contention for playoff spots. David Savard, another former Blue Jackets defenseman, credits Johnson with taking him under his wing. Their kids were born around the same time, and they had family dinners together.

None of that mattered to Penguins fans when Johnson struggled over a two-year tenure in Pittsburgh, where he signed after Columbus. He became such a point of contention among fans that Penguins general manager Jim Rutherford said in a 2020 interview with The Athletic that, "He's not as bad as all of the anti–Jack Johnson people think he is." Despite his defense of the player, Rutherford bought out the final three years of Johnson's contract two months after that interview. Then came the defenseman's injury-stricken season with the Rangers. His career, it seemed, was trending toward an unceremonious ending.

Johnson brought perspective with him to Avalanche training camp. Perhaps a tryout wasn't an ideal situation, but he had faced far more significant adversity than that in his life. In October 2014, he declared bankruptcy after his parents spent millions of his dollars, leaving him deep in debt.

"I'd say I picked the wrong people, who led me down the wrong path," Johnson told the Columbus Dispatch at the time.

That aspect of his life had stabilized by the time he arrived in Colorado, and he was ready to prove he still had good hockey left in him. The Avalanche played him in five of six preseason games to evaluate whether they should use a roster spot on him, and they liked what they saw. He could provide defensive sturdiness, likely in a bottom-pairing role.

After the final preseason game, a 4–2 win against the Stars, Johnson went with his wife's uncle to Chopper's, a sports bar in Cherry Creek, where many Avalanche players live. It was late in the evening and only a few days before the season opener, but Johnson still hadn't heard anything about his status.

"Hopefully, I'll hear something tomorrow," he thought to himself while eating a turkey club and vegetable soup.

Then his phone rang. His agent, Pat Brisson, told him the Avalanche wanted to keep him on board on a one-year contract. He had made the team. He was thrilled. His career was not only alive, but he also had a chance to play for a legitimate championship contender.

The Avalanche announced the signing the next day, then reassigned Barron to the minors a day later. With that, Sakic's roster was set. The Stanley Cup chase could begin.

5

BEHIND THE BENCH

AFTER THE 2020 bubble playoffs and a 2020–21 season featuring strict COVID-19 regulations and only divisional play, October marked a return to normalcy, at least in some ways. With Chicago in town for the opener and the Avalanche on the ice for morning skate, Landeskog chatted with childhood friend and Blackhawks defenseman Erik Gustafsson, who stood on the bench in a sweatshirt and red hat he wore backward. That sort of social interaction would have been out of the question the previous season.

The pandemic had prevented Alex Newhook's parents, Paula and Shawn, from traveling from their Newfoundland home to watch Alex's NHL debut or any of the games he played in the spring of 2021. But they were in town for the Colorado-Chicago game, seats secured in the lower bowl of Ball Arena, ready for their first in-person experience at one of their 20-year-old's NHL contests. His grandmother, Ann, made the trip, too, wearing a signed No. 18 jersey. "To Nan, Thanks for the support from Day 1," Alex had written in Sharpie.

There was anticipation for the game, driven in part by the approval to allow Ball Arena to be filled to capacity for the first time since before the start of the pandemic. Still, there were reminders that COVID-19 would continue to impact the hockey world. The day before the opener, Nathan MacKinnon—who, like everyone on the Avalanche, had received the vaccine—tested positive for the virus, forcing him to stay off the ice for more than a week. Journeyman Jayson Megna, a 31-year-old who had never played in a season opener, entered the lineup in the center's stead.

Bednar was out with COVID-19, too. He wasn't experiencing symptoms by the time the opener rolled around but still had to watch from home. His assistants Ray Bennett and Nolan Pratt handled in-game coaching duties.

The start of every season is about possibility and hope, and the Avalanche came in with the same championship expectations they had the season before. This year, the Ball Arena rafters featured a new flourish for the opener: a white 2021 Presidents' Trophy banner that jumped out next to the one from two decades earlier, which was yellowed by time. The team made no mention of it pregame, though. The goal wasn't a banner signifying regular season excellence. The Avalanche wanted a greater prize—the one awarded at the conclusion of the playoffs.

The Blackhawks, who had won three Stanley Cups in the 2010s, entered the season with a newfound excitement, too. They had revamped their roster after missing the playoffs the season before, trading for standout defenseman Seth Jones and star goalie Marc-André Fleury over the summer. Perhaps, the team thought, these veterans would be a winning cast around Patrick Kane, Alex DeBrincat, and Jonathan Toews.

The buzz built as each Avalanche player received an introduction during a pregame ceremony. Some, like Megna and youngster Sampo Ranta, soaked in the pageantry for the first time. Fan favorites like Cale Makar, Gabriel Landeskog, and Mikko Rantanen received raucous ovations. The excitement was fitting for one of the most talented, skill-heavy rosters in the league.

But once the game started, the player who struck first was among the final members of the Avalanche to make the team. Less than five minutes into the first period, Jack Johnson found himself alone with the puck in the offensive zone after Jake McCabe and Tyler Johnson tripped each other up at the blueline. The defenseman darted toward Fleury and showed off the offensive skill that had once helped make him a third-overall draft pick. He pulled the puck across his body, then backhanded it past Fleury and into the net. He threw his hands into the air as the goal horn rang through the arena. Nichushkin engulfed him with a hug.

"I've taken a few penalty shots in my day, so I wasn't totally lost on a breakaway," Johnson said. "If everyone falls down, I'm pretty good."

The first period also featured a career milestone, as 20-year-old Bowen Byram—whose dad, Shawn, appeared in one NHL game for the Blackhawks in 1991—joined an offensive rush. He received a pass from Landeskog and beat Fleury on the glove side with a shot, giving him his first NHL goal. The score might have been only one play, but the offensive burst showed what made Byram such a promising prospect for Colorado.

When the night was done, the Avalanche had a 4–2 win that featured three goals in the opening 10 minutes. A national TV audience got its first glimpse of how potent their offense could be.

The public address speaker announced Byram as the First Star of the game, so he stayed on the ice late for a postgame interview. In the locker room, Landeskog told his teammates to give Byram the silent treatment when he walked in. No one said a word to him until he'd put his helmet away. Then, finally, they burst into cheers, and Byram flashed his infectious, youthful grin. Landeskog handed him the game puck. The rookie joked afterward that his mom would probably steal it.

But the early-season excitement faded over the next few games. Some of that had to do with player availability. The Department of Player Safety suspended Landeskog for two games because of a boarding penalty on Kirby Dach against Chicago, and Valeri Nichushkin sprained his wrist against the Blackhawks. Jack Johnson tested positive for COVID-19, and Pavel Francouz (ankle) and Devon Toews (shoulder) were still out. Newhook, meanwhile, was sent down to the minors for a month, both to clear salary cap space and because Bednar believed he hadn't shown enough to stick.

All those players, as well as MacKinnon, missed the team's second game, a 5–3 loss to the Blues. The Avalanche had to play a man short because of salary cap restraints, and the lineup became even more shorthanded when Stefan Matteau, up from the minors, suffered a lower-body injury on his fifth shift of the game.

The loss was Nazem Kadri's first game against the Blues since the Faulk hit during the playoffs in the previous season, and he received an initial taste of what would be a testy relationship with St. Louis for the rest of the year. As he jumped onto the ice for his first shift of the game, Blues forward Brayden Schenn whacked him with his stick, challenging him to a fight. Knowing it would be against hockey code to decline, Kadri nodded and threw off his gloves. The two wrestled each other to the ice, then skated to the penalty box for offsetting five-minute fighting penalties.

Colorado nearly erased a three-goal deficit against the Blues, and an apparent goal from Tyson Jost that would have tied the game was waved off as the officials determined he'd kicked the puck into the net. Kadri collected two assists, and Bednar, cleared from COVID-19 protocol, said postgame he thought missing the Vegas series had stuck with Kadri. The center was determined to have a strong start.

MacKinnon returned for the next game, which came on the road against the Washington Capitals. But it was clear he'd been off the ice for a week, as he took an interference penalty and finished with a minus-five rating. The losing streak reached three when the Panthers beat the Avalanche two days later in Sunrise, Florida.

With a disappointing 1–3–0 record, Colorado flew across the state to play the Tampa Bay Lightning, winners of the two previous Stanley Cups. And in Amalie Arena, where they'd eventually hoist the Stanley Cup, the Avalanche seemed to find their game.

"Both teams knew there was a chance we'd be seeing each other down the road," Megna said. "We were the group that was up-and-coming, the challengers, and they were obviously on top, back-to-back champs. There was definitely an energy in that building."

With the score tied 2–2 in the third period, MacKinnon scored his first goal of the season, showing off his one-time slapshot on the power play. He lasered the puck in from the faceoff circle, a spot from which he frequently works on his shots at practices and morning skates. "I'm trying to make it a threat," he said. Sure enough, months later he would score a power play goal against the Lightning on a slap shot in the decisive game of the Stanley Cup Final.

Later in the period, Darcy Kuemper made his best save up to that point in an Avalanche sweater, leaning back and using his stick to keep a bouncing puck from crossing the goal line. But Tampa Bay standout Brayden Point sent the game to overtime with a perfectly placed shot through traffic in the dwindling minutes. When neither team scored in the five-minute three-on-three period, Cale Makar came through in the shootout, giving Colorado its first road win of the season.

"It's something we needed," Kadri said.

But it didn't spark a run. The Avalanche failed to win three of their next five as they integrated newcomers such as Kuemper, Jack Johnson, Darren Helm, and Ryan Murray into the mix. A loss to the talented Golden Knights, though disappointing, was at least understandable, but Colorado started November with back-to-back losses against lowly Columbus and blew third-period leads in both contests.

"Sometimes it looks like we're kind of effortless," the normally affable Rantanen said after the first Blue Jackets loss. "If you want to win in the playoffs, or if you even want to get in the playoffs, this is not how you play hockey."

Colorado had four off days before its next game, and Rantanen stressed that the Avalanche needed to evaluate themselves honestly during that time. Fortunately, they had the coach to help them do just that.

• • •

Bednar never appeared in an NHL game as a player, and he didn't spend a full season in the AHL, either. Most of his playing career came in the East Coast Hockey League, two tiers below the NHL, as a defenseman known to be unafraid to drop gloves and stand up for his teammates. After the 2001–02 season, at the age of 30, he knew his playing career wouldn't last much longer.

But Jason Fitzsimmons, one of Bednar's friends and former teammates, had an idea. Recently promoted from assistant to head coach of the South Carolina Stingrays, Fitzsimmons was in the process of assembling a staff. Bednar was one of the Stingrays' leaders, and Fitzsimmons, a younger coach, had relied on him for insights. What if Bednar joined him as an assistant?

The two friends lived only a few blocks from each other in Charleston, and one evening, while hanging out together in Fitzsimmons's backyard, the coach brought up the idea. Up until that point, Bednar had envisioned himself continuing to play, so he was unsure at first. But coaching had intrigued him as he'd gotten older. The thought grew on him.

"About six or seven beers later, I had an assistant coach," Fitzsimmons said in an interview with The Athletic's Ryan S. Clark.

Bednar talked to his wife, Susan, and officially decided to make the transition. With that, a playing career ended and a coaching life began. Bednar, a Saskatchewan native, spent five years as a Stingrays assistant, excelling at game-planning, before he was promoted to head coach for two years. In the second of those seasons, he led the Stingrays to a 2009 league championship. He had two quality goalies at his disposal during that playoff run—James Reimer, who has gone on to have a long NHL career, and Jonathan Boutin. The coach laid out an unorthodox but simple plan: if a goalie won a game, he'd stay in for the next contest. If he lost, the other would get a chance. The two came in and out for each other during the first two rounds, but then Boutin helped the Stingrays to a third-round sweep.

When Boutin dropped Game 2 of the Kelly Cup championship, Bednar had a decision to make. Should he stick with his original plan? Or would it be wise to let Boutin keep going, considering he'd won seven in a row before the loss? Bednar chose the former, subbing Reimer in for a Game 3 win and letting him play until he lost Game 5. Then he switched back to Boutin for Game 6, which the Stingrays lost, sending the series to a Game 7. Once again, Bednar stayed the course. He put Reimer in for Game 7. The goalie rewarded his coach's trust with a win against Alaska.

"He stuck to his word," Reimer told Sportsnet's Ken Wiebe years later. "In my mind, he didn't have to. That was pretty instrumental in my development."

Looking back on the championship now, Bednar can't imagine doing a goalie rotation like that again. But he trusted both players, and each responded well. Reimer and Boutin finished the playoffs with .929 and .910 save percentages, respectively.

His first coaching championship secured, Bednar accepted a job as an AHL assistant in the Flames organization. After one year, he got a head coaching opportunity at the AHL level and worked for Peoria (Illinois), Springfield (Massachusetts), and Lake Erie (Ohio) over the next six seasons. In 2015–16, Bednar led the Lake Erie Monsters, the Blue Jackets' AHL team, to a Calder Cup championship.

His wife and two kids, meanwhile, stayed in Charleston, which had become home and where he spent his off-seasons. His mother-in-law moved in to help Susan with his kids, and Bednar didn't take his family's sacrifices for granted. He was back during the summer but recognized that was the easy time of year to be a parent. Susan was the one getting the kids through the daily grind of the school year. It was tough for Jared not to be there, and it was tough for Susan not having him there.

"There's always a trade-off to anything you want to try and accomplish," Bednar said. "That was just one of the sacrifices we decided to make."

Shortly after Bednar coached the Calder Cup champs, the Avalanche were hit with Patrick Roy's resignation, which assistant general manager Chris MacFarland called a grenade. Training camp was set to begin the next month, and Colorado had no one to stand behind the bench. Joe Sakic had to find a head coach.

The Avalanche front office requested permission from other clubs to interview coaches in their organizations. Sakic brought in a mix of candidates, including Bednar; Capitals assistant Lane

Lambert; Blackhawks assistant Kevin Deineen; and Travis Green, head coach for AHL Utica.

MacFarland knew Bednar when they both were with the Blue Jackets organization, and he vouched for the coach when Sakic asked for his perspective. In MacFarland's mind, it was only a matter of time before Bednar became an NHL head coach. He liked his competitiveness and the way he connected with young players. Plus, Bednar's passion for coaching is apparent, whether he's talking through a play in a press conference or leading his players through one of his seemingly endless supply of end-of-practice games. During the 2022 playoffs, Bednar said that if the NHL had never come calling, he would happily still be coaching in the minors. Watching how he operates, that's 100 percent believable.

Colorado brought Bednar in for multiple interviews. He established a rapport with Sakic, and the conversations quickly went from question-and-answer sessions to broader discussions about hockey philosophy. The general manager appreciated the style of play Bednar encouraged. He coached teams to play an up-tempo, entertaining style. That's how Sakic likes watching games.

"You want fans to leave a building knowing they were excited watching their home team," he said.

Two weeks after Roy's resignation, Sakic hired Bednar. The coach was in South Carolina hunting with close friend Brett Marietti when he got the call. He stepped away to take it, then nonchalantly returned.

"It looks like I got the job in Colorado," Bednar said to his friend, as Clark detailed in his story for The Athletic. "Let's go hunting."

Bednar already had a Kelly Cup (ECHL) and Calder Cup (AHL) on his résumé. If he were to lead the Avalanche to the Stanley Cup, he would become the first head coach to win a title at all three affiliated levels. Colorado, though, wasn't close to a championship-caliber team in the disastrous 2016–17 campaign. At points during the year, Bednar worried Sakic would fire him. The NHL isn't always a forgiving league.

But the front office didn't consider making a change. The general manager knew his roster wasn't ready to contend that season, especially after injuries to Erik Johnson and goalie Semyon Varlamov. Colorado didn't have the organizational depth to fill holes left by injuries, plus MacKinnon, Landeskog, and Matt Duchene all were having down years. Everything that could go poorly, did. Sakic told his coach the team would just have to get through the year, that Bednar's main job was to keep the team's core players engaged. There were internal fixes to make, but changing head coaches wasn't one of them.

Colorado's patience proved fruitful. Bednar helped the team make a surprise playoff appearance in 2017–18, earning a nod as a coach of the year finalist.

"Seeing what we could accomplish in that year really kind of started driving our team forward," Bednar said.

That season also marked the start of Bednar's biggest office initiative. In April 2018, a bus crash in Saskatchewan killed 16 people, most of whom were members of the Humboldt Broncos junior hockey team. Bednar spent part of his childhood living in Humboldt, a small city in Saskatchewan, and played two seasons for the Broncos. The tragedy struck a personal chord; he had connections to the team's roster at the time of the crash. A son of one of his friends was a goalie on the Broncos. He survived the crash but was paralyzed from the waist down.

The crash shook the hockey community, and it brought back difficult memories for Sakic, who survived a bus crash in 1986 while playing major junior for the Swift Current Broncos. His team bus skidded on black ice that day and went off the road, hitting an embankment and going airborne. It then flipped onto its right side and continued sliding, eventually stopping in a ditch. Sakic climbed out of the front window unharmed, but four of his teammates lost their lives.

The general manager doesn't talk about the accident often. The pain is still there, and some of it resurfaced after the Humboldt crash. Sakic spoke to Bednar afterward and told The Athletic's Katie Strang

Jared Bednar, Colorado's coach since 2016, leads his team behind Darren Helm (43), J.T. Compher (37), and Kurtis MacDermid (56) during a game against the Arizona Coyotes in March 2022.

at the time that it was crushing to think others were going through what he'd experienced.

Less than a month after the accident, Sakic and Bednar both attended a country music concert in Saskatoon raising money for families affected by the crash. Sakic met with Broncos families and, late the night before leaving town, made a visit to a local hospital to see Kaleb Dahlgren, a Broncos forward who suffered a severe brain injury, fractured skull, broken neck, and broken back. Sakic talked to Dahlgren about his legendary wrist shot and at one point brought up the crash he survived while with Swift Current. Dahlgren relayed his message to *theScore's* Nick Faris: strive to fully honor the friends he lost.

Later that summer, Bednar helped organize the Humboldt Broncos Memorial Golf Tournament. It became an annual event to remember the victims and raise money for several local causes. The Avalanche coach still serves as co-host and has gotten to know many of the Broncos families through his efforts.

"It's been a healing process," he said.

And one he wants to be part of.

Bednar's help for Humboldt doesn't stop with the summer tournament. During the 2021 Colorado-Vegas series, he received a text message from Marty Richardson, the president and CEO of DAWG Nation, a Denver-based non-profit that helps hockey players and their families in times of crisis. Former Humboldt forward Graysen Cameron, one of the crash's survivors, was driving through Denver on a cross-country road trip, and Richardson was wondering if Cameron could watch a practice. Bednar told him to come by and, at the end of the skate, asked security to bring him to ice level. The coach talked to him for 15 minutes. Makar came out of the dressing room to sign a jersey for Cameron.

Hosting Cameron at practice wasn't something Bednar publicized or did for clout. But given his history with both Humboldt and the Broncos, it was important to him.

"You definitely see his character and the type of person he is," Cameron said. "He has a big heart and likes making people's days."

• • •

Bednar's style suits Colorado's speedy roster. He encourages defensemen to jump into play on the offensive side of the ice, which allows players such as Makar to flourish. He stresses relentless forechecking, too, to keep the puck in the offensive zone.

In the Golden Knights playoff series in the 2020–21 season, the Avalanche got away from Bednar's structure. They didn't recover quickly enough when Vegas proved more physical and limited opportunities for MacKinnon and Colorado's top line.

"We wanted it so bad," Bednar said. "We had a really good team that believed we could win and, when we lost a game, it stuck with us too long."

The series loss still bothered the coach as training camp got under way in 2021–22. But those bumps were part of a maturation process the Avalanche needed to go through if they were going to reach new heights.

• • •

At the practice after the first Columbus loss, Bednar held a meeting with his players. The coach believes in honesty. When the Avalanche play well, he recognizes that. When they struggle, he does the same thing. And everyone knew they played poorly against the Blue Jackets.

At points during the first Columbus game, the team's in-game work ethic dipped. That led to poor defense and five Blue Jackets goals, all of which Bednar believed were preventable. No team in the league matched up with the Avalanche's skill, but Colorado couldn't expect to rely exclusively on that advantage. The Columbus game showed what could happen if it did.

"I think we sort of took things for granted and just thought maybe we could skate our way through that game," O'Connor said. "They sort of handed it to us, outworked us the whole time."

Work. Skating. Effort. If the team was going to be successful, it had to rely on those things, not talent alone.

At the meeting, the players didn't watch much video. Bednar spoke, reminding his team that talent wasn't the issue. But they had to work harder. They had to decide which way their season was going to go. Jack Johnson saw it as a turning point. The coach left the responsibility on his players.

Not long after, the Avalanche hit their stride.

THE STEADY FORCE

DEVON TOEWS DOESN'T fill highlight reels or stat sheets like Cale Makar, and he doesn't skate with the elusiveness of Samuel Girard. He isn't as big as Erik Johnson, as talented as Bowen Byram, or as experienced as Jack Johnson. Unlike most of his fellow Avalanche defensemen, he wasn't a first-round pick, and though he grew up playing street hockey with his neighbors in British Columbia, he didn't give the sport his sole focus until he was a teenager.

None of that stopped Toews from becoming one of the most important players on Colorado's roster. The 27-year-old returned from his shoulder injury for the second Columbus game November 6 and, after that loss, the Avalanche rattled off six consecutive wins. That was no coincidence.

He's consistent as can be, and though he entered the season with only 169 career games under his belt, it seemed to Erik Johnson that Toews had been in 500. He has a veteran presence. "When he has the puck," Johnson said, "you feel like everything is in control."

Along with being the strongest defensive player among Colorado's blueliners, the 6'1", 191-pound Toews demonstrated the skating ability to keep up with his primary defensive partner, the speedy, skillful Makar. Add that with elite puck-moving abilities and a dangerous shot, and you've got a legitimate top-pairing defenseman: one of the most underrated in the NHL, in teammate Mikko Rantanen's eyes.

And when Toews returned to the lineup in November, recovered from that off-season shoulder surgery, he was the exact steadying presence Colorado needed.

• • •

During Toews' final junior season in the British Columbia Hockey League, Quinnipiac University coach Rand Pecknold talked to every NHL scout he knew, telling them to draft the defenseman. Unlike MLB, NFL, and NBA prospects, hockey players can go to college after getting drafted, then join their NHL organization when ready to turn professional. Toews was committed to Quinnipiac, and Pecknold had confidence he could develop him into a quality player. If an NHL club used a low-risk, seventh-round pick on the defenseman, the coach reasoned, it would be happy down the road.

But Toews lacked size and muscle—160 pounds soaking wet, he said—and NHL teams don't like small.

"His weakness is his strength," Pecknold told scouts. "We're going to fix that."

Seven rounds came and went without Toews hearing his name. None of the NHL clubs took Pecknold's advice. They would come to regret it, some returning to Pecknold later and telling him they should have listened.

While playing for the Surrey Eagles the season before college, Toews started to see the same potential in himself as the coach did. His game was trending in the right direction. About four years earlier, he had given up baseball, his other favorite sport, to focus solely on hockey. Now after hearing a bit of draft chatter, he started to wonder if he could someday reach the highest level.

Toews was an instant contributor with Quinnipiac, running the top power play unit his first year on campus and logging 17 points in 37 games. Pecknold met daily with assistant Reid Cashman, asking how they were going to coach Toews that day. "I'm not going to lie," Pecknold said later. "We don't do that for every player."

They saw what the defenseman could become.

By the end of the season, NHL teams saw it too. The Islanders drafted Toews in the fourth round, which shocked Pecknold. He thought his player would go in the third round, or maybe even the second.

As Pecknold had assured teams it would the summer before, Quinnipiac's staff worked with Toews on getting stronger. Sam Anas, a 5'8" forward and one of Toews's classmates, remembered lifting the same weights freshman year as his friend, despite being nearly half a foot shorter. But Toews flourished under strength and conditioning coach Brijesh Patel, and Anas said he "exploded" the summer after freshman year. You could see the new muscle.

Toews's on-ice play reflected his physical progress. He increased his point total his sophomore and junior seasons, helping Quinnipiac reach the 2016 NCAA title game. Pecknold called him "a Corsi machine," referencing the advanced statistic that tracks shot-attempt differential when a player is on the ice.

"We did other statistics that we keep for our team, and he blew some of them out of the water," Pecknold said. "Unlike anything we'd ever had in the past."

After Toews's junior year, he had the option to turn professional and play with the Bridgeport Sound Tigers, the Islanders' American Hockey League affiliate. Pecknold hated the thought of Toews leaving a year early, but he told his player the truth.

"You need to go," Pecknold said. "Believe me, I'd love to have you back, but you're ready for the American League, and it's not going to be long before you're in the NHL."

Once again, the coach was right. After a year in Bridgeport, New York brought up the defenseman who had once been passed over by every team in the draft. He immediately made his mark, helping the Islanders reach the second round of the playoffs in 2019. The next season, they reached the conference finals, losing to the eventual champion Lightning. During that playoff run, Toews made a point to honor Anas's mom, Deme, who was battling breast cancer, by writing her initials on his stick.

"It was one of her last days, so it was something that hits home for us," Anas said.

Shortly after the playoffs ended, Toews paid homage to Deme again, this time at his wedding in New Jersey. Anas arrived at the reception and found his seat at one of the dark wood tables. He didn't notice anything unusual until Toews came over and pushed a white bookmark across. There was one at every other seat.

"In lieu of a favor, a donation has been made to Hockey Fights Cancer in loving memory of Deme Anas," it read in purple lettering.

"We just kind of had a nice little moment there," Anas said later. "Not a whole lot of words spoken, but a big hug."

The rest of the night passed, Devon in a dark blue suit and his wife, Kerry, in her dress as they celebrated a new beginning. The wedding was only the start of major life changes ahead. Two days later, his agent, Ross Gurney, got the defenseman on the phone. He had been traded.

Avalanche defenseman Devon Toews, skating with the puck during a game at Denver's Ball Arena in March 2022, contributed 57 points and led the team with a plus-minus of 52 during the 2021–22 season.

• • •

The Islanders found themselves in a difficult situation after 2020. They were up against the salary cap, which hadn't increased because of the COVID-19 pandemic. Toews was a restricted free agent, and due a raise. Mathew Barzal and Ryan Pulock were restricted free agents, too. The Islanders didn't have cap space to keep all three players.

Sakic sensed an opportunity. With ample cap space, he took advantage, trading a pair of second-round picks to New York. Islanders general manager Lou Lamoriello gave an honest assessment of the deal. "We made a transaction we would have preferred not to make," he said. Sakic, on the other hand, had found someone the team would turn into a top-pairing defenseman. By the end of the month, he had signed Toews to a four-year extension worth $4.1 million annually.

The move to Denver wasn't easy on Toews. As he noted in an introductory press conference held over Zoom, he had an exciting hockey opportunity ahead of him, but there was an emotional side to the trade, too. He had to say good-bye to his friends and to the only professional organization he'd ever known.

Eventually, though, Toews started to feel excited. He and Kerry adopted their dog, Riggins, and Colorado offered plenty of outdoor space for the pup. When the young family arrived in Denver, Devon was reminded of his hometown of Abbotsford, British Columbia, just outside Vancouver.

"This kind of caters more to home than New York does to me," he said.

On the ice, he quickly settled in with a new defensive partner in Makar. They met up within a week of Toews arriving, and though he liked Makar right away, it took time to get the young, reserved defensemen out of his shell. Two years later, after plenty of time together, Toews bragged about his ability to do it: he claimed to be one of the best at making Makar "comfortable and smiley and having fun."

The two were potent together in games. Toews prides himself on his hockey sense. Both he and Makar are capable of jumping into offensive play. They scored at career-best rates in Toews's first season with the Avalanche, and Makar finished second in voting for the Norris Trophy, given to the league's top defenseman. Toews wasn't far behind at 11th.

By the time the 2021–22 season rolled around, they were arguably the best tandem of defensemen in the NHL. Sakic's opportunistic acquisition had already paid off, and it only looked better as more time passed.

"I'm not sure if the Islanders regret that [trade]," one NHL executive said. "But I suspect they do."

Toews was on the ice for more Avalanche goals scored than allowed in each of his first nine games in 2021–22. He picked up his first goal of the year on a long-range slap shot in his second contest. The Avalanche crushed the Canucks 7–1 that night, then rattled off wins against San Jose, Vancouver again, Seattle, Ottawa, and Anaheim.

With Toews, the pinnacle of reliability, back in the lineup, they looked like themselves again.

• • •

The Avalanche outscored opponents a combined 36–15 during their six-game win streak. Ball Arena DJ Craig Turney played the children's song "Baby Shark" during a 6–2 blowout against the Sharks.

During the high-scoring stretch, Colorado underwent key roster developments, one of which was cause for major concern. Bowen Byram took an accidental Bo Horvat elbow to the head in the first Canucks game, leaving him concussed. It was an alarming interruption to an encouraging start to Byram's first full NHL season, especially after a pair of head injuries ended his 2020–21 season early. Now 2021–22 was in doubt.

"There were many times throughout it I thought of not playing again," said Byram, who played only seven of Colorado's next 58 games.

Nathan MacKinnon also missed time in November, sitting out three weeks with a lower-body injury, and the Avalanche made an addition, claiming depth forward Nicolas Aubé-Kubel off waivers from Philadelphia. He had struggled with the Flyers, taking too many penalties and failing to produce offensively. But Colorado thought he had been on the right path earlier in his career. Aubé-Kubel had a promising 2019–20 season as a 23-year-old, establishing himself as a strong forechecking presence, and the Avalanche front office believed it could help bring along his offensive skill.

Sure enough, Aubé-Kubel scored against Seattle in his second game with the Avalanche, batting a rebound past former Colorado netminder Philipp Grubauer, who was off to a brutal start while adjusting to a new system and weaker supporting cast.

Sakic also signaled faith in Bednar, signing him to a two-year contract extension. The front office wasn't dissuaded by the disappointing loss in the Vegas series, and talks had started during training camp. Sakic doesn't look to make changes for the sake of change, and he viewed Bednar as someone with a good pulse on the team and whom players respected.

"You keep those guys," he said.

The general manager had taken care of an important piece of office business, but on the ice, his new goaltender still wasn't settled. Kuemper's numbers were better than Grubauer's—his save percentage was sitting at a respectable .915 after the November 19 Seattle game, compared to Grubauer's .875—but he was still adjusting to a new system, breaking down video and working with coach Jussi Parkkila at practice.

Colorado had yet to see Kuemper's best, and his equipment did him no favors. He started having trouble with his skate blade holder the week of Thanksgiving. The blade fell off against Ottawa, and with Pavel Francouz still recovering from his ankle injury, No. 3 netminder Jonas Johansson replaced the starter briefly. Kuemper returned to finish off the game but struggled, ending the night with five goals allowed in a narrow win.

In a turn of events that caused Bednar to laugh in exasperation, Kuemper's skate blade fell out again two nights later against Anaheim, causing him to lose his balance and allow a goal. "Again!?" Bednar said on the bench. He'd seen a goalie skate blade fall off before, but never in back-to-back games. Again Kuemper reentered the game, but the blade fell out once more before the second period. At that point, Bednar decided to let Johansson and his two working skate blade holders finish the contest, which the Avalanche won. Makar scored his sixth goal in four games, and Nazem Kadri continued his fast start to the season with a power play tally.

Kuemper switched to a different brand of skate blade holder. "Hopefully those holders don't give us some problems, or I don't know what the solution will be," Bednar laughed. Fortunately for the netminder, the blade issues were finally behind him, though the team lost to Dallas in his next start.

Behind a Mikko Rantanen hat trick and three Makar assists, Colorado closed out the month with a 6–2 win against the Predators. Since the back-to-back Columbus losses and the ensuing team meeting, the Avalanche were 7–1–0.

Firing on all cylinders? Perhaps not. But looking like a contender? Absolutely.

"UNIQUE IN HIS PACKAGE"

COLORADO CROSSED the border for an early December contest in hockey-crazed Toronto. Nathan MacKinnon returned from a lower-body injury for the game, and it was supposed to be an exciting matchup of elite teams. The Maple Leafs were off to one of the best starts in the league, featuring a roster headlined by Auston Matthews, who was in the midst of what would be an MVP season.

Instead, the day turned out to be a lopsided disaster for the Avalanche, starting with a deteriorating goalie situation in the morning that became extreme as puck-drop approached in the evening. Following morning skate, Jared Bednar learned Darcy Kuemper was dealing with an upper-body injury and wouldn't be available. With Pavel Francouz still recovering from his ankle injury, the coach penciled Jonas Johansson in as starter. The front office called on 21-year-old Justus Annunen from the minors to back up.

One problem: Annunen's flight didn't get in until around the start of the game. So while he rushed to the arena during the first period, the Avalanche turned to a University of Toronto goalie named Jett Alexander to back up Johansson. The NHL allows for an emergency backup if a team has an injured goaltender and a minor league goalie can't get to the arena in time. Alexander was the designated EBUG in Toronto for the evening.

An environmental science student, Alexander managed to finish a biology assignment in time to get to the rink on time, then took the ice for warm-ups, getting stick taps from MacKinnon and Gabriel Landeskog. When Johansson finished getting his pregame reps in, Alexander stood between the pipes, managing to save a

54

couple shots from Avalanche players warming up. After growing up a Leafs fan, he called it surreal being on the ice with both star-studded teams, as well as seeing himself on the jumbotron. He ended up backing up Johansson for one period until Annunen arrived at the rink.

Alexander, who sipped a beer from the upper bowl after changing out of his uniform, enjoyed the game much more than Colorado's regulars. Johansson allowed three goals to Toronto before the Avalanche got on the board, and Bednar's players never found their footing, losing 8–3. Landeskog called the loss a reality check—an example of what happens when a team doesn't prioritize its defensive game.

The Avalanche bounced back over the rest of the five-game road trip. They beat Montreal and collected an overtime point in a loss to Ottawa. With that, the Avalanche crossed the border for games in Philadelphia and New York.

The Flyers were off to a horrible start and fired coach Alain Vigneault the morning of the Avalanche game, leading a stadium worker to say to a reporter just arriving for the game, "The only thing that should be covering this team is a blanket." Colorado won easily in Annunen's first NHL start.

The New York Rangers were a tougher, playoff-bound opponent, and the Avalanche took it to them, tallying five second period goals. MacKinnon scored one of his most impressive regular season goals, darting around defenseman K'Andre Miller and using one hand to poke the puck through goalie Adam Huska's legs. It was a much-needed score for the star center, who was racking up assists but had only one goal in 12 games before the evening at Madison Square Garden.

Kuemper returned from his injury for the Rangers game. He'd had an up-and-down start to the season but, beginning with the game in Manhattan, appeared better adjusted to the Avalanche's style of play. From then on, he was one of the league's top goaltenders, posting a .926 save percentage the rest of the regular season—the second-best mark in the league. Teammate Erik Johnson saw the road trip as a turning point in his season.

Rick Tocchet coached Kuemper in Arizona and holds his former goalie in high regard. The coach noted that, since Colorado's team exceled at holding onto the puck, Kuemper often went through long stretches of inactivity. That was a change for the goalie, who came to Colorado from a Coyotes team that allowed the second-most shots in the league in 2020–21.

"He's adjusted as the year's gone on," said Tocchet, who fully endorsed the goaltender in a conversation with Joe Sakic heading into the season. "He just seems more comfortable."

And with as talented a group of skaters as the Avalanche had, more consistent goaltending was enough for the team to really start rolling. The Panthers, who would go on to win the Presidents' Trophy for the best regular season record, came to Denver midway through December, and Kuemper made 29 saves in a 3–2 Avalanche win. He robbed Patric Hornqvist while Colorado was on the penalty kill, then Owen Tippett in the slot during the second period. Bednar praised his goalie's rebound control after the game, and Colorado pulled out a win in a close contest.

"We can't score seven goals every game," Kuemper said. "That was a really good game of hockey tonight. You could see the urgency on both sides."

That urgency gave the game a playoff-type feel. The intensity ramped up after a Ryan Lomberg second-period hit knocked out Colorado's Jacob MacDonald. Nicolas Aubé-Kubel, who had been on the roster for less than a month, came to his teammate's defense, dropping his gloves to fight Lomberg and ultimately pinning the Florida forward to the ice.

McDonald, meanwhile, left the rink on a stretcher. By the letter of the rule, Lomberg's hit was legal, but it raised difficult questions. Could Lomberg have done something differently, or was MacDonald at fault for leaving himself in a vulnerable position? Are there ways to change the rules to lessen the risk of head injuries?

Physicality is an essential part of hockey, Erik Johnson said, but he added it's bad for the sport when hits force players to leave via stretcher. He didn't like Lomberg's hit and thought it might have warranted a charging penalty. But mostly he was worried for MacDonald. He felt sick to his stomach.

The hit added a level of emotion to the game, which was 0–0 when MacDonald left the rink. André Burakovsky showed how potent a scorer he can be when in the zone, putting Colorado up with a pair of goals. Then, after Florida tied the score in the third, Burakovsky scored with a shot MacKinnon said not many players in the league can pull off. The Swedish winger managed to create a slight shooting angle while defended by Florida star Aaron Ekblad, then fired a shot with enough precision and velocity to get past Sergei Bobrovsky. It was arguably Burakovsky's most impactful moment of the season, though that would change come the Stanley Cup Final.

That stood as the game-winning tally, in large part because of an Erik Johnson play in the game's final minute. During a scramble in front of the net with 12 seconds left, a Sam Reinhart shot squeaked behind Kuemper, but Johnson saw it just in time to bat it back, tucking it under his goalie's body to freeze play. The defenseman called his save a desperation play, the sort of competitive moment for which athletes live. But Johnson's postgame comments also indicated a mindset pervasive through the team. "Those are the types of games that you need to win come playoff time," he said. Every game like the Florida one had to be preparation for the most important time of year.

The Avalanche pulled out another close victory two nights later against the Rangers, giving the team five wins in a row. Colorado was rolling, and the only thing that seemed capable of slowing it down was the ongoing pandemic. With Devon Toews already in COVID-19 protocol, Burakovsky and J.T. Compher tested positive after the Rangers game. Colorado didn't have enough salary cap space to bring up enough players to fill a full lineup for its game December 16 against Nashville, so only 19 players were in the lineup, one fewer than normal.

That number soon got lower. As the Avalanche were at the rink preparing for the game, some of their rapid tests came back positive. Trainer Matt Sokolowski walked into the dressing room to inform players.

"It was like the grim reaper walking in the room," Jack Johnson said.

First, Kuemper tested positive, meaning the Avalanche had to dress another emergency backup goaltender, this time 33-year-old Dustin Smith, formerly of the Middle Tennessee State club hockey team. Then Sokolowski pulled Cale Makar and Jack Johnson from the dressing room with both players half-dressed in their gear. They had returned initial positive tests. The team tested them again, hoping they had returned false positives. Makar's second test came back positive, meaning he was out of the game, but Johnson tested negative two times, which allowed him to play.

The Predators also had players unavailable with positive tests, as well as their entire coaching staff. Nick Cousins, one of the Nashville players to miss the game with a positive test, tweeted that the NHL should pause the season until after Christmas. "[It's] not fair to players to play with this hanging over [their] heads," he told The Athletic's Adam Vingan.

But the teams played, with Nashville winning 5–2. There wasn't much to learn from a game between two COVID-19–riddled clubs, but on an encouraging note for Colorado, Francouz was able to make his first start of the year. His return spelled the end of Johansson's season in Colorado. The Avalanche put him on waivers, and Florida claimed him.

Before the game, as the Avalanche learned of their positive tests, the league alerted the team it could decide whether or not to play. Bednar relayed the choice to his already-dressed players. Their thought process was simple.

"If you ask a group of hockey players if you want to play the game or not, they're pretty much never going to say 'no,'" said Jack Johnson, who missed most of the first period while waiting for his COVID-19 test to come back. "You're going to need a third party to make an objective decision and end it."

That's what happened after the Predators game. The NHL shut down Colorado's season until January 2 as further positive COVID-19 tests flooded in. On December 26, the Avalanche announced 11 players had tested positive for the virus since December 16, the day of the game in Nashville.

So the Avalanche headed into an elongated holiday break with a 17–8–2 record. Nazem Kadri was off to a torrid start, first on the team with 38 points, and Valeri Nichushkin looked more than comfortable in a bigger role than he'd played the season before.

And leading the team with 14 goals was a player sometimes overshadowed by MacKinnon, Makar, and his other star teammates—one who had nevertheless developed into one of the most consistent wingers in the league: Mikko Rantanen.

• • •

In Denver, comparisons to Peter Forsberg aren't taken lightly. That's especially true when they come from the mouth of Joe Sakic, who played with the Swedish great for 10 seasons.

Forsberg's combination of force and skill made him a generational player. And while injuries limited him to only 708 NHL games, he made the most of his healthy days, winning two Stanley Cups with the Avalanche as well as the 2003 Hart Trophy for league MVP. That, combined with his international heroics for the Swedish National Team, made him a no-doubt Hall of Famer.

Knowing all of that, Sakic didn't hesitate to bring up his former teammate when discussing Rantanen. He sees similarities to Forsberg, especially in how difficult it is for defenders to separate him from the puck. The general manager raved about Rantanen's hockey sense entering the season, calling him one of the best players in the league. It wasn't an exaggeration, especially considering Rantanen led the league in plus-minus rating in 2020–21 and finished in the top 10 of the MVP voting.

Rantanen's contract reflects that level of play. Entering the 2019–20 season, Sakic signed him to a six-year, $55.5 million deal, and his $9.25 million annual hit against the salary cap was highest of anyone on the 2021–22 roster. He's been worth every cent.

Landeskog, who grew up idolizing Forsberg in Sweden, agrees with the parallels between Rantanen and the Hall of Famer, adding

Colorado right winger Mikko Rantanen, at Ball Arena in April 2022, led the Avalanche in 2021–22 with a career-high 92 points.

that, when watching his teammate, he also sees shades of Penguins star Evgeni Malkin, a three-time Cup champion and former MVP.

"But Mikko is his own player," Landeskog said, bringing up his skating, passing ability, and 6′4″ frame. "Mikko is so unique in his package."

Size wasn't always an advantage for Rantanen, who grew up just outside of Turku, Finland, the third-largest urban area in the country. He doesn't remember thinking much about playing in the NHL until he was a teenager, when he grew six inches in two years. The sudden growth spurt initially messed with his on-ice coordination, but he said he found his game around age 16. Around that time, he started playing in Finland's top professional league. Everyone knew he'd play in the NHL someday, remembers Ville Touru, a Finnish sports reporter.

Sure enough, the Avalanche picked Rantanen 10th overall in the 2015 NHL Draft, and he had one of his career highlights the following season. He played for the Finnish team that won the 2016 World Junior Championships, which were hosted in his native country. Within hockey-crazed countries, the World Junior Championships are a huge deal, similar to NCAA basketball's March Madness in the United States. Rantanen captained a star-studded Finnish roster that featured future NHL standouts Patrik Laine, Sebastian Aho, and Roope Hintz. In the gold medal game against Russia, he scored a go-ahead goal with two-minutes left, only to see the Russians tie the game with six seconds on the clock. His teammates recalled his poise heading into overtime, and that set the tone for the whole team, Aho said.

Sure enough, Finland kept its cool in overtime. Kasperi Kapanen scored the winner less than two minutes into the period. Rantanen won the Finnish player of the game award, and he smiled for a picture with Hall of Famer Teemu Selänne. Then, after the medal ceremony, he hoisted the championship trophy, the Helsinki crowd roaring behind him.

It was the best experience of his hockey career, he said, though that would change during the Avalanche's 2021–22 playoff run. Hoisting the Stanley Cup has that effect.

Bednar both trusts and respects Rantanen. When Erik Johnson, one of the team's alternate captains, was hurt for all but four games in 2020–21, the Avalanche coach put an *A* on his top-line right wing's jersey. Heading into 2021–22, Bednar called Rantanen to tell him that, even with Johnson coming back, the 25-year-old would continue as alternate captain.

Now the team's three top forwards—captain Gabriel Landeskog, alternates Nathan MacKinnon and Rantanen—all had letters. It was a subtle change but one that mattered.

"As a kid, you dream about the NHL, but you don't really think that you're ever going to play there," Rantanen said. "All of a sudden, you're a core player. Then you get an *A* on your sweater. It was a pretty special moment."

That meant Johnson, at the time the longest-tenured Denver athlete among Denvver's major league teams, no longer had a letter on his chest. But what could have been a thorny transition didn't carry any awkwardness. Rantanen said Johnson took the change well. The defenseman was simply excited to be back playing after missing the previous season.

Avalanche radio announcer Conor McGahey and TV broadcaster Marc Moser both regularly call Rantanen "the Moose" on the air, a nod to his large size. And at an open practice during the season, a young girl came to the rink wearing inflatable moose antlers in his honor.

When around teammates, Rantanen is an energetic, at times goofy presence. At one practice, he lifted a nifty backhand shot past Kuemper, then immediately skated toward a team photographer to ask if she had snapped pictures of his move. When she said she hadn't, he jokingly slapped the glass in front of them. Later in the skate, he poured water on André Burakovsky's head.

"He's like a little kid in a big boy's body," fellow Finn Artturi Lehkonen said.

Rantanen is principled, too. During the 2020–21 season, the NHL fined him $2,000 for embellishment. Rantanen had accepted a similar fine in 2018, and he didn't have a problem with that punishment. He knew he'd dived to try to draw a penalty. This time was different. He said he toepicked—meaning he fell because the toes of his skate hit the ice at a sharp angle—and did not intentionally flop.

So Rantanen took matters into his own hands. He didn't want people around the game to see him as someone who flopped in search of penalties. "It's not a good look for a hockey player to get an embellishment fine," Rantanen said. "It was not about the money."

It was about pride. He wrote an email back to the league, explaining the play and arguing his case. Sure enough, they saw his points and rescinded the fine. Rantanen's Avalanche teammates read through his email and were impressed, some joking that he could consider going to law school. An interesting idea, but hockey seems to be treating him just fine.

"WATCHING GREATNESS"

ENTERING THE 2021–22 season, no defenseman had scored more than 30 goals in a season since Washington's Mike Green in 2008–09. As the Avalanche climbed the standings, Cale Makar gave himself a chance to break that streak, buoyed by an explosive November. He missed the first two games of the month with an upper body injury, then put up 14 points, including seven goals, over the final eight. After one of those games, a win against Nashville, a fan threw a head of kale onto the ice. Grinning, the 23-year-old phenom picked it up and raised it for the crowd to see.

During Makar's first two full seasons in the league, Bednar encouraged him to shoot more. The coaching staff loves his wrist shot, and his elite skating ability helps create shooting lanes. The message seemed to get through to Makar early in 2021–22, as his shot attempts skyrocketed. When Bednar watched his scoring spree, he pointed to that as the main cause.

Through December, Makar had 13 goals in 23 games, a 46-goal pace for an 82-game season. He downplayed his gaudy numbers whenever they were brought up, but both Bednar and MacKinnon viewed the 30-goal plateau as within reach. Green did, too. The former Capitals defenseman thought he had a chance to go well beyond.

"I hope he gets 40, to be honest," he said. "And I think he's capable."

Makar wasn't simply putting up numbers. He was making opponents look like fools. During a December game in Philadelphia, he grabbed the puck behind the net, then galloped up ice. At center ice, he sped up, then cut past Ivan Provorov as he neared the net. At the last possible moment, he lifted the puck, beating goaltender Martin Jones to complete the end-to-end tally.

Nazem Kadri laughed, as if in disbelief, when he celebrated with Makar on ice after the goal. "Bobby!" Erik Johnson called from the bench, referencing Bobby Orr, widely considered the greatest defenseman ever. Makar, meanwhile, didn't even crack a smile. He simply breathed heavily and accepted his teammates' congratulations.

"We're lucky because we're watching greatness," Johnson said later in the season.

Less than a month later, in Colorado's second game back from its COVID-19 pause, Makar found a way to one-up the Philadelphia goal. With the Avalanche in overtime against Chicago, Makar skated behind the net, defended by Kirby Dach. He moved along the glass, past the offensive zone faceoff circle. As he skated with the puck, he noticed Dach's positioning. He was overcommitting in hopes of stopping Makar from cycling the puck toward the top of the offensive zone.

Makar saw a window which few skaters in the world would be able to open. He halted, then spun back to the net in one motion, leaving Dach in his wake. As he skated toward goaltender Marc-André Fleury, he looked for a chance to pass to MacKinnon. But Chicago's Philipp Kurashev was blocking the star center in front of the net.

That left only one option for Makar: beat Fleury and his Hall of Fame–caliber résumé by himself. As he approached the net, he shifted the puck from his forehand to his backhand, then lifted it past the goaltender. There was nothing Fleury could do.

Normally mild-mannered, Makar let out a celebration this time. As his momentum carried him behind the net, he dropped to a knee and uppercutted the air before turning with a smile to his teammates. Even opposing players made a nod toward the game-winning goal. Chicago's Calvin de Haan said it would be "all over NHL Network" the next day. He was right.

This wasn't a normal play. It was one befitting a generational talent.

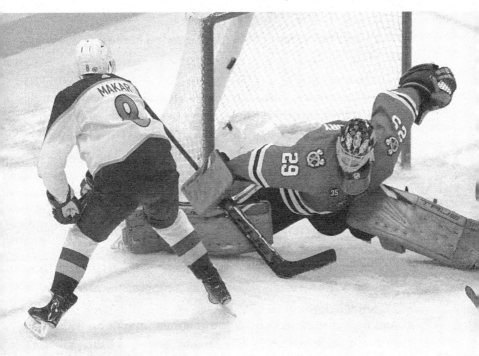

Colorado's Cale Makar lifts the puck past Blackhawks goalie Marc-André Fleury for the game-winner in overtime on January 4, 2022, in Chicago. Makar would win the 2022 Norris Trophy as the NHL's best defenseman.

• • •

"Not many teams have a No. 1 defenseman," MacKinnon said. "And we have the best one."

• • •

At Makar's childhood home in Calgary, his parents keep a school project he turned in when he was 10. It's an autobiography dated November 4, 2008, with a headshot of young Cale on the cover. He's smiling with closed lips, his hair neatly straightened across his forehead.

Cale's Amazing Life, it's called.

The typed, multi-page project is stapled twice in the upper left-hand corner and starts with an introduction detailing the pages to come.

"I have had a pretty great life so far and I'd like to tell you about it," Makar wrote.

His words provide insight into both his background and dreams. He was named for a hockey player—Cale Hulse, a Calgary Flames player at the time of his birth—and his writing makes sure to point out that the defenseman played 12 years in the NHL. Makar really liked his name; it's a shortened form of Caleb and "probably stands for faithful or loyal," he wrote.

The 10-year-old expressed interest in becoming an engineer, explaining that he enjoyed creativity, drawing, science, and math. He mentions the importance of getting good grades, then gets into the aspiration that truly gripped his heart.

"My real dream is to be a hockey player in the NHL, and I am working very hard on my skills to make it happen," the page reads.

On one page, Makar taped a hockey card of himself from his youth team, the Blackhawks, showing him in uniform with that same, closed-lipped smile. His parents, Gary and Laura, saw his love for hockey at a young age when they watched him play with mini sticks in the kitchen. That led them to put their youngster in organized hockey. "I still love it!" Makar made sure to note in the project.

But hockey wasn't his only sport. He played soccer in the spring and, at the time of his 10-year-old autobiography, had recently picked up badminton. The pictures he included, though, almost exclusively show him in skates. Along with the Blackhawks card, there is a 2008 youth hockey card from the Southern Alberta Selects, an action photo of him on the ice, and even a picture of Hulse in a Flames jersey, his face locked in concentration.

And when he got to the page about his collections, he listed three: medals (which he misspelled as "metals"), trophies, and hockey cards. He displayed his trophies and medals, won in tournaments and shootout competitions, on the shelves in his room, and his writing mentions why he enjoyed hockey cards: "because it's fun to look at the player's stats and picture and how many years they played for."

"Maybe one day," he wrote, "I'll play in the NHL and people will collect hockey cards of me."

• • •

Makar wasn't a prodigy. Hockey Canada didn't invite him to camps when he was young, and he wasn't drafted into major junior hockey until the eighth round of the 2013 Western Hockey League Bantam Draft. He was only around 125 pounds at the time and admitted in a post-draft interview that, given his size, he was surprised a team even selected him.

Though Makar's skating may be up there with the best in the world now, he didn't go to private skating coaches. Instead, he discovered his creativity as a kid on outdoor rinks. And he always played on teams that encouraged him to jump into offensive play as a defenseman.

"Even when I was young, it was pretty abnormal [for a defenseman] to be all over the ice," Makar said. "I was fortunate to have great coaches that allowed me to use my skating abilities and play the game I want rather than just being that stay-at-home guy."

If Makar had decided to play major junior hockey with Medicine Hat, the team that drafted him, he would have forfeited his eligibility to play NCAA hockey. But there was another option. He could play in the Alberta junior league, a step below major junior, without jeopardizing his ability to get a hockey scholarship in the U.S.

And fortunately for Makar, one of the best AJHL teams—the Bandits—was located in Brooks, Alberta, around two hours from his hometown of Calgary.

When Bandits coach Ryan Papaioannou went to scout a youth Calgary Flames game in 2014, he had no clue who Makar was. But in warmups, the coach saw something special in the small, rosy-cheeked defenseman. It didn't matter that he might have looked like somebody's younger brother. His skating popped. His hands were deceptive and quick. He simply wasn't like the other players.

Papaioannou saw enough to offer Makar a chance to join the team for the end of the 2014–15 season and playoffs. Mark Logan,

Makar's cousin, was on the team at the time and spoke highly of it, so Makar jumped at the opportunity. With a baby face, he took the ice in Brooks' bright red jerseys, standing a half-head shorter than Logan in pregame lineup introductions.

"Oh my God, he's going to get killed out there!" Gary thought when he saw his son on the ice.

Fortunately, you can't get killed if no one can catch you. That was the case with Makar. Papaioannou thought the youngster looked great in his callup, even if he was smaller than everyone around him. He had the confidence to try things most of his older teammates wouldn't think about, be it toe-dragging around players or going one-on-one with opponents at the blue line. He finished the post-season with seven points in 20 games to add to his five points in three regular season contests.

His confidence went up, Gary said. He saw he could play in this league.

That off-season marked an important decision for Makar. He could continue playing with Brooks, putting him in position to play NCAA hockey, or he could join Medicine Hat and play in the WHL. Though they took time to discuss it, the Makar family had already viewed continuing in the AJHL as the best route for Cale. Gary reasoned it gave his son a longer runway to develop. He would have his time in Brooks, then could spend up to four years in college to grow his game. He'd be exposed to scouts the whole time. And so Cale and Gary called Papaioannou, confirming he would continue with the Bandits.

Heading into the 2015–16 season, his first full year at the AJHL level, Makar committed to play collegiately at UMass Amherst. But with their new commit tracking their games from Alberta, the Minutemen had a miserable year, winning only eight games. They fired head coach John Micheletto, who had recruited Makar, and replaced him in March 2016 with Greg Carvel.

The UMass athletic director immediately told the new coach to get in touch with Makar, who still had a season left with the Bandits. So Carvel flew to Alberta to watch Makar play, and before warm-ups were over, the coach was on the phone with his assistants. Makar already reminded him of elite NHL defensemen.

"We have Erik Karlsson coming to our program," he said into his phone, referencing the then Senators star, who had already won the Norris Trophy twice as the top defenseman in the league.

Makar moved with ease across the ice, his speed too much for his poor AJHL opponents to handle. Goalies were no match for his wrist shot, and he averaged more than a point per game the first of his two full years in Brooks. During that time, he lived with billet parents Adam and Ashley Herman. Once, while the couple was out for a night, Makar and teammate Will Conley heard a loud bang outside the house. They called the Hermans, explaining the noise, and when Adam and Ashley came home, they found that a car had crashed into their fence.

Ashley showed a picture of the damage to Makar and Conley. They had yet to leave the basement where their bedrooms were. They were too scared. Makar might have been a rising hockey star, but he was still a teenager living away from his parents for the first time.

The next season, Makar's second and final with Brooks, he was joined at the Herman house by defenseman Dennis Cesana, who would go on to become a captain at Michigan State. Cesana first remembered watching Makar during summer training and had a thought shared by many who saw Makar play. He turned to teammate Joe O'Connor and asked, "Who is this guy?"

"You don't know Cale, bro?" O'Connor said. "He's pretty nasty."

That year, especially. In 54 games, Makar put up 75 points, including 24 goals, one of which in particular jumped out to his father. Playing on the road against Portage in May 2017, Makar and his Bandits teammates took the ice for a five-on-three power play. O'Connor fed a pass to a charging Makar in the faceoff circle, and the defenseman pulverized the puck with a one-time slapshot.

The rubber disk didn't simply fly past the goaltender. It lodged in the net. Two officials had to skate to the crease and pull the puck out from the twine.

"I remember him not really celebrating or anything," teammate Oliver Chau said. "That was one of the craziest things that I've seen." Though Makar was the league MVP that season and carried the Bandits all the way to the 2017 National Junior A Championship Game, he still had deficiencies, especially on the defensive end. His teammates didn't have much to criticize on the ice, but Chau recalled giving him grief for his poor gaps—the amount of distance between a defender and his opponent. Makar often played too far away from offensive players despite being, in Papaioannou eyes, the best skater in the country.

None of that deterred professional teams, especially when they watched Makar dominate at the 2016 World Junior A Challenge. He finished the tournament with eight points in four games for Team West Canada. His NHL Draft stock skyrocketed.

Papaioannou said he heard from interested NHL clubs as the season went on. Teams with top-15 picks in the first round started reaching out. Then teams in the top 10. By the time the draft rolled around, teams picking later in the first round didn't even bother calling. They knew he'd be long gone by then.

"Wow," the coach thought, "he must be better than we think."

And someday, time would tell, better than those teams could have imagined.

• • •

About 100 miles from Brooks, Wade Klippenstein had a decision to make as Makar entered his final season with the Bandits.

Forty-six years old at the time, Klippenstein had spent the past three years as director of scouting for the Brandon Wheat Kings in the Western Hockey major junior league. Now, with Kelly McCrimmon leaving for the Vegas Golden Knights front office, he had the chance to take over as Brandon's general manager. It was an excellent opportunity, one Klippenstein initially leaned toward accepting. But it didn't quite feel right. He didn't want to move from his home in Lethbridge, Alberta. He could stay there as a scout but would have to relocate to Brandon if he was named the Wheat Kings' GM.

The Avalanche were hiring around the same time, so Klippenstein interviewed for a scouting gig. The team offered him a job focused primarily on junior leagues in Western Canada. He accepted, saying good-bye to the Wheat Kings organization.

Colorado was lucky he did.

Klippenstein's house was only a 90-minute drive from where Makar played in Brooks, and the scout frequently zipped over to the nearby town, speeding enough to cut 15 minutes off the expected arrival time. Klippenstein quickly realized Makar was the best player on the ice, but the scout said it was hard to gauge his actual talent because of the inconsistent competition level in the AJHL. In a report emailed to then amateur scouting director Alan Heppel in September 2016, Klippenstein called him "a top-three round pick at first viewing." He wrote that Makar was undersized with defensive deficiencies, and his passing still had to progress. But he was dynamic with elite skating ability. That shined through from the beginning.

Makar wasn't playing against bunches of future NHLers, like he would have had he gone to Medicine Hat in the Western Hockey League. In Canada, Junior A players always have the burden of proof, Klippenstein said. They have to work their way into the top round. They have to push others out.

The Avalanche, meanwhile, were playing terribly, en route to the NHL's worst record and therefore the league's best draft lottery odds. Klippenstein knew they'd have a high pick, likely in the top 10. Makar wasn't someone he saw in that range.

But in December, 2016, the young defenseman started making waves representing Canada West at the Junior A Challenge. Then, one night in April, Klippenstein traveled to watch the defenseman play a game in Okotoks, Alberta, and he estimated there were 30 representatives from NHL clubs present. Not just area scouts, either. There were general managers and assistant general managers and head scouts for teams picking in the draft lottery. These weren't people who would waste their time on someone they weren't considering taking.

Makar showed out that night, and on his drive back to Lethbridge, Klippenstein thought to himself that the defenseman was a top-10 pick. In his report from the game, he wrote that Makar made nine good plays and only one bad one, a turnover under pressure. He had solidified himself as the No. 1 skilled defenseman in the draft.

"Nobody skates like this guy and no one can match his pace of play," Klippenstein's emailed Heppel. "Top-10 NHL pick right now!!!"

That meant he was in Colorado's draft range. Up to that point, Klippenstein had been cautious about banging the table too hard for Makar. It was his first year with the team, and he didn't want to come in blazing to meetings, telling his new coworkers they were going to fall in love with a Junior A player. But the scout's mindset shifted after the night in Okotoks.

This was a special player.

That occasionally put Klippenstein in uncomfortable situations. Cal Foote, son of Avalanche great Adam Foote, was one of the highest-rated defensemen in that year's draft class, and he was also in Klippenstein's scouting region, playing major junior in Kelowna.

"To confidently say, 'I feel Cale Makar is a better fit for what we need and I think he's a player we need to select,' that wasn't easy," said Klippenstein, who was promoted to director of amateur scouting ahead of the 2021–22 season.

The Avalanche also caught a break, though it didn't seem like it at the time. They lost the draft lottery and were awarded the fourth-overall pick, not the first. Makar's stock was trending up, and other Avalanche scouts had watched him play, but Colorado likely wouldn't have taken Makar had it received a higher pick. Klippenstein sensed that most of the team's scouts and decision-makers viewed Finnish standout Miro Heiskanen as the top defenseman in the draft.

"He wasn't in a lot of conversations when we thought we were picking No. 1," Klippenstein said. Heppel expressed a similar sentiment in an interview with NHL.com, saying he's not sure Colorado would have taken Makar first overall.

But Klippenstein's final report from a Makar game, written off a May 6, 2017, contest, reiterated that Makar was worthy of a top-10 selection. He was the first defenseman who should be selected out of western Canada, Klippenstein wrote. And maybe the world.

A month and a half later, Makar arrived at the draft at the United Center in Chicago wearing a blue suit purchased from O'Connors, a Calgary menswear store owned by the family of Logan O'Connor, Makar's future Avalanche teammate. And after Dallas drafted Heiskanen at No. 3, Heppel tapped Klippenstein on the shoulder and told him the Avalanche were taking the Brooks defenseman he scouted.

"All of a sudden things got very real for me," Klippenstein said.

Gary Makar's phone started blowing up as the pick was announced, and the Avalanche invited Cale and his family to a stadium suite. He posed for pictures with his dad and Sakic. Makar's smile was wide, and his cheeks were rosy as ever.

• • •

For as much of a show as Makar can put on while playing hockey, he doesn't consider himself particularly splashy away from the rink. He's reserved. It takes time and comfort for him to open up. But when he arrived at UMass, shortly after the Avalanche drafted him, he wanted to surprise his new teammates. Every year, the Minutemen have a bonding day during which the team plays a round of golf at a local country club, then, over a meal, holds a freshman talent show on the patio. A few days before the event, Makar called his dad for help. He wanted to throw playful jabs at his new teammates and coaches. And he wanted to do it in the form of a rap.

So together, father and son composed the lyrics, one of which ribbed a teammate for objecting when others touched his shoes. When he got on the stage and performed, his rap had the desired effect. Players were caught off guard. Makar spared no one, not even the coaches.

"It was honestly hilarious and was kind of what we needed to start to feel more comfortable and to feel integrated with the team more," said fellow freshman Oliver Chau, who played with Makar both in Brooks and at UMass.

Chau recognized Makar's brilliance early. Professor Richard Halgin, a clinical psychologist who met individually with UMass players, remembered Chau talking to him shortly after Makar arrived. Halgin found his words over the top at the time.

"I feel so privileged to play with the best player of my generation," Chau told him.

The statement was prescient.

Buoyed by Makar and a freshman class that also featured future NHLers in Chaffee, John Leonard, and Mario Ferraro, the Minutemen made strides in 2017–18, going 17–20–2, up from a five-win season the year before. Makar logged 21 points, second-best among team defensemen, and joined Team Canada at the 2018 World Junior Championships, where he won a gold medal. (The Canadian roster later came under scrutiny when, in 2022, a woman filed a statement of claim saying eight unnamed Canadian Hockey League Players, including members of the World Junior team, sexually assaulted her after a summer 2018 Hockey Canada award banquet. Makar never played in the Canadian Hockey League, going from Brooks to NCAA hockey, and told reporters he "wasn't one of the guys part of" the alleged assault. He added that he cooperated with Hockey Canada's investigation. At the time of this book's publication, the identities of the eight John Doe defendants were not known.)

During his freshman season, Makar also could have represented Canada at the 2018 Winter Olympics, but he turned down the opportunity. He believed that commitment, paired with World Juniors, would have been too much time away from UMass. Plus, he expected Team Canada would use him only for his offensive strengths, and it was key for his development to play in defensive situations, too. He could do that at UMass.

That wasn't the last time Makar prioritized development over a more glamorous opportunity. By the end of his freshman season, Colorado had seen enough to believe he was ready to turn professional. But Makar had talked with Carvel early his freshman year, and both agreed he'd likely need two college seasons before he was physically ready for the next level. He wanted to add strength and endurance. He had come to UMass as, in Carvel's words, "one of the weakest players on the team." The coach remembers his defenseman sometimes ran out of stamina playing back-to-back games his freshman year.

In Carvel's mind, a player should be over-ready before leaving college. After his freshman year, Makar was not. He listened to his coach and told the Avalanche he wanted to spend another year at UMass.

"Great decision by him," Colorado coach Jared Bednar said years later.

Along with being a key to his development, a second season on campus gave Makar another year as a college kid. He had fallen in love with stir fry at the Berkshire Dining Hall, usually having it with chicken and plenty of vegetables, and asked for it so much that the chef knew his order by heart. He enjoyed playing cribbage and cards with teammate Jake Gaudet, and he shot the breeze with John Leonard about *Hawaii Five-0*, a show they both liked.

And when freshman Colin Felix joined the team in Makar's second year, the two engaged in dorm room prank battles. The jokes started small but grew bigger and bigger. Once, Felix got into Makar's room and flipped over his bed, chair and everything on his desk. Makar rebutted by plastic-wrapping Felix's possessions, from his bed to his iPad.

"I swear I was finding things in my room wrapped up for a couple days," Felix said. "I never got him back after that. Pretty sure he was on the lookout."

Teammate Mitchell Chaffee said that, though you might not expect a fourth-overall NHL Draft pick to focus on his studies, Makar did. No one saw that more than his professor Halgin, who mentored Makar through independent study classes each semester during his sophomore year, the first on leadership and a second on self-understanding. The defenseman once walked through a snowstorm to meet with Halgin on time, even though campus was closed.

The professor was shocked as he opened his door to find the star hockey player in a maroon and gray winter hat.

Makar read six books for each independent study course, and analyzed each of them in a paper turned in to his professor. At the end of the semester, he wrote a research project about his findings.

Makar left for the Avalanche before the second semester of his sophomore year ended, but he made sure to stay on top of assignments from afar. Halgin said the defenseman emailed him the day after his NHL debut, earnestly asking for an extension. It had been a busy few days, he wrote in his message.

When Makar is invested in something, he gives it his full attention, whether it's hockey or schoolwork. He has an incredible capacity for focus, Halgin noticed in their time together. That went beyond the ice.

Hockey-wise, Makar took off during his sophomore season. In UMass' first game of the year, a 6–1 win against Rensselaer Polytechnic, Makar logged four points, but he seemed less than content postgame. He didn't believe he'd played to his standards.

"You could tell he wasn't satisfied," teammate Marc Del Gaizo said.

Satisfied or not, he kept filling up the statsheet, finishing the season with 49 points in 41 games and winning the Hobey Baker Trophy as college player of the year. Carvel had never seen a defenseman create so many breakaway attempts. Makar's speed made him a unicorn.

Students around campus took note. Once, someone approached Makar in the dining hall and asked him to sign a napkin. He wasn't yet famous, as he'd become with the Avalanche in the coming years, but he was starting to gain acclaim. This wasn't a typical athlete on a college campus. This was someone who could reach dramatic heights.

Led by Makar, the Minutemen reached the Frozen Four in Buffalo, an unthinkable feat given where the program was two years prior. But a storybook ending eluded the team. UMass reached the NCAA title game but fell to a better, more experienced Minnesota-Duluth squad.

"We were bright-eyed and not used to being there," Gaudet said. After the loss, Makar walked into his press conference still wearing his sweat-soaked maroon jersey. Though he deflected questions about whether he was turning professional, he knew his college career was done. He didn't want to take it off. To say good-bye.

• • •

As UMass players unwound in their Buffalo hotel following the Duluth defeat, they received a group text from Makar, inviting them to the building's conference room. The Avalanche, who were in the middle of their first-round playoff series, wanted their top prospect to go to Denver immediately. Now over-ready, like Carvel wanted, he was ready to sign the contract. But first he wanted his friends to come down for one final farewell.

Holding a blue pen, Makar wore a dark suit and sat at a small, circular table as his teammates gathered around him. They grinned for cameras as he prepared to sign his contract. In the wake of a disappointing loss, Makar's achievement gave the players reason to celebrate.

The next day, they went their separate ways. Makar's UMass teammates bussed back to Amherst as he flew to Denver, his professional career set to begin.

With the playoffs underway, the Avalanche were facing off with the Flames, Makar's hometown team. And as Bednar went through meetings with his new defenseman, he remembers sensing a quiet confidence. The 20-year-old calmly listened to the coach walk him through Colorado's style of play and game plan for Calgary. If he was overwhelmed, he didn't show it.

"It was just hockey," Makar said. "Just a different sweater."

Bednar put Makar in the lineup for Game 3, which took place only two days after the UMass-Duluth NCAA championship final. Ahead of Makar's debut, hordes of reporters swarmed his locker during interviews after morning skate. That night, the defenseman immediately proved the hype was warranted. Late in the first period, Nathan MacKinnon galloped through the neutral zone, then dropped the puck off to his new teammate in the slot. With Flames forward Mikael Backlund attempting to slow Makar, the Avalanche blueliner managed to get a shot on net. It slid through goaltender Mike Smith's pads.

"You can't write that stuff," Gary Makar said. "Somebody sprinkled magic lucky dust on you."

After the game, a little before midnight, as the elder Makar waited in the family room for his son, MacKinnon and Gabriel Landeskog walked in. Gary, a lifelong hockey fan, couldn't pass up the chance to ask them for a picture. As they posed together, Cale came around the corner. When he saw his dad, a mortified expression came to his face, one that—in Gary's eyes—read, "My dad, the biggest nerd on the planet, is taking a picture with MacKinnon and Landeskog."

Little did Gary know, his son's star might someday shine brighter than the franchise centerpieces posing next to him.

ALL THE SMALL THINGS

A TEAM'S LEVEL of play is never linear throughout a regular season. For clubs both good and bad, there are strings of losses mixed with stretches of eye-opening play with runs that make fans think their team might reach its ceiling.

But special groups usually leave hints of greatness along their regular season journey—moments to remember. They play games that show they have another gear, a level of talent or will or toughness that might not be normal, that might lead to trophies hoisted and dreams realized.

That's exactly what Colorado's home contest against Toronto was on January 8. The game's start was similar to the teams' matchup a month prior, with the Maple Leafs seizing a 3–0 lead 15 minutes in. A year earlier, the Avalanche likely would not have come back against this quality team. They didn't record a single comeback win when facing a three-goal deficit in 2020–21.

But with more than 17,000 fans watching at Ball Arena, the Avalanche showed they weren't the same team as the season before. They'd display that over and over in the month of January.

After the Leafs' third goal—superstar Auston Matthews's second of the evening—Jared Bednar pulled Darcy Kuemper from the game, replacing him with Pavel Francouz. The coach didn't blame Kuemper for the deficit; poor defensive play was the problem far more than the goalie. But the Leafs' skaters were playing with more competitive fire than Colorado was, and Bednar believed something needed to change. He thought a goalie swap might spark his team.

It did. The Avalanche picked up their intensity and tightened up defensively after the switch, limiting the shots Francouz faced. Nathan MacKinnon, who had lost Matthews in defensive coverage ahead of Toronto's second score, got a goal back late in the first. He beat Toronto goalie Jack Campbell from the slot, and that cut the deficit to two, giving the Avalanche a chance.

After trading goals with Toronto in the second period, Colorado entered the final 20 minutes of regulation down 4–2. That score stood until midway through the third, in large part because of Campbell, who laid out like a baseball outfielder to snatch a Devon Toews shot. Nazem Kadri, positioned next to the Maple Leafs' net, put his hands on his head and doubled over in disbelief. Speaking to reporters postgame, he called Campbell's play the save of the year.

But the Avalanche kept pushing. Less than a minute after Campbell robbed Toews, Gabriel Landeskog pulled the Avalanche to within a goal by barely squeaking a Mikko Rantanen pass over the goal line.

The score gave Rantanen his second assist of the game, and his third was even prettier. With 8:20 remaining in regulation, he grabbed the puck along the boards behind Campbell's net. Somehow, with his back facing the rest of the ice, he backhanded a pass between his legs, right to a waiting J.T. Compher. The center grew up playing baseball in the Chicago suburbs, and he one-timed the sliding puck as if it were a fastball in the batting cage. His shot hit Campbell in the back and went in. Rantanen is such a dynamic scorer that his playmaking sometimes gets overlooked, but it was on full display on Compher's goal.

The game was tied, until Toews got overtime revenge for his almost-goal. He got the puck from Rantanen at the top of the offensive zone, then noticed the Leafs still had tired skaters on the ice. With Matthews defending him, Toews passed to Kadri and darted toward the net, dusting the Leafs forward, and received the puck back from Kadri. Crossing the faceoff circle, Toews ripped a shot through Campbell's legs. The Avalanche had won 5–4.

"There's not many teams in the league that are able to keep these guys below four [goals] these days," Toronto coach Sheldon Keefe said.

The comeback was a lesson for the rest of the league: the Avalanche were rarely out of a game. In the COVID-19–truncated 2020–21, they logged comeback wins in 28 percent (11 of 39) of their victories. In 2021–22, Colorado finished its 56-win season with 23 comebacks (41 percent of their victories). It added another three-goal comeback in a February game against Winnipeg.

"Sometimes you just have that swagger," Landeskog said.

That mentality paid dividends—including in the playoffs.

Two nights after beating Toronto, the Avalanche completed another multi-goal comeback to upend Seattle. Then the team traveled to Nashville, the site of the bizarre, COVID-19–stricken game in December. Perhaps Colorado simply wasn't fated to have normal regular season games in Tennessee, because this one had its share of controversy and confusion, too.

Regulation went by normally enough. The Avalanche battled back from 2–0, 3–2, and 4–3 deficits, and the game went to a five-minute, three-on-three overtime period. But midway through it, referee Dean Morton raised his hand and blew his whistle to call a penalty, a bench minor on the Avalanche for having too many men on the ice. Morton said Rantanen hopped over the boards before MacKinnon was within five feet of the Avalanche bench.

Colorado's players were livid. André Burakovsky, who called the penalty "a terrible decision" by the referee, raised his arms from the bench, yelling at the officials. An exasperated Erik Johnson pleaded his case with Morton. Cale Makar said it was the most frustrated the Avalanche had been all year.

Dave Jackson, a former NHL referee now working as ESPN's rules analyst, tweeted his thoughts on the sequence. He pointed out that Rantanen had hopped onto the ice when MacKinnon was still 10–15 feet away. It's technically a penalty, he said, but one that is often ignored.

"Sixty to 70 percent of the [line] changes made in that game or any game are that bad or worse," Bednar said.

But Morton's call stood, and the Predators took the ice for a four-on-three power play. Roman Josi fired a shot on net, and when J.T. Compher blocked the puck, it bounced right to former Avalanche forward Matt Duchene. The veteran fired it past Kuemper, ending the game.

Normally, MacKinnon said, the Avalanche locker room is quiet after a loss. That night it wasn't. "What the hell just happened?!" players asked each other.

"We didn't know what was going on," MacKinnon said.

The Avalanche didn't know it at the time, but months down the line, they would find themselves in another "Too Many Men" controversy—one that favored Colorado. It would come at a far, far more consequential moment.

• • •

Kurtis MacDermid wasn't the Avalanche's best hockey player in 2021–22. He was among the team's slowest and least-skilled skaters, and he ranked low on the team in scoring and most advanced statistical categories.

None of that mattered to his teammates. Joe Sakic acquired him ahead of the season, sending the Seattle Kraken a fourth-round pick in return, and MacDermid's work ethic, toughness, and loyalty quickly made him a beloved figure in the Colorado dressing room. "Dermy loves violence," MacKinnon said after MacDermid fought Ryan Reaves earlier in the season, and the stat sheet reflected as much. The 6'5" bruiser led the Avalanche with 89 penalty minutes and six fights in 2021–22.

The son of longtime NHLer Paul MacDermid, Kurtis knew his role on the Avalanche's star-studded roster. He rotated between forward and defenseman depending on what Bednar needed, never complaining about his low ice time (7:24 a game, a career low, in 58 games). After practices, he frequently stayed out late to work on refining his skating and technique. Once, younger teammates Alex

Newhook and Compher even went to him for fighting tips. He showed them how to position their bodies and where to grip an opponent's jersey.

MacDermid's fit with his teammates was so seamless that when he scored his first goal of the season, Colorado's players went nuts. The Avalanche were hosting Boston in a late-January contest, and MacDermid received a pass from Burakovsky midway through the first period. With Valeri Nichushkin blocking Bruins goaltender Linus Ullmark's vision, MacDermid wristed a shot from the slot into the net.

Burakovsky and Samuel Girard mobbed him. The Avalanche bench erupted. MacDermid roared with glee.

The Avalanche led 1–0 in what had already been an emotional game. Two minutes into the contest, Bruins forward Taylor Hall hit MacKinnon as he entered the neutral zone. During the collision, Hall's shoulder knocked MacKinnon's stick straight into his face, breaking his nose and leaving him with a concussion. MacKinnon fell straight to the ice, his feet kicking up and down in pain. Blood gushed from his nose.

Though Landeskog later acknowledged Hall didn't mean to hurt MacKinnon, he charged after his opponent. Officials separated the Avalanche captain from Hall, then handed the Boston forward a five-minute major penalty. After reviewing the play and seeing MacKinnon's stick did the damage, they reduced the penalty to a two-minute interference call.

Colorado's star center skated off with help from a trainer. The play hung like a canopy over the game. The team was rattled. And MacDermid's goal, welcome as it was, didn't snap players out of their shock. Colorado spent the next stretch of game time trying to avenge the hit. MacDermid nudged Hall at the end of the first, and Landeskog tried to fight him in the second. Hall declined to drop his gloves, saying two days later that he didn't want to fight on someone else's terms. He believed his play on MacKinnon was a clean hit, just one with an unfortunate outcome.

The Avalanche's focus on Hall proved costly. With the score tied 1–1 and Boston on the power play midway through the second period, Erik Johnson hit Hall with multiple cross checks, knocking him to the ice. The officials didn't seem to want to call a penalty and hand Boston a five-on-three advantage, but Johnson gave them no choice. Referee Steve Kozari emphasized that when announcing the two-minute penalty to the crowd. "Three cross-checks," he said.

Boston scored on the 5-on-3 power play, and then again right as the defenseman's penalty expired. The cross-checking led directly to a 3–1 Avalanche deficit, and Bednar benched his veteran defenseman for most of the rest of the game. His message was clear: that was the type of mistake that can cost a team a win.

But thanks to the Avalanche's resolve—"stick-to-it-iveness," as Bednar calls it—their recklessness didn't cost them the Boston game. Colorado logged twice as many shot attempts as the Bruins in the third period, and with eight minutes left, Girard scored with a shot that bounced awkwardly off the ice. It squeezed past Ullmark.

Down one, the Avalanche pushed for the rest of the game, desperate for an equalizer. Finally, with less than a minute to go, they broke through. Bednar pulled Kuemper for an extra skater, and when Kadri found Landeskog with a perfect cross-ice pass, the captain one-timed the puck into the net. He held his hands above his head in celebration. A wide grin crossed his face. In overtime, Makar struck, extending Colorado's home win streak to 17 games.

"It's the belief. They're buying into what we're trying to do," Bednar said after the victory. "That's our biggest win of the year, I would say."

Colorado rattled off wins against Chicago and Buffalo to finish January with a 15–0–1 record, tying the 2014 Bruins and 2013 Penguins for the most wins in a month. During that stretch, Colorado outscored opponents 66–35.

And though the team cooled slightly as February arrived, it still started the month with a 4–1–1 record. MacKinnon's concussion and broken nose forced him to miss the All-Star Game, but Makar and Kadri both went. So did Bednar, who coached the Central Division squad.

The Avalanche were riding high, which meant fans had plenty to sing about at home games. More than two years earlier, Ball Arena DJ Craig Turney played blink-182's "All the Small Things," a catchy pop single. Part of Turney's job is reading the crowd, and he noticed fans engaged and singing along. The DJ liked the vibe, so he continued playing the song.

Before long, it was a staple. Turney would play the song in the third period, usually when the Avalanche were leading and trying to close out a game. The crowd would belt out the lyrics and, when the music cut out so play could resume, they would continue singing. Ball Arena became an a cappella venue, not just a sports arena.

The tradition made it through the COVID-19 pandemic shutdown and was in full force during the 2021–22 season. With Colorado humming along like an engine, the jam rang through the arena frequently as the calendar flipped to 2022. The team was doing all the small things needed to pull out wins.

MUSCLE AND DEPTH

WEARING A PURPLE TIE and white shirt, Jared Bednar entered a small visiting media room in Boston and took a seat in front of the microphone. Though his voice remained steady, his dissatisfaction was clear. Aside from the top line, he said, the team didn't get enough out of its forwards in a 5–1 trouncing at the hands of the Bruins.

With the March 21 trade deadline exactly one month away, the Avalanche had come out flat as a plateau. It was an all-around disappointing game for the Avalanche, who let Taylor Hall tally three assists and David Pastrnak score twice. None of the Colorado players had positive ratings, and MacKinnon showed his frustration after a third-period faceoff, trying to whack at Boston center Tomas Nosek and instead hitting a linesman.

The MacKinnon swipe caused a minor stir—the NHL's Department of Hockey Operations talked to on-ice officials and found any contact with the linesman was unintentional—but that wasn't on Bednar's mind postgame. Far more concerned about the game, he gave an honest, unhappy assessment of his bottom two forward lines.

"We've got guys playing six, seven minutes because we're trying to scrap together one line out of two lines that we have," Bednar said. "Other teams are playing four lines, and we have to be able to put them together and make sure we can play four lines. I find as a coach on some nights I'm not getting that."

The implications of Bednar's frustrations were clear. The Avalanche, high in the standings as they might have been, still had holes. The trade deadline offered a chance to fix that.

• • •

Colorado rediscovered its mojo before making any moves, rattling off four wins, two of which came with a heavy dose of emotion. Darren Helm returned to Detroit for the first time after 14 years with the Red Wings, and Bednar put him on the top line so he could start the game. He collected an assist on a Gabriel Landeskog goal the first shift, then teared up later in the game when the Red Wings played a tribute video on the jumbotron.

A week later, the Avalanche were back in Denver to play the Islanders. It was Jack Johnson's 1,000th game, a major accomplishment in the NHL. The night before the game, his wife organized a surprise dinner with a plethora of loved ones, including his younger brother and former college teammates. Johnson thought he was simply going to a steak dinner with immediate family members at Denver ChopHouse, but when he walked in, he was blown away by the number of people there. The big, bruising defenseman's eyes grew wet. He didn't feel deserving, he told reporters the next morning.

The Avalanche prepared a video for the game, showing highlights from his draft night and the previous four NHL teams for which he'd played. The Avalanche presented him with gifts, including a No. 1000 jersey signed by all his teammates, handed over by Landeskog. Erik Johnson, whom he medaled with at the 2010 Olympics, brought him a silver hockey stick.

"What the organization did for me, the way they treated me on my 1,000th game night, I never would have expected that," said Jack Johnson, who had played only 50 of his 1,000 games with the Avalanche, all during the 2021–22 season. "They treated me like I had been playing there for 10 years."

The Avalanche won only one of their next five contests and failed to score at all on the road against Carolina. It was the only time Colorado got shut out all season or postseason. Landeskog was frustrated after the game, teeing off on how the officials handled two plays involving Nazem Kadri. The Avalanche believed Nino

Niederreiter flopped in the third period, resulting in Kadri getting a hooking penalty, then felt Niederreiter got away with a hook on Kadri ahead of Carolina's go-ahead goal later in the period. Landeskog started venting his frustration on the ice, getting a 10-minute misconduct penalty with less than a minute left for arguing with officials. "I guess [referee TJ Luxmore] didn't like that I said he had a tough night," the captain said. And in his postgame interview, he questioned if Kadri was being officiated fairly (Landeskog and the players believed he wasn't) or if multiple suspensions on his record were working against him.

"Whether a guy has been suspended numerous times or not, is he going to be carrying around that heavy baggage forever?" said Landeskog, who did not receive a fine for his comments.

With his message sent, Landeskog flew back to Colorado with the team and promptly underwent surgery on his knee, which had been bothering him since before the season started. The pain had gradually gotten worse, and by the Carolina game, Landeskog didn't think he'd be able to make it through the rest of the regular season plus the entire postseason unless he underwent surgery.

"I didn't want to be good in the first round and maybe a little bit into June," he said. "I wanted to make sure I was healthy for the end of June because I had a feeling that we were going to go on a deep run."

The procedure ended his regular season and was a surprise to the public, but it wasn't a point of concern for his teammates. They were confident he'd be back by the postseason. Jack Johnson spoke to Landeskog ahead of the surgery; the plan all along was for him to be ready for when the games mattered most.

Because the postseason was the team's focus. And with that in mind, Sakic, at long last, made one of the league's first big moves at the deadline.

• • •

The forward position might have seemed like Colorado's most glaring need, especially considering Bednar's postgame comments in Boston, but it wasn't the position Sakic addressed first on the trade market. Instead he went for a defenseman: Josh Manson, the son of longtime NHL tough guy Dave Manson, who played more than 1,000 NHL games and logged more than 2,700 career penalty minutes.

Drafted in 2011 by Anaheim, the 6'3" Manson had given his whole professional career to the Ducks organization. He played a key role on the 2016–17 club that made the Western Conference Finals, and he appeared on a pair of Norris Trophy ballots the next season. Considering his history with both the team and city, Manson didn't want to leave Anaheim, where he'd met his wife, Julie, had a daughter, and put down roots.

"We were just well set up," Manson said. "You get comfortable there, and that's kind of where we were. And I was hoping it was going to work out."

Back when Manson entered the league, Bruce Boudreau, his first NHL coach, was instantly impressed with his ability to play strong defense against other teams' top players. The Ducks allowed the fewest goals in the league during 2015–16, Manson's first full season. "Josh was steady, steady," Boudreau told The Athletic's Michael Russo.

Manson also made an early impression on fellow blueliner Cam Fowler, who broke into the league in 2010. During the 2015 preseason, with only 28 NHL games under his belt, Manson took exception to a Milan Lucic hit on teammate Chris Wagner. Lucic is widely regarded as one of the toughest players in the league: not someone to mess with. But Manson dropped his gloves and squared off with the 6'4" forward, lasting for nearly a minute before getting brought to the ice. The fight blew Fowler away, and he applauded with the rest of his teammates. Most players wouldn't consider fighting Lucic.

"It kind of set the tone for what he was willing to do for our team and what he continued to do up until the day he ended up going somewhere else," said Fowler, Manson's primary defensive partner before the trade.

Though the Ducks had playoff success in the mid 2010s, their fortunes fell later in the decade. They started to rebuild and, midway through the 2021–22 season, were on pace to miss the playoffs for a fourth consecutive year. Manson was in the final season of his contract, so he made sense as a trade candidate, even if those around the team saw him as a potential successor to the retiring captain Ryan Getzlaf.

That's how Pat Verbeek saw it. Hired as Ducks general manager in February, he had a conversation with Manson a couple weeks after taking over. He didn't bring up a potential contract extension, instead informing the defenseman that he'd likely be traded.

"I didn't really want to get moved, if I'm being honest," Manson said. "It's tough to say good-bye."

As February turned into March and the weeks went by, the uncertainty proved to be the hardest part. But it came to an end a week ahead of the March 21 trade deadline. With the Ducks in New York for a road trip, Verbeek called Manson and, in a short conversation, told him he'd been dealt to Colorado. Sakic sent a second-round pick and a quality prospect in Drew Helleson, who had represented the U.S. at that winter's Olympics, back to Anaheim. The Avalanche believed they needed a player like Manson, one who could thrive against big, physical teams they might face in the playoffs.

Manson packed his bags and left the hotel, no longer a Duck for the first time as an NHL player. He didn't get the chance to say good-bye to teammates; Fowler heard about the deal from an autograph seeker as he left the hotel for dinner.

Manson boarded a cross-country flight to meet his new team in Los Angeles. His uncertainty about a trade destination evaporated, and his excitement grew knowing he was on a team with a chance to win a championship. He played against the Kings the next night, registering a team-high 10 hits and playing more than a minute on the penalty kill.

"It was the type of guy we'd probably been missing," said Bednar, who was ecstatic when Sakic told him about the move. "They're hard to find. Teams generally don't move guys of his caliber."

And when teams do, they usually expect a strong return. The Manson deal was the first time in Sakic's tenure as general manager that he paid that kind of price in a pre-deadline move. The Avalanche had a window. The trade for Manson was a sure signal—to the fans, to the league, and to the Avalanche players—that the front office was going to do everything it could to maximize it.

• • •

Trades involve sacrifice. When something new arrives, something else leaves.

But not all trade chips carry the same emotional connection. A college or junior hockey prospect, however promising he might be, hasn't formed deep relationships with players on the NHL roster. Neither, obviously, has a future draft pick—an abstraction more than a human being.

Then there's someone like Tyson Jost. He grew up with the Avalanche core, coming up as a 19-year-old with the dreadful 2016–17 team. He was beloved in the dressing room and involved in the community, speaking to the Boys & Girls Club of Metro Denver during the 2020–21 season and encouraging members to follow their passions. Bednar said he never doubted how much Jost cared during his Avalanche tenure, and the forward showed as much as the trade deadline neared, not missing a single game after breaking his jaw in an early March contest against Calgary.

On March 14, Pi Day as well as Jost's 24th birthday, the Avalanche flew to Los Angeles ahead of a game with the Kings. As he walked across the tarmac ahead of the flight, he grinned and accepted a piece of Whole Foods pie from Madeleine McCarty, the Avalanche's social media manager. He climbed into the private plane, not knowing he wouldn't be flying back with his teammates.

A day later, as Jost prepared on his own ahead of the Kings game, his phone rang. He saw Joe Sakic's name on the caller ID, and though he hadn't been expecting a trade, he instantly knew something was happening. Sure enough, Sakic told Jost the Avalanche were trading him to Minnesota. It was a phone call Sakic hated to make, but he remembered what the late Pierre Lacroix, Colorado's general manager for its two previous Cup wins, used to say: "Do what's best for the logo." Sakic believed that was moving on from Jost. He acquired

26-year-old forward Nico Sturm in the deal, giving the Avalanche a defensive-minded center who brought more size than Jost to the fourth line.

The Avalanche had drafted Jost 10th overall in 2016, but his offensive game hadn't developed like the team hoped. Perhaps he could have benefitted from a second year of NCAA hockey at the University of North Dakota, where he averaged more than a point per game, but instead he turned pro after his freshman season. He never logged more than 26 points in a season with Colorado, and by the end of his tenure was playing in a bottom-six, penalty-kill role, averaging the second-fewest minutes per game of his career.

In some ways, the trade was a blessing for Jost, who carried no ill will toward either Sakic or Bednar. He called the move to Minnesota "a nice fresh start" and saw it as an opportunity to play in more offensive situations. Plus, the Wild were playoff-bound. He wasn't going from the Western Conference's best club to a bottom feeder.

That didn't make the move painless. Shortly after his call with Sakic, Jost's phone rang again. This time, Gabriel Landeskog, the only NHL captain he'd ever known, was on the line. "Holy smokes," Jost thought.

"That was really tough," he said. "That was where the emotions kind of hit."

That night, after a 3–0 win against the Kings, players reflected on their friend's departure. Jost's closest buddy on the team, J.T. Compher, wished him the best and acknowledged that trades are part of the job, and Darcy Kuemper called him a locker room favorite. Bednar said the trade was "a tough one." He and Jost were both newcomers with the Avalanche in 2016–17, and now the forward was gone before the team had reached its goal of winning the Cup.

When the Avalanche eventually won the championship in June, Jost sat on his couch and sobbed. He avoided Instagram; it was too hard to look at the pictures of his friends celebrating. "I should be there," he couldn't help but think.

"[With] how many years Jost was here, you see the team building and building and building, and then we finally accomplish it, [and] he's not a part of it," O'Connor said after the season. "It's tough. He was loved throughout the whole team."

But as Sakic said after the deadline passed, you have to give to get. And sometimes giving hurts.

• • •

On the other end of the Jost deal was Sturm, who met the Avalanche in San Jose, shaking every one of his new teammates' hands as they walked into the rink. He perhaps didn't have as high an offensive ceiling as Jost—the trade didn't fix Colorado's need for another scoring threat—but he brought a style of play the Avalanche saw as better suited for a grinding fourth-line player. He also had a salary cap hit worth $1.275 million less than Jost, giving Colorado added cap flexibility to make additional trades.

Sturm's road to the Avalanche wasn't conventional. He grew up in Germany—the home of only six skaters who appeared in NHL games in 2021–22—and went undrafted. But, in three seasons playing college hockey at Clarkson University, he caught the attention of NHL clubs around the league. The Wild signed him as a college free agent, and he debuted toward the end of the 2018–19 season.

"He has a pretty inspiring story," said Oilers superstar Leon Draisaitl, who played with Sturm on junior German national teams growing up. "When he was younger, maybe his path never showed the NHL for him, but he obviously worked his tail off."

That's who Sturm is. His girlfriend, professional hockey player Taylor Turnquist, describes him as intense when it comes to his sport. He dials into everything that will make him better on the ice, whether that's nutrition or keeping a healthy sleep schedule. At Clarkson, where he met Turnquist, there were times he didn't go out on weekends, knowing his body needed to recover for the week ahead.

"I have to remind him sometimes that there is an off switch," Turnquist said. "He wants to be the best version of himself that he can."

During the 2020–21 season, Sturm claimed a regular spot in the Wild lineup, and he got off to a good start with the club in 2021–22, logging 16 points through the team's first 42 games: respectable totals, considering he was playing fourth-line minutes without time on the power play.

But shortly after February's All-Star break, the Wild hit a skid, and Sturm's ice time dropped. He played more than 10 minutes in only one of his final 11 games with Minnesota, putting up only one point in that span, and coach Dean Evason left him out of the lineup on multiple occasions. He watched from above with the healthy scratches. Everything felt like it was going downhill, both for the team and for Sturm.

Sturm loved the group of Minnesota players and called general manager Billy Guerin a great guy, noting that he received a congratulatory text from his old boss after the 2022 playoffs. But he wondered if the Wild still viewed him the same way it did when he arrived fresh out of college, "as that young kid that maybe can't be relied upon in certain situations," he said. The post–All-Star break stretch took a toll on him. His mental health took a downturn, and he found himself full of dread as he drove to the rink. "I was just depressed every day about not being the player that I know I can be, that I was the past five months," he said. He talked to his agent and looked over stats, trying to figure out solutions. He didn't know why, all of a sudden, he was doing so poorly.

With Sturm's contract set to expire at season's end, Guerin approached him about signing an extension. Sturm said the team made a good, fair offer, but he didn't take it. His decision wasn't about money or term but about fit. He had already decided he wasn't planning to re-sign after the season; he wanted a new opportunity.

His wait for a change turned out to be shorter than expected. Following the Wild's practice March 15, he took a shower and dressed to head home. Then he saw Guerin walk around a corner and, just as Jost knew he'd been traded when he saw Sakic's name on his phone, the reality hit Sturm. He was going somewhere new.

"We made a deal with Colorado," Guerin said.

A flood of emotions hit the forward. Questions set in. He'd never been traded before, and his life in Minnesota was getting uprooted.

His mind racing, he said a series of painful good-byes to Wild players still at the rink. He gave hugs to Kevin Fiala, Cam Talbot, Jonas Brodin, and various staffers. As he left the building, though, he couldn't shake his feeling of excitement. "I was in a very tough spot, and the trade probably saved me," he said.

Sturm isn't at ease being the new guy, and he needs to be comfortable off the ice to perform on it. That was one source of nerves. He received texts from Landeskog and MacKinnon almost immediately after the trade, though, and during his first skate in San Jose, he felt as if he'd never played for any other team. Looking back, he's surprised at how quickly he felt comfortable. He credited the Avalanche players with making him feel welcome from the jump.

Sturm wore No. 7 in Minnesota, which was taken in Colorado by Devon Toews. Makar wore No. 8, the next number up. No. 77 didn't work—it's retired for Ray Bourque—and Sturm didn't want to take Jost's No. 17, his college number at Clarkson, out of respect for the player he was replacing. The move was too fresh. That left him stuck, so he turned to his brother Timo, who had an obscure suggestion: No. 78, in honor of their hometown team in Germany, Augsburger EV, which was founded in 1878. No one in Avalanche history had ever worn it. He had a new number, a new start, and a Stanley Cup–contending team he felt believed in him.

"Sometimes, as much as it hurts, change in your career is necessary: to go into a new spot where people see you in a little different light," he said. "I'm happy it turned out the way it did."

TENACITY AND LEADERSHIP

A SEASON EARLIER, Sakic had made four in-season deals within a month of the 2020–21 trade deadline. Neither goalie Jonas Johansson nor goalie Devan Dubnyk, both acquired for late-round draft picks, appeared in a playoff game. Carl Söderberg, who came over for two minor leaguers, played in only four and had a –2 rating. And though Patrik Nemeth, acquired for a 2022 fourth-round pick, was on the ice for every postseason contest, he struggled mightily, committing penalties and costly turnovers during Colorado's collapse against Vegas.

The Avalanche had tried making moves around the edges, building depth rather than adding game-changers, partially due to limited salary-cap flexibility. And it bit them. They couldn't overcome Kadri's suspension, and with Erik Johnson and Byram hurt, they didn't have six reliable defensemen.

Sakic, working with more cap space at the 2022 deadline than he did in 2021, wasn't going to let that happen again. With the Manson addition, the Avalanche had solidified its defense. And though Sturm provided bottom-six depth, the Avalanche wanted a top-six-level forward to bolster their forward group. Someone who could put them over the top.

Philadelphia's Claude Giroux was the big fish. Set to become a free agent after the season, the 34-year-old was no longer on the same timeline as the struggling Flyers club. The captain wanted to win, and his team wasn't in a position to do so.

The Avalanche inquired about Giroux. Sakic was in contact with Flyers general manager Chuck Fletcher for "a couple months" heading into the trade deadline. But, with a full no-movement clause in his contract, Giroux had control over his next destination. He decided he'd only accept a deal to the offensive juggernaut Florida Panthers. Colorado might have been able to beat the Panthers' offer for Giroux, but it wouldn't have mattered.

"At the end of the day Claude wanted to go to Florida," Sakic said.

So Sakic's push continued. He still needed another forward.

• • •

In the days leading up to the deadline, Montreal general manager Kent Hughes pulled Artturi Lehkonen aside, as detailed in a Pierre LeBrun story in The Athletic. Hughes wanted to know how his winger was holding up.

Less than a year earlier, Lehkonen had scored the biggest Canadiens goal in decades, potting an overtime winner to knock off Vegas in the conference finals and send his team to the Stanley Cup Final. But times in Montreal hadn't stayed sunny. The loss of free agent Phillip Danault, a defensive stalwart, and injuries to Carey Price and Shea Weber had forced the team back to earth. They were an Eastern Conference bottom feeder, and Hughes had already begun trading contributors off their roster, sending Tyler Toffoli to Calgary and Ben Chiarot to Florida.

With the firesale underway, Lehkonen's name emerged in trade rumors. He didn't pay much mind to it. It comes with the territory when you play in a market like Montreal, he said. Plus, he joked, he often couldn't understand the speculation because it was in French.

Hughes wasn't looking to trade Lehkonen, who would still be under team control as a restricted free agent after the season, and he told his young forward as much.

"But I can't tell you I wouldn't, either," Hughes said. "It would have to be something really good."

The Avalanche, meanwhile, had their eyes on Lehkonen. Sakic frequently checked in with Hughes. He kept asking if different offers would work, and the Canadiens general manager kept saying no.

But with the deadline creeping closer, Sakic upped the offer, and it was one Hughes felt he couldn't pass up: a 2024 second-round pick and promising young defenseman Justin Barron, a 2020 first-rounder who had debuted with Colorado earlier in the season and had impressed the coaching staff at training camp. The Avalanche organization was high on Barron, and Sakic said he only would have moved him for someone who would be more than a rental. Lehkonen fit the bill.

The Finnish forward was taking a pregame nap when the ring of his phone woke him. The call was from Hughes, who told him the team got a deal it needed to make. The Canadiens would miss him, he said. Coach Martin St. Louis, who loved Lehkonen's game, was crestfallen.

"I think there's some good news," Hughes said during his conversation with Lehkonen. "Let me ask you: if you were to pick where you would want to get traded to have the best chance at winning the Stanley Cup, where would you want to go?"

"Colorado," Lehkonen replied.

He had his wish.

• • •

To see where Lehkonen got his passion for hockey, look no further than his father, Ismo.

Ismo played professional hockey in Finland, and he coached in the country's highest professional league. He turned 60 the month before the Canadiens traded Artturi, and he trains professional players in the off-season, including both his son and Mikko Rantanen. He's also a hockey analyst for the Finnish Broadcasting Company. During the NHL regular season, he tapes three or four games a night and watches them when he wakes up in the morning. The Lightning and Avalanche were among the teams he watched the most, even before Sakic traded for Artturi.

"Almost every Finnish hockey fan knows Ismo," laughed Ville Touru, a Finnish hockey reporter. "Maybe more people know Ismo than Artturi."

Artturi, the middle of five children, tried multiple sports growing up. Soccer. Basketball. Tennis. But hockey was his passion. When
Artturi was a baby, Ismo bought mini sticks for the house and set up
a small net in the living room. Young Artturi would crawl around,
smiling with a stick in his hands, and whack at balls his dad rolled his
way. He took slapshots before his first steps.

His passion for hockey didn't diminish with age. He'd watch
his dad break down film of his team's games and pepper him with
questions. Why was one player in a certain position? What was the
mistake someone else made? He watched NHL footage, too. Ismo
showed him VHS tapes of the 1990s Philadelphia Flyers teams,
which featured the "Legion of Doom" line in Philadelphia.

"There was a lot of forechecking and there were a lot of battles,"
his dad said.

That made Artturi like the Flyers. Perhaps it impacted his style
of play, too, considering the aggressiveness with which he hounds
opponents on the forecheck.

Growing up, Artturi—"Arsi," as his family called him—hated
losing, and not just on the ice. Coming up short in street hockey
games with his friends, or even in other activities with family, infuri-
ated him. He'd sometimes run to the woods near their house and cry.

Ismo developed a strategy for calming down his son. He told
him about Teemu Selänne, a Hockey Hall of Famer and Finnish legend, and how he would reflect on a painful loss for a short period of
time, let himself feel his emotions, and then move on. Ismo called it
the five-minute rule, and he knew how to make his son remember it.

"The magic word is 'Teemu Selänne,'" Ismo said.

Montreal drafted Artturi in the second round of the 2013 draft,
and he spent two seasons playing professionally in Sweden before
coming to North America. His club in Sweden, Frölunda, was instrumental in his growth. The coach, Roger Rönnberg, pushed him to
kill penalties, forecheck, and grow defensively, and the team played
a similar style to what he'd ultimately play in Colorado, Ismo said.

When Artturi arrived in Montreal, he stood out to veteran forward Tomáš Plekanec, who became a mentor and dinner buddy to

the young Finn. Plekanec was a player who paid close attention to details, and he quickly saw Lehkonen was the same way. Lehkonen had good positioning and stick placement. As a coach's son, he knew the importance of doing small aspects of the game well. He finished his Canadiens tenure with 149 points in 396 games, as well as a reputation as a strong two-way player. Danault said he had "one of the best sticks defensively" he'd seen and frequently used the phrase, "Good stick, Lehky!" which Canadiens fans and the team social media accounts picked up on, tweeting it whenever Lehkonen made big plays.

With the trade to Colorado, Artturi was going to a place where losing would be much less frequent than in Montreal. He also had a preexisting connection with Rantanen, who grew up in Nousiainen, Finland, a town less than 30 minutes from where Lehkonen grew up in Turku. The two occasionally played on the same tournament teams, and Lehkonen saw Rantanen grow from a tiny, blond-haired player to the giant, 6'4" force he is today.

"He's one of the smarter players I know, defensively and offensively," said Rantanen, who immediately texted his friend after the trade. "Exactly what we need."

Headlined by Lehkonen and Manson, Sakic's deadline additions had high approval throughout the dressing room, starting with the top of the roster.

"We need to win now," Nathan MacKinnon said. "That's the message Joe is sending to all of us."

The Avalanche were all in.

• • •

The Colorado general manager snuck in one final trade before the deadline, and he asked MacKinnon for input before making it. What would he think about adding veteran Andrew Cogliano from San Jose? MacKinnon had trained with the Sharks forward in past off-seasons and responded without hesitation.

"You have to get this guy."

Other people Sakic spoke to said the same thing. Within an hour of the deadline, Sakic finalized a deal to send San Jose a fifth-round pick for Cogliano. The move wasn't flashy or expensive, but it proved invaluable. It was made possible, assistant general manager Chris MacFarland said, because of the cap space cleared in the Jost-Sturm swap.

Cogliano had already played 1,122 NHL games when Colorado acquired him, and he was old enough to have played against Sakic. In Bob McKenzie and Jim Lang's book *Everyday Hockey Heroes*, Cogliano shared a story from the 2007–08 season, his rookie year with the Oilers. With Edmonton visiting Denver late in the season, the game went to a shootout. Dwayne Roloson was in net for the Oilers, and Cogliano was within earshot of Sakic—one of his heroes growing up—on the Edmonton bench. Suddenly, Sakic turned to Cogliano.

"Hey, kid, where should I shoot on Roloson?" he said.

Shocked, the rookie didn't say a word. Sakic hopped onto the ice and scored with a backhand, and as he skated back to the bench, he winked at Cogliano.

"I sat there, speechless that I had just witnessed a guy I idolized pull off a move like that," Cogliano said in McKenzie and Lang's book.

Now, after Colorado's final move at the 2022 deadline, the two were on the same team.

Widely respected around the league, Cogliano held the seventh-longest Iron Man streak in league history, suiting up for 830 consecutive games from October 2007—his NHL debut—to January 2018, when he was suspended for two contests for an interference penalty. The 2005 Oilers first-round pick scored as many as 21 goals in a season (2013–14 with Anaheim) and also received votes for the Calder (rookie of the year), Selke (best defensive forward), and Lady Byng (gentlemanly conduct) trophies at points in his career.

At 34, he had as respectable a non-star résumé as a player could have.

But he'd never won a Stanley Cup. He got close, reaching Game 6 of the Final with Dallas in 2020, but the Stars weren't able to upend the powerhouse Lightning. And with the deadline approaching and the Sharks well out of contention, he still wanted a chance to chase the famed trophy.

Away from the ice, Cogliano had gone through difficult stretches during his lone season in San Jose. His daughter, Olive, born in January 2021, had to go to the hospital multiple times while being diagnosed with asthma, forcing him to take time away from the team. But while around his teammates, Cogliano had a positive presence. Mario Ferraro, a young defenseman on the Sharks, told the *San Jose Mercury News* that the veteran helped keep him engaged and was someone younger teammates could learn from.

That's been a trend wherever Cogliano has been.

"He was one of the guys who changed our dressing room," said Stars general manager Jim Nill, who traded for Cogliano during the 2018–19 season. "What he brings to the dressing room, how he plays the game the right way, helps with young kids, how he helps older guys. He's been there and done that. You can never have enough of those guys.

From the veteran's understanding, San Jose was pleased at what he'd done for the team's culture and approached him to ask if he'd want to be moved.

"They wanted to give me an opportunity if I wanted," Cogliano said. "Colorado was a team that I basically said, 'If there was interest from their side, I'd really want to go there.'"

On deadline day, Cogliano heard from his agent that a move could be in the works. Sure enough, while he was in the gym with some teammates, Sharks assistant general manager Joe Will came down and informed him of the move.

Cogliano already knew a few members of the Avalanche. He had also trained with Erik Johnson during summers and had, in a fun twist, lived with a couple Colorado players at different points in his career. He and Jack Johnson were college roommates at Michigan,

Joe Sakic traded a fifth-round 2024 draft pick to San Jose for Andrew Cogliano on March 21, 2022, and got a forward whose leadership would play a significant role in Colorado's championship run.

and he housed Manson, his fellow deadline addition, in Anaheim as the defenseman got settled in the NHL.

"I used to make him drive me everywhere," Cogliano said. "He was my personal chauffeur."

Colorado's trade acquisitions had plenty of time to bond after the deadline, as all four initially lived out of a Residence Inn in Cherry Creek, a wealthy Denver suburb. They went to Elway's shortly after arriving in Denver, enjoying the steakhouse opened by Broncos legend John Elway. Traded guys, Manson believes, have to stick together early on.

"You're shooting the shit about your old team or your old guys and the new guys and your expectations," Sturm said.

By the end of his first practice with the Avalanche, Cogliano believed his new team could do something special. Though Sakic had thought the 2020–21 post-deadline Avalanche was as deep a team as Colorado would have, the general manager had one-upped himself. The talent and speed was unlike anything Cogliano had seen before. He loved the pace of play and energy, and he could see players' inner drive. The veteran could tell they wanted to take the next step.

"I'm a small piece of the puzzle," he said in his first press conference with Colorado. "But I think to have success you're going to need to have different pieces and people and personalities. Usually that's how winning teams work."

By the end of the season, Cogliano's puzzle piece wasn't small. And perhaps his biggest impact came away from the ice and at a moment when the Avalanche needed it most.

GUT CHECK

JARED BEDNAR DOESN'T see any use in trying to contain Nathan MacKinnon's fire. You want players to have MacKinnon's passion, he believes. It's far better having someone with too much than too little. But uncontained fire can sometimes lead to burns, as a MacKinnon decision shortly after the trade deadline showed.

Early in the third period of a game in Minnesota, Wild defenseman Matt Dumba laid a legal but high hit on Mikko Rantanen. MacKinnon took objection. Without hesitation, he threw off his gloves for a fight, landed a couple licks and brought Dumba to the ice.

Standing up for teammates is widely praised around the sport, but fighting also brings the risk of injury. That's why teams often don't like their star players doing it. Sure enough, MacKinnon hurt one of his fingers while throwing a haymaker.

A day after the Minnesota game, Erik Johnson said, "We definitely don't want him to do that," noting that enforcer Kurtis MacDermid would have been on the ice shortly to handle it. But as Johnson knew from nine years as MacKinnon's teammate, the center will take matters into his own hands. That kind of fire is why he's one of the world's best.

"That's what makes Nathan, Nathan," Bednar said. "It's not just that he's a good skater, has a good skill set, good hockey IQ. It's the way he plays the game. He's a bull in a china shop."

MacKinnon didn't regret the fight, later saying he would do it again, even if it led to a more serious injury. And though Bednar initially described the team's concern about the injury as "high," MacKinnon ended up missing only one game, a 2–1 Colorado road win against a strong Calgary club. Artturi Lehkonen's immigration paperwork cleared ahead of the contest, allowing him to make his Avalanche debut; Darcy Kuemper starred in net; and Valeri Nichushkin scored a pair of goals in the win. It was one of Colorado's most impressive efforts of the season, considering the team was missing MacKinnon, Gabriel Landeskog, Samuel Girard, Ryan Murray, and Bowen Byram to injury. Kuemper had fully rounded into form, and Nichushkin was continuing to prove himself not only as a strong defensive forward but as one who could score at a high level, too.

Meanwhile, Byram was nearing a return. He had missed nearly three months recovering from lingering concussion issues which forced him to go on personal leave, but he was finally ready to return to game action. He played a pair of games in the AHL on a conditioning stint and then, on April 5, returned to the NHL ice. He suited up against a Penguins team captained by the great Sidney Crosby, one of the players he admired most growing up.

"I tried not to fanboy when I was out there against him," Byram said. "But it was pretty cool."

He was back, hopeful his issues were fully behind him.

Colorado's positioning as top seed in the Western Conference was all but locked up at this point, so solidifying the roster for playoff success was the team's main focus. Byram's status had been a question mark since he went on leave. But if he was healthy and playing as well as he had early in the season, he was a ceiling-raiser. The coming months would tell just how much.

• • •

Sitting at Colorado's table during the 2019 NHL Draft, scout Wade Klippenstein didn't think the Avalanche would have a chance to take Byram with the fourth overall pick. Surely one of the three teams ahead of them would pick the explosive, smooth-skating defenseman from British Columbia. Playing for the Vancouver Giants the year before, he had dominated the Western Hockey League, solidifying his spot as one of the top prospects in the draft class. He was arguably the best Canadian prospect in the draft.

New Jersey, as expected, took Jack Hughes, an American, first overall. Then came the Rangers, who picked Kaapo Kakko out of Finland. Also expected. After that, a break fell in Colorado's favor. The Athletic's Corey Pronman, one of the industry's foremost draft experts, had projected the Blackhawks to take Byram. Klippenstein anticipated the same thing.

Then he heard Chicago announce its pick: "Kirby Dach."

Klippenstein was shocked and elated. The player he wanted was still on the board.

"We're getting Bo Byram," he thought to himself. "We got Cale Makar. Now we're getting Bo Byram!?"

Moments later, Sakic announced the pick. Byram hugged his parents and walked to the stage, where he pulled on an Avalanche jersey for the first time. Colorado had the No. 4 pick from Ottawa as part of Sakic's Matt Duchene masterpiece trade, and the team also found a useful player with its original pick: Alex Newhook at No. 16 overall. In the second round, Sakic snagged Drew Helleson, the defensive prospect he later used as a trade chip to acquire Josh Manson.

It was a fruitful draft. Fingerprints of the players the Avalanche acquired in it were all over Colorado's eventual Stanley Cup run. Byram was the jewel.

Unlike Makar, who went to UMass expecting to play two years of college hockey, Byram reported to the Avalanche immediately after the draft. Bednar thought he looked hesitant at training camp, though, so the team sent him back to play another season in the WHL. Byram was disappointed, but his father, Shawn, found it evident he wasn't quite ready for the NHL.

Byram put too much pressure on himself when he first returned to junior hockey, Giants general manager Barclay Parneta told The Athletic's Ryan Clark, and the defenseman later admitted he wasn't having much fun at the start of the season. But a positive experience at World Junior Championships, in which Canada won gold, reignited his passion. He showed how dynamic he could be after the tournament, totaling 33 points in his final 23 games before the

COVID-19 shutdown. He was playing the best hockey of his life, Shawn said.

The young defenseman put on muscle, too, hitting the gym after games. He didn't simply want to maintain his strength during the season. He wanted to add to it. By the time the 2020–21 season rolled around, Byram was physically ready for the NHL. He made his debut early in the year with his parents watching from their couch in their Cranbrook, British Columbia, home because of COVID-19 restrictions. And though the defenseman wasn't a star out of the gate, he didn't look out of place, either. At only 19 years old, his offensive potential was apparent.

Then came the setbacks. He suffered a concussion in February 2021, so his mother, Stacey, drove 17 hours from Cranbrook to stay with him in Denver. Byram recovered and returned to the lineup after 19 days. Shortly after, he took a hit along the boards from Vegas's Keegan Kolesar, who made contact with his head.

Stacey wasn't at the game because the league still wasn't allowing fans in the building. At first, she was relieved to see her son return to the action, but the feeling evaporated the moment he got home. She could see on his face that he wasn't okay. He admitted he wasn't feeling well. He went to bed, saying he would see how he felt in the morning.

When Byram woke, there was no improvement. He felt foggy. The team diagnosed him with another concussion, his second in less than a month. He didn't feel like himself, a sensation that would return again and again in the coming months.

• • •

Byram sat in his Toyota Tacoma, feeling lost and scared. He had turned 20 earlier in the summer and was in Vancouver, where he was training for the 2021–22 season with Colorado. He called his mom.

Things still weren't right. Byram hadn't played a game since the Kolesar hit. He had been nearing a return, only to come down with COVID-19 in April 2021. He thought he'd recovered fine from the virus—he had experienced symptoms for a few days, but nothing he couldn't manage—yet when he'd gotten back on the ice, everything was off.

"I felt like I was a corpse," he said.

It felt as if someone was pounding on his head. He was dizzy, too. To make matters worse, he started having vertigo episodes after his second concussion. Those increased in frequency after he got COVID-19. He didn't always know which symptoms were caused by the virus and which were caused by his concussions.

Eventually, he improved enough for the Avalanche to clear him during the 2021 playoffs. But he didn't appear in any games. After all the time Byram had missed, Bednar wasn't comfortable playing him in the biggest contests of the year.

When Byram got to Vancouver for summer training, his mental and physical state took a swing for the worse once again. He still didn't feel like himself. He worried something was wrong for good, that he had lost the sport he always wanted to play. Trainer Jordan Mackenzie noticed Byram's recovery times were slower than normal. The defenseman had less energy.

Something was just ... *off*.

"What am I going to do?" he asked his mom over the phone, while sitting alone in his car. He feared the worst.

"I can't play hockey anymore."

Stacey's heart dropped. She mostly listened during the conversation, letting Byram vent. But she also offered perspective. Just because he was injured in that moment, she said, didn't mean he always would be.

Byram tried checking every box to get better. He got massages on the soft tissue around his neck and saw a specialist in post-concussion management. The young defenseman also saw a therapist, which he found beneficial.

At the end of July, he and his father went on a 10-day trip into the Yukon wilderness, where they camped, unplugged, and lived off the land. They hiked more than a dozen miles some days. Byram dealt with occasional symptoms during the trip, but when he returned, he felt rejuvenated and ready for his second pro season. He looked dynamic early on for the Avalanche, scoring his first NHL goal early in the year and playing fearlessly on offense. He was unafraid to jump into the rush or take shots in big moments. Erik Johnson said his young teammate looked like a contender for the Calder Trophy given to the league's top rookie. Byram was still eligible for the award because he hadn't played enough to qualify the season before.

Then came the next hit. Just as it appeared he had made it through his concussion issues, Byram took an accidental Bo Horvat elbow to the head in a November game against Vancouver. He was concussed for the third time in less than a year.

After all the progress, he had to start the process over.

Colorado defenseman Bowen Byram in action against Winnipeg during a game on January 6, 2022, in Denver. A first-round pick in the 2019 draft, Byram was sidelined by concussion issues in 2021 but returned to the club in 2022 to make a big impact in the playoffs.

Byram initially returned two weeks later, scoring in his first game back. But even though he'd been medically cleared, his symptoms lingered. After his second game back in early December, he came out of the lineup again, missing another month. He tried to return again when the calendar flipped to 2022, and though he played well, he still didn't feel right.

Ahead of a January game against Nashville, Byram called his parents. He wasn't eating much and wasn't sleeping well. He needed a pause to figure out what was going on with his body. The team granted him a personal leave. Hockey wasn't his focus; he thought about shutting things down for the year. He simply wanted to feel better.

With time, he did. He started to think about playing again. He took the ice by himself, then worked his way into group skates. His excitement returned. Maybe, just maybe, he could make it back to the lineup.

And now, after the AHL conditioning stint, he was back, just in time to play Crosby. For the rest of the season, nothing concussion-related would keep him from the lineup. He was back.

• • •

It was a feel-good time for Colorado. The Avalanche knocked off a strong Edmonton team in a shootout four days after Byram returned to the lineup. Kuemper made the winning save then pressed his stick through his glove as if sheathing a sword. The Avalanche even collected a win off the ice during the post-deadline stretch, nabbing the top undrafted college free agent, Ben Meyers, from the University of Minnesota—a player the rival Wild desperately wanted.

Meyers was ineligible for the postseason because the Avalanche didn't have his rights ahead of the trade deadline, but he could suit up for regular season action. Bednar gave him a shot, and the rookie scored in his first game, a 7–4 Colorado win against Carolina. Nichushkin and André Burakovsky mobbed the rookie when he skated to the bench. The victory was the Avalanche's ninth in a row. They were rolling.

Streaks are fickle, though. As soon as one snaps, another kind can begin. The Avalanche dropped a tight game against Washington two nights after beating Carolina. Then came a disastrous road trip that included losses to lowly Seattle and Winnipeg.

Was Colorado just coasting, waiting for the playoffs to start before going all-in? Would the Avalanche be able to flip the switch that easily? As the postseason approached, the team had to figure that out. Landeskog, who was still recovering from knee surgery, debated how to address the poor play. He thought about calling his first players-only meeting of the year but decided against it. The team would simply have to push through the funk.

It's hard to keep up the intensity when there's nothing at stake, and the Avalanche knew they were in the playoffs as the top seed in the Western Conference. Whether it was because players were trying to avoid injury or because they were subconsciously relaxing, they seemed to play with less desperation in their game. Logan O'Connor ended up thinking the skid was beneficial long-term. It served as a reminder that they had to do the little, hard-nosed things. They couldn't just rely on their elite skill.

"It was a good gut check," O'Connor said.

Devon Toews—whose absence the Avalanche felt every time he missed games—didn't go on the road trip, to let some nagging injuries heal ahead of the playoffs, but he was back on the ice when Colorado returned home to play St. Louis. The Avalanche had three games left in the regular season, and Toews saw them as an opportunity to dial in and make sure the team's mindset was right.

Sure enough, the Avalanche played exactly the kind of game they needed against the Blues. After goals by Nichushkin and Erik Johnson started the second period, Colorado got a score from a player who was overdue for something to go right. Newly acquired Josh Manson, who had been struggling to adjust to the Avalanche style of play after the trade deadline, took a long wrist shot that slithered through traffic and into the net.

Manson went for a haircut ahead of the game and joked that "it had everything to do" with his goal. Bednar had talked to the defenseman about letting the game come to him, and it helped Manson grow more comfortable. It was an important development; Sakic didn't acquire him to play a small role come the postseason.

Colorado ended up clinching the Blues win with an empty-net goal from Nazem Kadri. To answer the bell for his hit on Justin Faulk the previous postseason, Kadri had two goals and two assists in three regular season games against the Blues in 2021–22, as well as two fights to answer the bell for his hit on Justin Faulk the previous postseason. It was a fitting precursor for the eventual matchup in the playoffs.

The win reminded the players, and perhaps some panicked fans, that the Avalanche had the talent and poise to thrive in big games. As Toews said, they were ready to go.

A BULL IN A CHINA SHOP

YOU'RE NEVER FAR from water in the Halifax area of Nova Scotia. Nathan MacKinnon, who lived by a small lake between the towns of Dartmouth and Cole Harbour, was never far from ice in the winter.

MacKinnon describes his younger self as "a bit of a psychopath." He first put on skates as a two-year-old, wearing a turtleneck, balancing on the blades indoors, and smiling for the camera. Before long, the dream of making it to the NHL had consumed him. He would accept nothing less. There was no Plan B, said Jon Greenwood, who coached him at the peewee and bantam levels. So he was always working, whether at organized practices or on the lake, which was small enough to freeze quickly. He spent hours out there, sometimes with friends and sometimes alone, firing puck after puck at the first net he ever owned. He'd come home for lunch in elementary school and eat on the lake. He'd have dinner on the snow bank, then play until dark.

The net's weathered posts now look ready to collapse, and the back is full of holes, barely still attached. MacKinnon hung a blanket behind the twine as a backup, but that's tattered now, too. His parents kept it: a symbol of their son's dedication.

Cole Harbour Place, a local rink and community center, was only a five-minute drive from his family's house. The building has expanded since it opened in the late 1980s and now has two sheets of ice, but the original rink features a mural of an idyllic-looking outdoor hockey game. This was where MacKinnon grew up playing.

Nowadays, the wall bordering the main rink's bleachers has a pair of display cases filled with old gear and photos that honor both

MacKinnon and Sidney Crosby, Cole Harbour's most famous son. Two banners hang over the rink itself. The newer one reads HOME OF NATHAN MACKINNON. The older one says HOME OF SIDNEY CROSBY.

Greenwood first heard about MacKinnon when the forward was dominating the under-11 age group, then started coaching him as a peewee player. He was struck by his focus and competitiveness. The youngster would get mad at himself for missing the net during skates, and he'd challenge Greenwood, who was 25 at the time, to post-practice shooting competitions. That would put the coach in somewhat of a catch-22. If MacKinnon lost, he'd be furious at himself. If he was victorious, he'd immediately ask if the coach had let him win.

Greenwood saw no choice but to try his hardest.

"I might have beat him once or twice when he was that age," he said while looking over the Cole Harbour Place rink. "But I'm sure that stopped shortly after."

Their hometown will always link MacKinnon and Crosby, who is eight years older. It isn't often two Hall of Fame–level talents grow up playing at the same community rink. But MacKinnon followed his idol's footsteps beyond Cole Harbour. When he was entering high school, he left Nova Scotia—and Canada altogether—to go to Shattuck–St. Mary's, the same boarding school in Faribault, Minnesota, that Crosby attended before playing major junior hockey. The highly regarded hockey program helped develop the Penguins captain, as well as NHL standouts Jonathan Toews and Zach Parise. It worked for MacKinnon, too.

• • •

To hold a proper tournament, Nathan MacKinnon needed a proper prize. He was a freshman in high school at Shattuck and was organizing a two-on-two knee hockey tournament with Danny Tirone, his closest friend at school. Jody Koch, their dorm mom in Breck residence hall, took the two friends to Walmart to buy supplies so they could make a trophy. They picked out a wood base and silver lettering. Back at the dorm, they painted the wood maroon to match Shattuck's colors, then used the letters to spell out "Breck Knee Hockey Champs." On top, they glued a miniature Stanley Cup.

Koch remembers how proud the two buddies were of the trophy. The tournament was to take place in Breck's basement, which was complete with a carpeted floor and NHL pennants on the wall. To MacKinnon and Tirone, it was inevitable that they would get to hoist the prize they created.

But as classmates watched from along the wall, the games didn't go as planned. MacKinnon and Tirone lost, sending both of them into a rage. The way Koch remembers it, MacKinnon had to be separated from one of his opponents, and Tirone's face went red with anger. Both left the basement to cool off before returning to watch the end of the tournament.

MacKinnon was just as fierce on the ice. Shattuck defenseman Willie Raskob remembers his forceful skating more than anything else. There was a sound to it, even back then: a *bam, bam, bam* to his first three strides. Some of hockey's fastest skaters are graceful, like Connor McDavid, who looks effortless gliding across the ice. That isn't MacKinnon. His speed comes from power. You can see the work he puts into every stride.

The hype around MacKinnon had already started by the time he reached Shattuck. His teammate at the time, Garrett Cecere, saw him at their dorm meeting the first night and noticed he had muscles unlike the other teenagers. Reid Brown, who knew the then freshman as a messy roommate he helped with math homework, once typed, "Nathan MacKinnon hockey" into his Google search bar. He found he was already being projected as a top pick in the 2013 NHL Draft. ESPN ran a story in 2010 called "Nate the Kid" comparing his rise to his favorite player, Sid the Kid.

"He's worn that crown of thorns pretty well," said Tom Ward, Shattuck's director of player development.

Raskob keeps up with MacKinnon's NHL career now, but the two butted heads as short-tempered, ultra-competitive teenagers. MacKinnon was on a different level than his teammates, said John

LaFontaine, his freshman coach. Sometimes he couldn't seem to comprehend that they simply didn't have the ability to do what he could on the ice.

"Willie, play D!" he'd snap at Raskob.

"Nate, mind your own business," the defenseman would reply.

Once during freshman year, Raskob grew so frustrated that he went to LaFontaine's office to talk. MacKinnon was driving him up the wall, he told the coach, and he wasn't alone. The players could never do anything right in their star teammate's eyes, Raskob said. The coach told his defenseman that MacKinnon was trying to set a high bar, that his attitude will help them. But, he added, someone might need to stand up to him. To tell him to back off.

The next day at practice, perhaps on his own or perhaps after a conversation with Raskob, defenseman Ian McCoshen knocked MacKinnon to the ice with a clean but hard check. McCoshen, who went on to play in the NHL with the Panthers, then held his stick over MacKinnon's chest, not allowing him to get up for a few extra seconds. MacKinnon skated to LaFontaine, furious, and asked if he saw the play.

"You play really hard, and you're pretty tough on your teammates," the coach told him, adding that McCoshen's hit was clean. "I think he was just trying to make sure he was tough on you in the same way."

MacKinnon was trying to make everyone better with his hardnosed nature. He does the same thing at Avalanche practices, driven by a deep desire to win. But at Shattuck, playing with those who didn't share his physical gifts, perhaps he needed to be less harsh. The McCoshen hit put MacKinnon in his place, at least to an extent, LaFontaine said.

As much as MacKinnon expected from others, he expected the same, if not more, from himself. He and Tirone, a goaltender and his sophomore year roommate, shared an intensity to improve. They did extra workouts and even tried yoga in their room. MacKinnon was an early riser, and he'd invite Tirone on walks, which they both found cleared their minds. They'd go to the rink together so MacKinnon could shoot pucks at Tirone, and the goalie remembers his friend once asking him not to tell anyone. He loved working when others weren't. It made him feel like he was gaining an edge.

Then there was food, which he and Tirone both took seriously, perhaps to an unhealthy extent. They prided themselves on passing up dessert, viewing every sweet they refused as an advantage gained on someone who indulged. MacKinnon didn't even want cake on his birthday, Koch remembers. She started making yogurt parfaits for the pair because they kept declining the cookies and brownies she baked for residents. The approach was certainly over the top, Tirone said years later, but nevertheless an example of how badly each wanted to maximize his potential.

"Nathan MacKinnon is no fluke," he said.

Now that he's an NHL veteran, MacKinnon competes with the same fierceness—albeit better contained—as he did at Shattuck. His coaches at the school worked with him to try to channel his frustrations in positive ways, sometimes with more success than others.

Multiple Shattuck teammates described MacKinnon as the most competitive person they've been around, and his need to win extended beyond the ice. Tirone, for example, arrived at school as a better Ping-Pong player than his friend, which irritated MacKinnon to the point that he practiced over and over until he could win. Students were required to play sports year round, so MacKinnon was on the tennis team during his freshman year. He'd be frustrated when he lost. It didn't matter that hockey was his focus—losing was infuriating.

MacKinnon even found a way to compete in the classroom. During sophomore year history class, he would have his computer out, as if taking notes. In reality, he'd found another competitive outlet: playing Tetris against other hockey players in the room.

He got by academically, but classes were far from his passion. He once asked Koch to home-school him so he could spend more time practicing hockey. He was joking—at least partially. And though he was intense on the ice, those around him at Shattuck found him approachable, genuine, and goofy away from competitive environments. Koch, for one, saw his sweet side. They'd sit together and chat, talking through things if he had a bad day, and he wrote her a thank-you note at the end of his second and final year at the school. Kathy MacKinnon, Nathan's mother, bought Koch a pair of earrings as a farewell gift.

Baie-Comeau Drakkar chose MacKinnon first in the Quebec Major Junior Hockey League draft, but the team knew it would have a hard time convincing an English-speaking player to come to a small town northeast of Quebec City. Sure enough, MacKinnon didn't report, so Baie-Comeau traded his rights to the Halifax Mooseheads, the Quebec league team for which he grew up rooting. His family had even hosted Mooseheads player Frédérik Cabana when Nathan was young, and he chose to wear Cabana's former No. 22 when he started his major junior career.

Though Baie-Comeau fans booed MacKinnon when he played road games there, calling him MacChicken, his decision to go to the Mooseheads was a good one. He lived at home and went to school with his childhood friends. He drove teammates Jonathan Drouin and Zach Fucale, both future NHLers themselves, to the rink in his black Ford Escape. The Mooseheads won the Memorial Cup—a national championship involving the winners of all three Canadian Hockey League titles—and MacKinnon dominated in their postseason run, scoring 11 goals and adding 22 assists in 33 games. When he scored an empty-net goal to clinch the final game against the Portland Winterhawks, who were led by defenseman Seth Jones, he skipped through the air and leapt onto the bench, where his teammates mobbed him. It was his third goal of the game—but as he'd show in the 2022 playoffs, not his last hat trick in a big moment.

MacKinnon and Jones, the defenseman he beat in the Memorial Cup Final, entered 2013 NHL Draft week as arguably the top two prospects. The Avalanche were also interested in Finnish center Aleksander Barkov, but after the Memorial Cup, Joe Sakic and the front office saw MacKinnon as the clear-cut No. 1. In his TSN on-set interview moments after announcing MacKinnon as Colorado's pick, Sakic mentioned the forward had played under a microscope for a long time. He shouldered the pressures that came with Crosby comparisons, then came through as the No. 1 pick in the Quebec league draft.

Now he'd have lofty expectations on him once again. He'd be ready to meet them, too.

• • •

Crosby assumed MacKinnon wouldn't make it to their workout with trainer Andy O'Brien. The young centerman had returned to Canada the night before from his trip to the U.S. for the NHL Draft. O'Brien's workout was scheduled for 9:00 AM on Prince Edward Island, which is a three-hour drive from Halifax and has good beaches for running. No one would have blamed MacKinnon for missing it.

But when Crosby arrived at the beach, MacKinnon was in the parking lot with his father.

"He got back at 2:00 AM, jumped in the car at 5:00 or 6:00 AM," Crosby remembered.

"What are you doing here?" the Pittsburgh captain asked.

"I'm not missing a workout," MacKinnon replied.

They sprinted in the sand, mixing in lunges and other speed footwork. O'Brien pushed them to go at a good pace. Crosby was gassed; he wondered how MacKinnon was holding up. With five minutes to go in the workout, he found out. MacKinnon started puking everywhere.

Crosby had thought MacKinnon simply showing up was remarkable. When he saw how hard he pushed himself, he was even more impressed. The success of going No. 1 overall wasn't going to deter his work ethic. MacKinnon went on to be the NHL rookie of the year the following season, though Crosby offered him an early reminder of how far he had to go. In his ninth NHL game, as MacKinnon defended Crosby in the Avalanche defensive zone, the Penguins star deked him. MacKinnon nearly fell to the ice.

When MacKinnon was growing up, Jon Greenwood always wondered when he'd hit the inevitable speedbumps. But they never seemed to come. He thrived against kids from bigger provinces.

He dominated at Shattuck. He took major junior hockey by storm. Now, after MacKinnon's Calder Trophy win, it looked like the NHL would be the same.

But then the young forward stagnated, failing to match his rookie point total over his next three seasons. Colorado missed the playoffs in all three of those years. He had to adjust. He had to mature.

• • •

MacKinnon's stubbornness shone through early in his professional career. He didn't believe he needed to go through extra treatment or invest additional resources on his body when he was banged up. Mental fortitude was all he needed, he thought. He could push through.

"I was an idiot," he said.

MacKinnon knew he was better than he had shown since winning the Calder Trophy. He was sick of being average. Something had to change.

That led him to an all-encompassing approach aimed at optimizing his body and mind. He started seeing a sports psychologist, aware that he has a tendency to get down on himself and let his emotions get the best of him. He dialed even more into nutrition— he'd been eating chips and drinking soda on team flights early in his career—and focused on treatment, too. Performance rehabilitation specialist Marcin Goszczynski, who has worked with the likes of Crosby, Maria Sharapova, and Andre De Grasse, played a big role in that. MacKinnon first met Goszczynski through Crosby early in his career, and he started working with the trainer more as he started taking off-ice recovery more seriously. Midway through the 2017–18 season, he talked to Goszczynski about moving to Denver so they could work together more regularly. Sharapova, though, had recently hired him to help her in Los Angeles, but she said Goszczynski could travel to MacKinnon and Crosby on his off days.

Then, when Sharapova retired from professional tennis midway through the 2019–20 hockey season, MacKinnon paid for Goszczynski to move into a downtown Denver apartment. The center loves how his body feels after their sessions, which can involve anything from massages to soft-tissue work to actual exercises. He pays Goszczynski a premium and gets treatment from him after home games. "I look at it as an investment in my body," MacKinnon said going into the 2021–22 season. "That's the best thing I can invest in—my body and mind."

Avalanche captain Gabriel Landeskog compared MacKinnon's focus on his body to how Formula 1 racers take care of their cars. It has paid off. After leading the team with 53 points in Colorado's abysmal 2016–17 season, MacKinnon scored 97 in 2017–18, finishing second to Taylor Hall in MVP voting. He's been one of the league's top players since.

As he developed into a superstar, MacKinnon's contract became a bigger and bigger bargain for the Avalanche. He signed a seven-year deal worth $44.1 million ($6.3 million average annual value) heading into 2016–17. It seemed fair at the time, if not a little pricey for the Avalanche. But when MacKinnon exploded, it became one of the most team-friendly deals in the league and gave Colorado added financial flexibility.

MacKinnon's serious approach to preparation, on-ice performance, and recovery rubbed off on his teammates, many of whom now also pay for Goszczynski's services. Heading into the 2021–22 season, former Avalanche defenseman Nikita Zadorov gave an interview in Russia saying MacKinnon removed desserts from the dressing room and started eating chickpea pasta to get more protein. The tone of Zadorov's interview was complimentary—he said MacKinnon's increased focus was a key factor in the team's growth—but it also led to a series of memes ribbing the forward for his intensity.

MacKinnon himself found them funny but added that some of Zadorov's comments were a bit exaggerated or perhaps lost in translation. He made a point to say he'll sometimes eat at In-N-Out Burger during West Coast road trips.

No one wanted a title more than Colorado's top-line center, Nathan MacKinnon, seen here in Game 6 of the Stanley Cup Final vs. Tampa Bay. MacKinnon tied for the most goals scored (13) in the 2022 playoffs.

That doesn't mean there wasn't some truth in Zadorov's comments, though. MacKinnon is strict with himself, and he expects his teammates to be committed to their performance, too.

"He's definitely on a couple guys about diets and what's the right thing to eat before games," André Burakovsky added in a 2020 interview with The Athletic.

He also chides players for on-ice mistakes at practice. That includes the team's best players, including Cale Makar. MacKinnon's intensity jumped out to Manson as soon as Colorado acquired him at the deadline, but the defenseman believed it was good for the team.

"In a lot of situations, people don't really have the ability or the bravery to come out of their comfort zone and say that awkward thing," Manson said. "He doesn't really have that. He's just like, 'Hey, I don't like this and I'm gonna tell you about it.' I think it's great."

He cares about his teammates, too. When Bowen Byram was dealing with his concussion issues in the 2020–21 season, for example, MacKinnon paid for him to work with Goszczynski, his trainer.

MacKinnon, whose fierceness is balanced out by Landeskog's calm head, was 26 years old entering the postseason. He already had three top-three MVP finishes in his career, as well as a World Championship gold medal, a Lady Byng Trophy, and a Calder Trophy. But he still lacked what he craved the most: playoff success.

He had grown into a more poised presence after Colorado's 2021 disappointment, speaking with added perspective after in-season disappointments. But though he perhaps wouldn't have used the same harsh tones he did after the Vegas loss—"I haven't won shit"— he still believed he had more to prove. In his eyes, anything less than an Avalanche championship would mean disappointment.

MOVING ON

THE AVALANCHE'S FIRST-ROUND matchup with Nashville was a collision between their present and a key member of their past, one whose departure shaped the team for years to come.

On November 5, 2017, the Avalanche were in the midst of a road game against the Islanders when Matt Duchene slipped off the ice, heading to the dressing room behind injured teammate Blake Comeau. Duchene had played only a pair of shifts and fewer than two minutes that night. Those moments on the ice turned out to be his last with the Avalanche, the team that drafted him third overall in 2009.

Around Christmas the year before, Duchene had approached Sakic, his childhood idol, to request a trade. He called it the hardest thing he'd ever done, but he suspected a rebuild was coming in Colorado and wanted to play postseason hockey. He'd been through multiple rebuilds already. He didn't want to do it again.

John Mitchell, who was on the 2016–17 team, said the trade request caused some turmoil during the Avalanche's dismal, last-place campaign. It wasn't the main reason the season fell apart, but it was, Mitchell believed, certainly a small component. "When one of your better players is like, 'Hey, I want out of here,' it's like, 'Okay, well you don't think we're good enough,'" he said. "All those things run through your mind."

Sakic didn't fulfill his player's request immediately, and he drew some criticism for it nationally as the process drew out. Insider Pierre LeBrun, for one, thought the general manager missed key windows to trade the standout forward. But Sakic was showing the hockey world his patience. He wasn't going to trade Duchene for less than his value, and so the disgruntled forward started 2017 training camp still with the team. Duchene told reporters he was there to honor his contract and out of respect for his fans and teammates. He hadn't expected to still be in Avalanche colors.

Sakic told Duchene to remain patient, and the center played the first 14 games of the year with Colorado. He logged 10 points and helped the team to an 8–6–0 start. Teammates credited him with going about his business professionally.

The trade request remained, though, until Colorado finally worked out a three-team blockbuster with the Senators and Predators. The deal was finalized during the Islanders game and, when Duchene saw staffers talking on the bench during play, he figured something was going down. Sure enough, the coaches pulled the forward from the contest.

Sakic waited for Duchene as he left the ice, and the two met one final time, the 26-year-old still wearing skates. The general manager said he could tell his former player was happy. Relieved.

"There's no such thing as a perfect human being, but for me, Joe Sakic is pretty close," Duchene said the next day during his Senators introductory press conference. "We both had a tear in our eye yesterday when he talked to me."

Duchene showered, put on a black, collared shirt, and left the dressing room before the end of the first period. The year-long saga was over.

"At the end of the day, we all want to play for the Colorado Avalanche and do great things here," Erik Johnson told reporters after the game. "He didn't, and we wish him well."

Bednar viewed the trade as a changing of the guard. With Duchene, at that point the longest-tenured Colorado player, traded away, the team was officially in the hands of its young core players: captain Gabriel Landeskog, Mikko Rantanen, and Nathan MacKinnon, who finished the season second in MVP voting.

"It became their team with the older group leaving," Bednar said. "Basically everything has changed since then."

In the short term, it relieved a stressor that had been hanging over the team's head. Two months later, when asked by Sportsnet how the trade changed the dressing room culture, MacKinnon said, "It did a lot." He didn't blame Duchene—"it wasn't like a crazy breakup or anything," he said—but the move ensured everyone on the roster wanted to be there. Comeau called it a reset, and Rantanen believed it made the dressing room looser. The situation had been weighing on the team.

In a cruel twist of fate for Duchene, the Senators missed the postseason, going from a near–Stanley Cup Final berth in 2016–17 to the next-to-worst team in the East in 2017–18. The Avalanche, meanwhile, underwent a massive turnaround from their 48-point season, going 35–24–9 after the Duchene trade to clinch a playoff spot.

Ottawa struggled again the next year and ended up moving Duchene at the trade deadline to Columbus, where he finally appeared in playoff hockey games. He helped the Blue Jackets upset Tampa Bay in the first round and notched 10 points in 10 games, then signed a seven-year, $56 million deal with Nashville in the off-season. Ultimately, the situation worked out for Duchene. He received a massive contract and was on playoff teams four of the five years after leaving Colorado.

But the trade may have worked out better for Sakic. In the three-team deal, the Avalanche received Samuel Girard, a draft pick that became Bowen Byram, and another pick used to acquire Justus Annunen, who debuted in December 2021 as the team's top goaltending prospect. All three were available to Colorado entering the 2022 playoffs, and both Byram and Girard played top-four defensive minutes at points during the regular season.

Girard, Byram, and Annunen weren't the only players Sakic acquired in the deal. The Avalanche also got goalie Andrew Hammond (who appeared in postseason games for Colorado in 2018), 2017 first-round pick Shane Bowers, and a 2019 third-round selection eventually used on Matthew Stienburg. But none of those players were with the NHL club during the 2021–22 regular season. Additionally, the Avalanche acquired a 2018 second-round pick, which they traded to Pittsburgh for two later picks, one of which was used to acquire Annunen.

"As you're watching it, it seemed like a never-ending soap opera," Blues general manager Doug Armstrong told The Athletic's Pierre LeBrun. "And then all of a sudden he makes that three-way trade and solidifies his organization for a decade."

"That was a Picasso by Joe," said Erik Johnson, adding he holds nothing against Duchene, whom he called a great guy. "In a way, we should be thanking him because we got some pieces that helped us win the Stanley Cup."

Duchene had a career-best season with Nashville in 2021–22, scoring 43 goals and averaging more than a point per game. His days in Colorado felt like a distant era, and MacKinnon downplayed the connection going into the series.

"He just needed a change of scenery," he said. "Dutchy is a great player, having an awesome year. That's really about it."

To players, perhaps. But to fans, many of whom jeer Duchene whenever he returns to Denver as a visiting player, his presence in the first round was a reminder of an uncomfortable departure. A reminder of how situations change, sometimes for the better.

• • •

Darryl Sutter never shies away from speaking his mind. And in mid-March, when discussing the importance of avoiding a wild-card playoff spot, the 63-year-old Flames coach brought up the Avalanche.

"If you are a wild-card team, I sure as hell don't want to play Colorado in the first round," Sutter said. "Because it's going to be a waste of eight days."

The Calgary media room laughed, but his point didn't seem like an exaggeration as the Nashville series began. The Predators were without star goaltender Juuse Saros, who suffered a late-season ankle injury. Even with Saros, they lacked both the starpower and depth of the Avalanche. To make matters worse for Nashville, Landeskog returned from his knee injury in time for the Predators' series, playing on the second line with Artturi Lehkonen and Nazem

Kadri. Any concerns about the team's late-season funk evaporated early in Game 1.

After one period, Colorado led 5–0, scoring on the power play, penalty kill, and at even strength within the first nine minutes of the game. Makar added to his season-long highlight reel midway through the period with a play reminiscent of his Chicago overtime winner in January. With the puck on his stick, he backed toward the blue line, looking at partner Devon Toews. When he noticed Tanner Jeannot shifting over, he reversed direction as quickly as a match lights, sidestepping the helpless Nashville forward. That gave him enough room to get to the net, zooming at goalie David Rittich from an awkward angle. At the last second, he switched the puck from his backhand to his forehand and released it on net. The shot bounced off the goalie's helmet and in. Makar, who had barely missed the 30-goal mark during the regular season, finishing with 28, let his calm façade down for an instant, punching the air.

He called the play "a little bit of a lucky one," but when a player has Makar's skating ability and explosiveness, he sometimes benefits from fortunate bounces.

Rittich, who went to the 2020 All-Star Game representing Calgary but struggled as Saros's backup, didn't make it through the period. Nashville coach John Hynes pulled him 15 minutes into the game, immediately after his fifth goal allowed. In came Connor Ingram, who had only three games of NHL experience. But he hung in admirably in Game 1 relief duty, halting all but two of the 32 shots he faced.

The 25-year-old Ingram was actually one of the reasons Nashville drew top-seeded Colorado in the first place, though not because of strong play. The Predators had games on back-to-back nights to end the regular season, and with Rittich between the pipes in the penultimate contest, Hynes gave Ingram the start in the finale. A win against the lowly Coyotes would have given Nashville the top wild-card spot and a first-round date with Sutter's Calgary Flames. But Ingram and the Predators blew a 4–0 lead, setting up their playoff matchup with the Avalanche.

Duchene scored Nashville's first goal of the playoffs with a power play tally late in the second to cut Colorado's lead to 6–1, then added a third period goal to make the score 7–2. That stood as the final. His former home fans reacted less than warmly to his presence, booing him when he touched the puck and at times starting a "Duchene sucks!" chant.

"It's playoffs. The fans are into it," he said after the game. "They've always had an amazing fan base here. They're backing their team well."

As Nashville's chances of a comeback dwindled from slim to none, the Predators picked up their physicality. Landeskog said postgame, "If the result is not going your way, then you try to impact the game in a different way." By night's end, the Predators collected 34 penalty minutes. And, perhaps aware of Kadri's history of losing his composure in playoff games, they seemed to try getting under the center's skin. At the end of the second period, Artturi Lehkonen got in a scuffle behind the net, and when Kadri skated toward the crowd, Luke Kunin knocked him to the ice and pulled off his gloves, as if he wanted to fight. Manson saw what happened and, not wanting Kunin and Kadri to fight, he grabbed the Predators forward and threw him to the ice. A step too far? Maybe, he told reporters, but he wanted to send a message.

"I'm not going to let him step in against Naz," he said. "We're not going to fall into that trap that they're trying to get us to."

Kadri, meanwhile, didn't lose his cool. It was an example of his maturation, Bednar said the next day. Playoffs aren't about ego, to the coach. They're about winning.

• • •

Any NHL-level goaltender can have a day in which everything works. That's why Ingram could go from letting a huge lead slip away against the Coyotes to stopping just about everything in front of him in Game 2 of the first round, the highest-pressure game of his young NHL career.

"Against a high-powered offensive team, you're going to need excellent goaltending to win games," Hynes, the Predators coach, said after the game. "He certainly provided that tonight."

But that wasn't how it looked early. MacKinnon darted up ice five minutes into the first period and buried a shot shortside from the faceoff dot. "Let's fucking go," he yelled to Byram as the rookie skated toward him to celebrate.

Ingram, wearing a white mask, planted his stick upside down on the ice and reached for his water bottle, the goal horn still ringing overhead. He wouldn't hear that sound again for several more hours.

Of the Avalanche's next 49 shots, zero got past Ingram, aside from a Valeri Nichushkin putback waved off for interference on Artturi Lehkonen. The Nashville goalie snatched a dangerous J.T. Compher shot from the circle in the first period. He used his pads to stop a Makar power play chance in the second and his glove to stop the defenseman on a shorthanded rush in the third. Arguably his best save came when Bowen Byram teed Kadri up for a one-timer right in front of the net. Ingram lunged and somehow halted the puck with his left pad.

"He stood on his head big-time," Toews said. "We peppered him with everything. We were hitting seams, which a lot of times are open nets because our guys make such good plays down low, and finding open guys. We just couldn't get something past him."

As Colorado heaped shots on Ingram to no avail, Nashville found a way to tie the game. With five minutes left in the first period, star defenseman Roman Josi sent a puck up ice. Girard made a smart read, jumping in front of the puck in the neutral zone. But the puck took a funky bounce and went off the defenseman's body—right to Yakov Trenin. With Girard behind on the play after dropping to a knee to try to block the initial pass, the Russian forward darted toward Kuemper on a two-on-one rush and zinged the puck into the net. He jumped into the glass with glee.

The game went to overtime with Colorado having more than twice as many shots as the visiting team. The Predators generated chances in the extra period, but Kuemper did his best Ingram impression and stood firm, snatching a Mikael Granlund deflection 17 seconds into overtime and later gobbling up a Granlund rebound before Duchene could crash the net.

Players joked that their scouting report on Ingram was "completely false," according to Toews. "It had us shooting glove side a lot, and that wasn't the play," he laughed when looking back at the game. But the defenseman never sensed frustration. The team believed it could sneak one past the netminder.

Sure enough, midway through the first overtime period, Helm won a puck battle behind the net, passing it along the boards. Nico Sturm kept the puck moving, getting it to Toews, who found Makar. The defenseman surveyed the ice, which drew Predators forward Michael McCarron out of the slot, allowing Sturm to zip into the dangerous scoring area. Makar found his teammate. Sturm got a shot off, but Josi sprawled in front of it, blocking the chance.

Unfortunately for Nashville, the puck bounced off Josi's body and went right to Makar, the most dangerous player in that night's game. He fired a quick shot on net. O'Connor, who stood directly in front of Ingram, said he instinctually thought Makar would shoot low, so he jumped. His dad, former NHLer Myles O'Connor, later asked why he didn't try to tip the shot, to which O'Connor replied, "It's Cale shooting the puck. I'll trust him."

Good call. O'Connor's positioning blocked Ingram's sight line—the goalie said it was the first shot all game he didn't have his eyes on—and Makar's shot went through his legs and into the back of the net. It wasn't the flashiest goal of the defenseman's season but, up to that point, it was the most important.

Raising his left arm to the sky, Sturm was first to reach Makar along the glass, starting the celebratory mob. MacKinnon and Artturi Lehkonen were last to leave the bench; they were too busy hugging. And back in Calgary, Gary Makar let out a scream he joked could be heard 1,000 miles away in Ball Arena.

It capped a brilliant game by the defenseman. He collected 12 shots, a team record in a playoff game, and Colorado dominated in scoring chances when he was on the ice.

"His vision is as good as anybody I've seen," Hall of Fame defenseman Paul Coffey said after watching the game. "His first two steps on the opposing blue line and getting away from guys, I've never seen anything like it."

And while Makar was a likely hero, the other contributors on the play were not. After leading the Avalanche with 81 regular season games played, Logan O'Connor was a healthy scratch in Game 1. Frankly, he said, it sucked sitting out. "But if you want to be on a winning team, I think you've got to sort of understand what may come with it."

O'Connor knew that, with the toll playoff games take, he'd eventually reenter the lineup. Sure enough, Andrew Cogliano suffered an upper-body injury in Game 1, which kept him from playing the rest of the series, and Bednar chose O'Connor over Alex Newhook as his replacement.

Sturm, meanwhile, was battling through a serious injury. He'd dinged up his elbow in the regular season finale against Minnesota, and in Game 1 against the Predators, Nashville defenseman Matt Benning hit him with what Sturm called "a tiny cross-check that happens a thousand times every game." Unfortunately for Sturm, Benning's stick went right into his already weakened left elbow. He felt it snap.

"The joint was probably already damaged in a way that it was really weak," Sturm said. "Then it just happened right there."

The next day, the forward got an MRI. When Scott Woodward, the director of rehabilitation, called to tell him the results, his tone sounded grim and made Sturm worry he was out for the year. It turned out he had torn his UCL—what major league pitchers need Tommy John Surgery to fix—but the training staff believed that, because hockey is a non-throwing sport, the ligament could heal on its own.

Sturm said that, as an athlete, it's difficult being in a position to decide whether or not you're able to play. He could barely bend his arm in the brace the doctors gave him, and he didn't want to take the spot of a fully healthy teammate who could perform better. He asked himself if he was hurting the team by playing, if it would be a self-ish choice. Ultimately, he decided it wasn't, much to the Avalanche's benefit. He went from uncertainty to assisting an overtime winner.

"That's the playoffs," he said. "It's incredible, the stories that come out of there, right?"

• • •

Some stories are incredible. And sometimes stories, incredible or otherwise, are jarring. The Avalanche saw that firsthand in Game 3, when Ryan Johansen battled with MacKinnon for positioning in front of the Avalanche net late in the opening period. As he did, his stick got caught on Kuemper's mask, sending him sprawling backwards. It was a freak accident, one unlike anything Bednar had ever seen.

Kuemper stood up, his glove over his eye, and tried skating to the bench. He didn't get far, falling down in the faceoff circle. Trainers rushed onto the ice and immediately took him to the dressing room.

"Eye things are so scary," Josh Manson said. "You only have two of them, and you need them both."

Especially as a goalie.

Kuemper's teammates heard at intermission that, though he was ruled out for the rest of the game, he would at least be okay. He eventually joined the healthy scratches by the locker room for the rest of the day, his eye purple with bruising and swollen shut.

Kuemper would battle the impact of the injury through the remainder of the playoffs. Bednar said later on that the goalie went to an optometrist two to three times through the playoffs to "retrain his eye," and did vision and depth perception exercises at his locker.

"He had like a little string with knots on them of different colors that he had attached to his change stall," Jack Johnson said. "Nine times out of 10, I'd walk by and he'd be in there doing his vision exercises." ·

But that would come later. Back on the ice in the Nashville series, Colorado turned to Pavel Francouz for the remainder of the series. And, with the swelling around Kuemper's eye not down enough for

Avs goalie Darcy Kuemper, acquired before the season, anchored the team's defense in 2021–22 and, despite an eye injury suffered in Game 3 against the Predators, posted a 2.57 goals-against average in the playoffs.

him to play in Game 4, Annunen dressed for his first career play-off contest. That meant three of the Avalanche's 20 players on the bench for the clincher were either directly or indirectly a part of the Duchene trade.

Francouz wasn't perfect, allowing two goals in his first full period of action and another three in Game 4, but finished the series with an acceptable .902 save percentage. That was more than enough for Colorado's high-powered offense. Landeskog scored twice in Game 3 and helped the Avalanche to a 7–3 win, and early in Game 4, André Burakovsky fired a wrist shot so hard that it broke through the net.

With their season on the line, the Predators had one final gasp in Game 4, taking a third-period lead after a Filip Forsberg goal. But Colorado wasn't to be denied. Erik Johnson found Toews in the slot midway through the period, and the defenseman ripped a shot past Ingram. Then, three minutes later, Makar had another Makar moment when Trenin skated toward him along the boards in Colorado's offensive zone. That was a mistake.

"The one thing you can't do is run at him, and he had a guy just bull rush him," Toews said. "That probably put a smile on his face."

Makar easily got around Trenin. Knowing that Nashville mainly played man-to-man and that he had his man beat, Makar figured someone would be open. Sure enough, he had Nichushkin alone on the other side of the net. He whipped the puck across the ice, and the Russian winger clapped it home. The Avalanche never relinquished the lead.

A MacKinnon empty-net tally clinched the game, giving the Avalanche a series win and a week-long break, which the star center used to play video games and hang out with his parents' dogs. But first he went through the handshake line, stopping to talk to Duchene and patting his former teammate on the chest. Rantanen told the Predators forward that he was happy for his success in Nashville. Duchene had averaged a point per game in the sweep, and Rantanen believed he was the Predators' best player during the series.

Before leaving the ice, Duchene raised his stick to salute Nashville's home crowd—a farewell heading into a summer apart. Colorado players happily shuffled to the dressing room, their business completed and championship dreams still alive.

15

THE SECOND ROUND

THE SWEEP OF the Predators was lopsided, just like the Avalanche's Round 1 series against the Blues had been a year earlier. Colorado won each of those 2021 games by at least three goals. There were no overtime periods and barely any hold-your-breath moments for Avalanche fans. It was one-sided hockey: a star-filled team against an overmatched one.

First-round dominance far from guarantees a long playoff run, though, as the Avalanche saw in their series loss to Vegas. Now the team was back to the spot it met its match each of the previous three seasons—the second round—set to face a much-improved St. Louis team. After the Avalanche swept them in 2021, the Blues had an active off-season. General manager Doug Armstrong acquired Pavel Buchnevich in a trade with the New York Rangers, and he signed Brandon Saad away from the Avalanche. That gave St. Louis two new players capable of filling top-six forward roles. When the season rolled around, young players took leaps—Robert Thomas and Jordan Kyrou both averaged more than a point per game—and an old star in Vladimir Tarasenko bounced back from a pair of injury-riddled seasons.

By the playoffs, St. Louis was healthier than the year before, when key forward David Perron missed the Avalanche series with COVID-19. In the first round, the Blues dropped two of the first three games against Minnesota, then rattled off three consecutive wins, outscoring the Wild by a combined 15–5 to take the series. Set for a postseason rematch with the Avalanche, this wasn't the same St. Louis club Colorado swept a year earlier.

The Avalanche weren't the same team, either, icing a roster with more health and depth at all positions. Blues coach Craig Berube shrugged off the Avalanche's struggles late in the regular season, and when asked what made Colorado different from the year before, he answered with a laugh.

"They're pretty good still," he said.

Pretty good, but yet to get over the hump, as St. Louis had with a Stanley Cup win in 2019.

Not all of Colorado's Round 2 series losses were created equal. San Jose was a better, more experienced club than the Avalanche in 2019; it was an accomplishment for Colorado to make it to Game 7. In 2020, the Avalanche were playing their third-string goaltender by the end of their series with Dallas, and Gabriel Landeskog, Joonas Donskoi, Erik Johnson, and Matt Calvert all missed the final game with injuries.

Then, in 2021, there were the four consecutive losses after taking a 2–0 lead against Vegas—a choke no matter how it was framed. "The Vegas one was our fault," Nathan MacKinnon said later. "One hundred percent. That was on us."

Fair or unfair, after three years of heartbreak, the second-round narrative was in full force. It started early in the season. "Get out of the second round, why don't you?" a Vegas player chirped at the Avalanche bench.

Entering the Blues series, Jared Bednar and his players shrugged off questions about the Round 2 hump. But they heard the chatter, even as they tried to keep it out of focus. Logan O'Connor remembers walking past TVs and hearing talk about the team's second-round shortcomings. "We knew what was going on," he said.

The Avalanche were back where they'd met their match the past three seasons. The Blues series offered a chance to remedy those mistakes, or else Colorado would have to live with the consequences.

"It ain't going to be an easy ride," Nico Sturm said hours before Game 1. "That's for sure."

• • •

As Cale Makar was breaking into the league during 2019–20, his first regular season, Bednar learned the defenseman sometimes needed to reestablish his feel for the game after he'd taken time off. With a week between the end of the Nashville series and Game 1 against St. Louis, Makar didn't feel like he had his legs.

Perhaps that's what led to his costly early mistake. Midway through the first period of Game 1, he tried to pass out of the defensive zone to MacKinnon. Instead, the puck bounced off Ryan O'Reilly's skate, ricocheted off Brayden Schenn, and fell at O'Reilly's feet, alone in front of the net. The Blues captain moved the puck slightly to his right, then backhanded it past Darcy Kuemper, giving his team an early lead.

Against Nashville, the Avalanche went into every intermission either tied or leading. St. Louis needed only one period to snap that streak. Blues goaltender Jordan Binnington looked sharp early and was helped by three Colorado shots hitting the post in the period.

Still, Josh Manson sensed no change in mentality among his teammates. The Avalanche kept pushing, and as new Broncos quarterback Russell Wilson watched from the stands, the game shifted after the first.

"The second period was probably our best," Bednar said. "We were really dangerous."

The Avalanche peppered Binnington with shots and were rewarded early. Mikko Rantanen fired a puck on net that touched MacKinnon, who was blocking the goal. It bounced off the Blues goalie, right to Valeri Nichushkin. The winger, an effective presence when near the crease, slammed it into the net and screamed, throwing his arms down in celebration as if pushing on ski poles.

Fewer than 10 minutes later, it was Samuel Girard's turn. The defenseman, generously listed at 5'10", had struggled against Vegas in the 2021 second-round loss and faced questions about his size and ability to hold up in a physical series. But after an up-and-down regular season, he had settled into a pairing with Josh Manson. Girard liked the way his defensive partner drew opponents by holding the puck, sometimes only for a split second, before passing.

That created extra space for Girard, whose elusive skating already made life difficult for opposing teams.

That space on the ice led to a Girard second-period goal. He received the puck from Manson just in front of the blue line and skated toward the faceoff circle. He unleashed a slapper past Binnington, snapping a personal 21-game goalless drought in the playoffs. It was a new year, Landeskog told reporters postgame. What happened against Vegas no longer mattered. All that did was that Girard was moving well against St. Louis.

The whole team did for most of the game, dominating the Blues in just about every statistical category, including shots, shot attempts, scoring chances, and expected goals. But St. Louis stayed within a tally, in part because of Avalanche missed opportunities, including those shots that hit the post. And then, with 12 minutes left in the second, Erik Johnson couldn't take advantage of a Bowen Byram feed that set him up with an empty net. He didn't make solid contact with the puck, and his shot trickled toward the goal line, giving Binnington enough time to recover and make the save. That embodied the night for Colorado. Bednar was pleased with the way his players got into dangerous scoring areas, but he also felt they could have shot the puck better.

The Avalanche finished the game 0-for-3 on the power play, and though they mostly stayed out of the penalty box, the opportunistic Blues capitalized on their one chance with a man advantage. With only five minutes left in the game, as time expired on a lackluster Colorado power play attempt, Devon Toews was called for holding Ivan Barbashev. Normally composed on the ice, the Avalanche defenseman complained in exasperation as he skated to the box.

Colorado's penalty kill nearly avoided any damage, but the Blues' Justin Faulk caught the unit in a change, firing a puck to Kyrou at the blue line. The young forward toe-dragged around two Colorado players, and when Nico Sturm's stick couldn't quite separate him from the puck, Kyrou scorched a shot past Kuemper. With the clock reading 3:14—matching St. Louis' 314 area code—the Blues tied the game.

As they had in regulation, the Avalanche dominated the scoring chances in overtime. But even with Binnington keeping the puck out of his net, Landeskog didn't feel Colorado's focus waver. The Avalanche believed a goal would come if they kept to their process.

But overtime games aren't always won by the more deserving team, especially when a hot goaltender is involved. Colorado needed someone to break through.

The postseason is a perfect time for unlikely heroes.

• • •

Joe Sakic played against Manson's dad, Dave, and knew how tough he was, how hard he was to face. Manson, who made All-Star Games with the Blackhawks and Oilers and played for four other teams, was a player known for both his strength and physicality. Only 12 players in NHL history racked up more career penalty minutes.

Like his father, Josh, too, is a difficult match-up (though perhaps not as well acquainted with the penalty box). Moments from his dad's hockey career shaped the player he became. He recalled the eye-opening experience when Dave, a member of the Dallas Stars at the time, lost the 2000 Stanley Cup in six games to New Jersey. The series showed the younger Manson how hard it was to win four playoff rounds. You need fortunate bounces and goals at the right time. So much needs to go right, and it's devastating getting as close as Dave Manson did, only to come up short.

Though Dave's impact on his son is clear, he never pushed the sport on Josh. The younger Manson didn't even play his dad's position—defense—until he was 19, when his junior hockey coach suggested he try it.

"His dad was really letting him create his own path and do things how he wanted," said Devin Gannon, his teammate in the British Columbia league.

Sometimes that path had detours. At one potential crossroads, it was Manson's mom, Lana, who kept him on track. As a 12-year-old, Manson found slopes more fun than skates. He didn't live near mountains growing up in Prince Albert, Saskatchewan, but there was a nearby hill where he could take his snowboard. He loved it. Hockey, on the other hand, wasn't doing much for him. He didn't know if he would like the coach, Trevor Gunnville, on the team he was set to join, and he told his mom he planned to quit. Lana wasn't having it. She believed an organized sport would benefit him more than hanging on a hill. She also felt that he should at least give his new coach a shot.

"No chance, buddy," she told him. "You've got to see this thing through."

"Thank goodness she did," Manson said years later. "That was the year I ended up loving my coach. That was the year hockey grasped me."

After two years playing with his buddy Gannon for the Salmon Arm Silverbacks in the BCHL, Manson went to Northeastern University in Boston. The summer before his freshman year, the Ducks drafted him in the sixth round, a nod to his potential. As Manson broke into the Northeastern lineup quickly as a freshman, Gannon saw "an insane amount of growth" from his friend.

"The player he was in Salmon Arm to when he came back after that freshman year was like a completely different player," Gannon said. "It felt like he'd grown five inches and put on 25 pounds."

That progression continued, and he became the strong, physical defenseman Colorado coveted at the trade deadline. His childhood hobby was far behind him. In the gym shortly after getting to Denver, Manson looked out at the mountains. He felt no longing for snowboarding, his old passion.

He was a hockey player, through and through.

• • •

The Avalanche had been throwing all they could at Binnington when Manson took the ice for a shift midway through overtime. Less than a minute earlier, the Blues goaltender speared a point blank Nichushkin shot, causing the winger to shake his head slightly. If dangerous chances like that weren't going in, what would? MacKinnon put a shot on net moments later, and when Binnington froze the puck, Bednar sent out Manson and Girard to play with his second line.

After play resumed, a forechecking Landeskog darted toward Binnington, then grabbed the puck when Kyrou nudged it behind the net. It was the type of play the captain made all playoffs—a hard-nosed burst of effort to retain possession. He then cycled the puck to Manson, who moved it to Girard, whose shot Binnington managed to deflect, setting up the game's crucial stretch. Kadri seized possession. He passed to Landeskog, who cycled up to Manson once again.

"He did it in such a way to give me time," Manson said. "He beat his guy, so the forward had to come down a little bit on him."

Manson, standing between the blue line and the O-zone faceoff circle, scanned the bodies in front of him. No Blues were near him, and the path to the net was filled with both teammates and opponents. Manson saw it as the perfect screen.

He faked a wind-up, buying a few extra seconds, then weaved a long-range shot through traffic. Landeskog, who had been active and effective his entire shift, stood directly in front of Binnington's eyes. The puck sailed past the netminder and found the twine at the back of the goal.

Binnington fell to his knees in disappointment, finally defeated. Manson leapt in excitement, hands raised, and Girard flew toward him, going airborne into his defensive partner's arms. Manson joked he had to hold his ground to stay upright as 6'4" defenseman Erik Johnson rushed in from the bench.

"EJ was three feet off the ground when he got to me, and that's a big guy," Manson said.

Dave Manson, now an assistant for the Oilers, was on the road for his own second-round series, so Lana watched alone at home. Like the son she convinced to stay in the sport, she threw her hands in the air.

• • •

As the Avalanche waited to learn who they'd be playing in the second round, Manson thought to himself that Minnesota would be a tougher matchup than the Blues. When the St. Louis series began, he quickly learned that wasn't the case.

"They gave us everything we could handle," he said. "[I] had underestimated them a bit, how good they really were."

Berube made adjustments after Game 1. Toews felt like the Colorado defensemen got plenty of shot attempts in the series opener from outside, and those opportunities vanished in Game 2 as Blues players stepped up their game. Perron said the team "probably had two or three players that had good games" in Game 1. That was it. St. Louis was much sharper in the second contest, knowing the dangers of going down 2–0 to a team as dangerous as Colorado.

Looking back, some Avalanche players referred to Game 2 as the only game in which they didn't play well all postseason. The Blues both outshot and outchanced the home team. Kyrou put St. Louis on the board halfway into the game, and the Blues scored again on a five-on-three power play late in the second period. For the first time, the Avalanche faced a multi-goal playoff deficit.

"We were bad," MacKinnon said. "We were really bad."

The Avalanche's execution was off—Mikko Rantanen said they did a poor job breaking out of the defensive zone, and MacKinnon added that, for whatever reason, the team didn't have its normal jump. Bednar told reporters his club got outworked.

Colorado came within striking distance in the third period after a Landeskog goal. But it wasn't enough. David Perron scored his second of the night after a turnover handed St. Louis a two-on-one rush, and Saad ended any hope of a comeback with an empty-netter.

"They answered back after a bad night in Game 1," Bednar said postgame. "Now the onus is on us. We have to do the exact same thing."

Against Vegas the year before, one loss in the second round sent the Avalanche spiraling. Because Colorado players had stressed their collective growth throughout the regular season, this Game 2 loss birthed a new opportunity—to show their maturity when games mattered most.

BLUES, BOOS, AND BIG GOALS

TRADES ARE WEBS that touch more people than meet the eye, all in different ways. Take the Nazem Kadri deal, for example. Acquiring the forward from the Maple Leafs was a huge win for Joe Sakic and the Avalanche front office in the summer of 2019. They found their second-line center—a position they desperately needed to bolster—and the main player they gave up, defenseman and power play quarterback Tyson Barrie, was expendable with the emergence of Cale Makar.

But for Kadri and his family, the trade cut deeply. Nazem's wife, Ashley, was in the midst of her nesting phase at the time of the deal, less than a week away from giving birth to their soon-to-be-daughter, Naylah. She had folded infant-sized clothes into drawers in the family's Toronto condo, and she had the baby's room decorated with pink polka-dot wallpaper. It was early July. The couple was on the couch watching TV, not ready for their lives to be uprooted.

Then Nazem's phone rang. He stood and left the room, which struck Ashley as odd, considering he normally did that only when his agent or dad called. Her confusion didn't last long, though. Nazem was back within a minute, bringing jarring news. Kyle Dubas, Toronto's general manager, had called, he told his wife. He had traded Nazem. They were going to Colorado, far from the only country or professional team he'd ever known.

Ashley watched her husband walk into their bedroom and close the door. She gave him some time to himself before entering. She found him on their bed. He was holding back tears. Heartbroken.

To make matters worse, the cause of the trade was clear, and it could've been prevented. In each of Toronto's previous two first-round playoff series, Kadri had lost his cool and been disciplined by the league. He boarded Boston's Tommy Wingels in 2018, earning a three-game suspension. In 2019, after going back and forth with Boston's Jake DeBrusk throughout Game 2, Kadri cross-checked him in the head. For that one, he received a five-game suspension.

The Leafs lost both series in seven games. Would they have advanced if Kadri had been available? It's possible. And though Leafs coaches credited Kadri's energy and edge for getting Toronto engaged in games throughout his tenure with the team, management seemed to lose trust in him after his pair of suspensions. If he couldn't stay on the ice, what good was he in a playoff series?

Dubas had already tried to trade Kadri to Calgary during the 2019 off-season, but the Flames were on the no-trade list Kadri had in his contract. He blocked the move, thinking it would allow him to stay in Toronto. But the front office pivoted. With Sakic interested, Dubas found a new trade partner in Colorado.

The deal done, Kadri's life was uprooted. And he wasn't alone. Ashley had to start anew, too, and their daughter would start her life more than a thousand miles from her grandparents in Kadri's hometown of London, Ontario, only a two-hour drive from Toronto.

The trade split Kadri from a city he loves, one where hockey takes center stage. The sport's hall of fame is in downtown Toronto, and the Maple Leafs are the biggest show in town. Kadri was a prominent figure there, sitting courtside at Raptors games and getting "Happy Birthday" tweets from Leafs superfan Justin Bieber. Supporters latched onto him; he remembers some almost fainting when they met him. A couple even named their newborn child "Kadri," and once, when Kadri was in the passenger seat at a stoplight as a friend drove him through downtown, someone banged on his tinted window. For a moment, both Kadri and his buddy thought they were being robbed. Then they heard the person screaming: "Kadri! Kadri!"

Privacy and pressure could be problems in Toronto. After fans found out he was dating Ashley, she deleted her Instagram account because of the volume of comments. Nazem took heat for his body weight early in his career, and Kadri's father, Sam, said anyone who plays in Toronto or Montreal should be paid a premium because of the spotlight and pressure. But Kadri embraced it.

"You asked for my heart and I gave you my soul," he typed on Instagram shortly after he found out about the deal.

The trade stung, but it turned out to be the best thing that could've happened to Kadri. He rented Barrie's house, and the traded defenseman left behind a gift basket with baked goods and a pamphlet about things to do in Denver. His new teammates were welcoming, as were the sunny skies and nice weather. He and Ashley found it a good spot to be when the COVID-19 pandemic hit; they could ride bikes around Washington Park and eat outside at restaurants.

Kadri's game fit with the Avalanche, too. He contributed a respectable 68 points in 107 games over his first two seasons. The team needed a capable No. 2 center behind superstar Nathan MacKinnon, and he fit that to a T. That is, at least until the league suspended him again in the playoffs, this time for his hit on Justin Faulk in the 2021 Blues series. It was the third time in four postseasons he missed time because of a discipline from the Department of Player Safety.

Sakic stuck with him, though, and Kadri rewarded the Avalanche's trust with a career-best 87-point season in 2021–22, all while playing strong defense. It was good enough for him to make his first All-Star Game.

"I can't see Kyle Dubas sitting back, thinking this was one of the better trades in his career," Ashley said during her husband's breakout season.

But Kadri couldn't fully answer the questions about his game until the playoffs, when he was about to find himself in yet another controversy. This time, though, it was through no fault of his own.

• • •

Game 3 started with a crunch. Less than two minutes into the first period, as Samuel Girard chased a puck behind the Avalanche net, Blues forward Ivan Barbashev hit him hard into the boards. The defenseman stayed down, face bloodied from ramming into the wall. He had avoided a concussion, but the hit from Barbashev broke his sternum. By the end of the game, he was at a St. Louis hospital, his season done. Colorado had players miss games earlier in the playoffs, but this was its first long-term test without a primary contributor.

Girard's injury wasn't the last of the night, or even of the first period. Perhaps the most consequential play of the series came less than seven minutes into the game, and it involved Kadri. When Blues goaltender Jordan Binnington allowed a rebound, the Avalanche center flew toward the loose puck. St. Louis defenseman Calle Rosen—who, ironically, had been traded along with Kadri from Toronto to Colorado in 2019—also went for the rebound, hoping to shoo it out of a dangerous scoring area. He and Kadri collided.

Both players went flying into Binnington, who had led the Blues to a Stanley Cup three years earlier and was off to an excellent start in the 2022 playoffs. The three-player tangle knocked the net off its pegs, and officials stopped play. Kadri and Rosen both got up easily, but Binnington stayed down. Boos started to rain down on Kadri.

After half a minute, Binnington got to his feet and tested his range of motion. Eventually, he left the ice. The collision had injured his left knee, putting him out for the series. It was a devastating blow for the Blues, even if their backup goalie, Ville Husso, had been the team's No. 1 for most of the regular season. Binnington was looking like the goalie that had carried a team to a championship. Against a star-powered Colorado team, he was the St. Louis player most capable of turning the series.

Now he was done, all because of a collision that started with Kadri's hard-nosed rush to the puck. The forward insisted he didn't intend to injure his opponent; the puck was loose in front of the net, he said, and he was trying to poke it in. The on-ice officials seemed to see it the same way. They didn't call a penalty on the play, and no Blues players charged at Kadri to defend their teammate, which would have been the expected reaction after a questionable hit. After the game, the league didn't levy any discipline against Kadri.

If any other player had been involved, the play likely would have been viewed as unfortunate but not controversial. Kadri isn't any other player, though, especially in the eyes of the Blues, who had players fight him twice during the regular season after his hit on Justin Faulk during the previous postseason. For the rest of the game, the St. Louis fans booed Kadri every time he touched the puck.

"Look at Kadri's reputation," Blues coach Craig Berube said. "That's all I've got to say."

Berube's comment frustrated coach Jared Bednar, who called Kadri's play a legal one with an undesirable result. It also angered Kadri, who added two nights later that, "I guess he's never heard of bulletin board material."

But all of that would come later. Husso now in net, Game 3 continued. With the Avalanche trailing 1–0. As they finished off a penalty kill, Darren Helm flipped a puck high in the air, sending it up ice. Defenseman Josh Manson was exiting the penalty box at the same time, and he snatched the puck from midair as he entered the offensive zone. He passed to Logan O'Connor, who had a step on Faulk. O'Connor moved the puck from his backhand to his forehand, then put it past Husso to tie the game.

O'Connor, whom Bednar had scratched the first two games of the series, grinned as teammates approached him. He isn't one of the Avalanche's most offensively gifted forwards, but he showed flashes during the regular season, especially early on when his confidence was high. Now he had come through in a key moment.

Or had he? The Blues coaches quickly began watching replays of the goal, wondering if Manson was offside when he first caught the puck. They weren't alone; the Colorado defenseman, for one, didn't think he had stayed onside. But Helm had thrown the puck so high in the air that the arena cameras didn't get a definitive angle of where it was in relation to the blue line. Not wanting to risk giving the Avalanche another power play, which would have happened had Berube lost a challenge, the coach decided not to have officials review the play. The game resumed, and the goal stood.

"I wasn't expecting it to count the whole time," Manson said. "But when it did, I was obviously elated."

Midway through the second period, Kadri made his presence known on the scoresheet, tipping in a Cale Makar shot. He punched the air as MacKinnon hugged him from behind. The St. Louis crowd greeted it with a stony silence. Not only had the Blues surrendered the lead, the least popular player among their fanbase had done the damage.

Kadri wasn't done. Later in the period, he fed Artturi Lehkonen a pass off the boards, setting up a two-on-one. The winger moved up ice with Bowen Byram, then zipped a shot past Husso, his former teammate on Finnish national junior teams. And though the Blues pulled to within one at the end of the period, they never tied the game. With two minutes left before the final buzzer, Gabriel Landeskog scored to clinch the win.

The Avalanche had a 2–1 series lead. But the night's drama was far from over.

• • •

Binnington limped through the bowels of the Enterprise Center as the third period ended. His injury had been evaluated during the game, and now he was heading down the hallway, an Eternal brand water bottle in his hand and a brace on his knee.

As the goalie made his way toward the Blues locker room, he saw Kadri standing in front of a TNT backdrop. The Avalanche center was doing an interview on national TV, smiling and laughing in response to questions.

The goalie was frustrated. He later said he felt he had a God-given opportunity to make Kadri look him "in the eye and understand what's going on." So he flicked his wrist, throwing the mostly-empty water bottle in Kadri's direction. It landed on the floor near the TV backdrop.

Kadri, coincidently, was in the midst of answering a question about the Binnington collision. He paused for five seconds when he heard the water bottle hit the ground, looking to his left. "I'm not sure if he just threw a water bottle at me or not," he said, perplexed.

Indeed, Binnington had, and it wasn't the first time he'd let his emotion dictate his actions. During the regular season, he swung his stick at Kadri during a game, earning a 10-minute misconduct penalty, and during the playoffs the year before, he'd skated down ice and seemingly tried to engage Philipp Grubauer in a fight. "If he feels the need to come down and do that stuff and fake punch guys, so be it," the then Avalanche goalie said. "I worry about stopping the pucks." And earlier in 2021, Binnington went after multiple San Jose players after he'd been pulled from a game.

He had earned a reputation as a hothead.

"He's an idiot," one Avalanche player said shortly after the water bottle toss.

Colorado players talked about and laughed at the incident, but in the end, the bottle was mostly empty and didn't hurt Kadri. Was it childish? Sure. Harmful? No.

The same couldn't be said for what happened next.

• • •

Half of the time Kadri doesn't notice boos, and he doesn't mind them when he does. He likes playing in environments where fans are engaged.

But there's a line, and people crossed it following Game 3. Sometime around 3:00 AM, a call from the St. Louis police department woke Brendan McNicholas, the Avalanche's vice president of media and player relations. In the aftermath of the Binnington collision, the department was monitoring online threats—many of which used Islamophobic language—toward Kadri, who is a practicing Muslim and of Lebanese descent. The police wanted to make Colorado and its team security aware of the threats. The cops sent additional patrols to the hotel that night.

The Avalanche weren't scheduled to skate the next day. After meeting with police the next morning, McNicholas approached Kadri to tell him what was going on. The center then met with police at the hotel. He also talked to former NHLer Akim Aliu, a founding member and the chair of the Hockey Diversity Alliance, an organization with which Kadri is involved.

Aliu brought the issue to the public's attention with a tweet, and the Avalanche followed with a statement of their own. The team was aware of the threats, it read, and were working with local law enforcement to investigate.

Kadri's wife, Ashley, shared screenshots of some messages on an Instagram page used to post photos of their cat, Jazzy. She wanted to shine light on what the family experienced.

"I'm going to find out your every move," one read.

"You Muslim son of a bitch," said another.

"Towel head."

"Hang yourself."

"You should've never come to America you fucking immigrant."

"They're just ignorant people," said Kadri's father, Sam.

Ignorance, racism, and Islamophobia are nothing new for Nazem. He first heard a slur directed at him when he was 11 or 12. It came not from an opposing player, but from a parent—a striking reminder that prejudice is passed down between generations. He continued to hear racist remarks as he got older, including while he was playing major junior in the Ontario Hockey League. His dark skin often jumped out in a largely white sport. Sam helped teach him to ignore the insults he never should've had to endure. In St. Louis, accompanied to the arena by added security the day after the threats, he told reporters that people need to be aware that "this still happens, and it's hurtful." The threats could have been empty—people looking for the most hurtful words possible—but that wasn't a risk anyone wanted to take.

"I know what was said isn't a reflection on every single fan in St. Louis," Kadri said. "But for those that wasted their time sending messages like that, I feel sorry for them."

Sam talked to his son ahead of Game 4. Nazem had struggled to sleep the night before, wound up from everything going on. His dad told him to stick to his style of play, to be himself on the ice. That, more than anything else, would make a statement, he said. Nazem had a chance to show he wasn't going anywhere.

Bednar sensed a readiness among his players entering the game. His only concern was Kadri, considering what had transpired since the previous game's conclusion. But he needn't have worried. The center was prepared. As his skate blades made contact with the ice, he felt the stress from the previous 48 hours fade away.

• • •

With Girard out, Bednar changed his defensive lineup for the first time in the playoffs. The night before, the coach had texted Jack Johnson, telling him he was in. The veteran—who watched Girard leave Game 3 from a weight room in the Enterprise Center, where the healthy scratches were in the middle of a workout—was set to make his first career appearance beyond Round 1 of the playoffs.

But this night was about Kadri. Early in the second period, shortly after Erik Johnson tied the game 1–1, the center darted up ice with boos raining down from the St. Louis crowd. Five strides into the offensive zone, he fired a shot under Husso's glove for his first goal of the night. He held his hand over his ears in celebration, looking into the still-booing stands. The message was clear: *I can't hear you.*

Toews scored 20 seconds later, Colorado's third goal in a span of less than two minutes. The Blues players were frustrated, and Kadri kept goading them. He bumped David Perron after a whistle, and an angry Pavel Buchnevich then shoved him to the ice. As Kadri started to get up, Perron charged at him, cross-checking him in the back and jumping on top of his opponent until linesmen split them up. Assigned roughing and cross-checking penalties, respectively, Buchnevich and Perron went to the penalty box, handing the Avalanche a five-on-three power play.

St. Louis nearly escaped it without damage, but as the power play expired and the Blues players rushed out of the penalty box,

Bowen Byram snatched a rebound and surveyed the ice. After two seconds, he zipped a backdoor pass to Kadri, who put the puck past Husso. The center let out a whoop and, as St. Louis fans flipped him off from the seats in the lower bowl, he stared in their direction and nodded.

The goal, which essentially came on a power play caused by what Kadri called "stupid penalties," was the difference in the final score. "If you lose your cool, we'll make you pay," Kadri said.

St. Louis pulled to within a goal after a pair of power play scores, but Kadri made sure they got no closer. Midway through the third period, he seized a loose puck in the offensive zone faceoff circle and fired it past Husso. The night after the threats had come to light, he had a hat trick, and the Avalanche held on for a win.

After the game, Erik Johnson went out of his way to praise Kadri. The team was proud of him, he said. Kadri had walked into a building where fans saw him as a villain, where he was booed every time he touched the puck. Some players might have been intimidated. But not Kadri. He used it as fuel. He embraced it. He came out on top.

AT THE HELM

AS MACKINNON BANGED the glass twice with his stick and the goal horn sounded, it looked as if he'd just achieved the defining moment of his Avalanche tenure. With time winding down and the score tied in Game 5, he grabbed the puck behind his own net and burst up ice, dusting Jordan Kyrou, swooping around Nick Leddy and creating just enough space to lift a shot past Ville Husso.

"I don't know if I'll be able to repeat that one," he said.

It was a world-class play from a world-class player. It was a moment that blended his stickhandling with his finishing ability and the elite skating he worked to perfect for all those hours on the lake behind his childhood home.

Ball Arena erupted. Gabriel Landeskog, who had endured the bleak 2016–17 season with MacKinnon, nearly knocked his friend down in celebration. Bowen Byram jumped up and down on the ice, then leaned over the bench wall to hug Jack Johnson and Andrew Cogliano. MacKinnon's goal was his third of the night, and hats came down from the stands like leaves in autumn.

Could it have been more fitting? The man drafted No. 1 overall—the player tasked with revitalizing a franchise and then meeting those expectations—helping his team over that pesky second-round hump with the goal of his life. If there was a hockey God, Sportsnet's Jeff Marek said on the widely listened to 32 *Thoughts* podcast, that would have decided the game.

All the Avalanche had to do was hold on for 2:46. Then the story would end neatly. The talk of second-round demons would be left behind them. They'd reach the Western Conference Finals for the first time in two decades. They'd be halfway through the postseason without any serious threats or doubt-raising moments.

But that's rarely how the Stanley Cup playoffs work, and it isn't how the Avalanche's path unfolded. The 2:46 left on the clock was too much time. MacKinnon would have to wait a little longer to have his moment.

And yet the star center—as competitive a player as there is in the league, the one who lost his temper over a dorm room knee hockey tournament—is thankful his team didn't win that night. Even in the moment, as the Blues injected uncertainty into the city of Denver, the thought crossed his mind.

"Our group really needed that adversity," MacKinnon said. "It would have been too easy."

The Avalanche had yet to face significant hardship in the post-season. They were about to.

• • •

Around three hours before MacKinnon's magic, as Kadri took the ice for Game 5 warm-ups, he skated into the polar opposite of the reaction he had received in St. Louis. The jumbotron flashed to him, and fans burst into applause, growing even louder when he saluted them. One supporter, Adrienne Ruth, printed off hundreds of signs reading STAND WITH NAZ for others to hold and, during the game, Kadri nodded his approval when fans started a "Kad-ri! Kad-ri!" chant. He found it both overwhelming and incredible.

For Sam Kadri, seeing the signs supporting his son meant as much as winning the Cup ultimately would, if not more. Christian Murdock, a photographer for the *Colorado Springs Gazette*, captured a picture during warm-ups of Nazem skating in front of a crowd of fans standing in front of the glass. Some held the signs Ruth printed, and others brought their own.

"It was pretty emotional for me," Nazem Kadri said.

After Kadri's pregame reception, the Avalanche gave the already engaged crowd no opportunity to calm down. Less than four minutes into the game, Byram used his glove to intercept a flying pass from David Perron, whom Colorado fans booed throughout the night, presumably for his Game 4 penalty on Kadri. Byram zipped the puck through the neutral zone to Artturi Lehkonen, who skated alongside Landeskog into the offensive zone. MacKinnon trailed his linemates, slapping the ice to ask for a pass. Lehkonen listened, and when MacKinnon got the puck, he angled a shot around Leddy. It beat Husso to hand the Avalanche a 1–0 lead.

MacKinnon gave Lehkonen's helmet an appreciative slap as the Avalanche celebrated, and he wasn't done. He scored on the power play later in the period, then assisted a Landeskog goal early in the second. The contest looked on its way to being a rout: a second-round coronation more than a hard-fought close-out game.

But, as in Game 4, the Avalanche let St. Louis chip away. The Blues fired off six more shot attempts at even strength than Colorado in the second period, creating a greater number of high-danger chances. They broke through before intermission when Vladimir Tarasenko, goalless in the series to this point, whipped a Leddy rebound past Kuemper.

The Avalanche entered the third period with a two-goal lead. But, from Landeskog's perspective, they grew tight as they came closer to closing out the series. Perhaps they wanted a win too badly, MacKinnon thought. Bednar believed his players' level of effort was appropriate, but the Blues out-worked them in front of the net. The Blues were more desperate and showed it with their play.

"As the game went on there, they had a little bit extra in the battle, and we didn't," said Bednar, also lamenting the Avalanche's poor puck decisions, which led to extra Blues chances. MacKinnon, for example, lost track of a puck at his feet in the offensive zone, leading to a Ryan O'Reilly shot midway through the third.

Still, Colorado had a two-goal lead with 10 minutes to go in the game. That changed when Pavel Buchnevich burst into the offensive zone, made a move around Byram and fed Robert Thomas in the slot. Without settling the puck, the young, skilled centerman whacked a shot past Kuemper's blocker. Then, with five minutes left, Jordan Kyrou batted in a loose puck in front of the net, tying the game.

MacKinnon's end-to-end tally—which Bednar described as "one of the prettiest goals that I've seen in a long time"—nearly spoiled the St. Louis comeback. It should have.

But the goal turned out to be a precursor to a setback. First came a missed opportunity. With under two minutes remaining and Husso on the bench for an extra attacker, Makar passed to Landeskog after Colorado won a faceoff in the defensive zone. The crowd noise swelled as the captain appeared to have a split-second chance to shoot at the empty net, but that opportunity disappeared as Justin Faulk rushed to cut off his angle. Landeskog held onto the puck until he crossed the halfway line, ensuring the Avalanche wouldn't be called for icing, but by then Faulk's positioning prevented any chance at a quality shot. It skipped down the ice, where the Blues regained possession.

Robert Thomas carried possession into the offensive zone, and the St. Louis forecheck forced both Makar and MacKinnon to commit turnovers. With 1:08 remaining, Toews nearly cleared the puck out of the Avalanche defensive zone, but Faulk managed to corral it inches in front of the blue line. He passed to Tarasenko, and the Blues began to cycle the puck, looking for a scoring chance. "One minute remaining," the Ball Arena public address announcer called out.

As he finished speaking, Tarasenko received a pass from Buchnevich and threw a shot on Kuemper from an odd angle. The goaltender made the save, but a rebound squeaked away from him. The puck sat in the crease for a millisecond. Both Makar and Thomas swung for it.

The Blues forward was a little bit quicker. He propelled the puck forward, over the goal line. The game was tied once again, this time with 56 seconds left. The Avalanche players had gotten on their heels. Now they'd fallen on their faces.

So the game went to overtime. When he walked into the Avalanche's dressing room between the third period and overtime, Bednar liked the chatter he heard, and he didn't mind the team's start to the extra period. A Landeskog one-timer had Husso beat and would have gone in the net had it not hit St. Louis defenseman

Robert Bortuzzo's hip, and the fourth line generated a couple of chances. Byram fired a dangerous shot from the outer slot. Husso made the save.

Colorado's style of play was in action, but overtime can be unforgiving. Good chances mean nothing unless they result in goals. And a little over three minutes into the period, Blues forward Tyler Bozak unleashed a shot from the high slot. It flew past Kuemper and in. Game over. The Avalanche's golden chance to advance to the conference finals had vanished.

"It's starting to look like you're either the hammer or the nail in this series," Bednar said after the game. "We have to go out and be the hammer."

Facing the adversity MacKinnon thought the Avalanche needed, the players needed to figure out how to follow their coach's advice. Weeks later, when the journey was complete, players would refer to the loss as a turning point.

• • •

Toews didn't sense doubt after the Game 5 loss, but there was frustration. The defenseman didn't want to board another two-hour flight back to St. Louis or spend another day away from home.

"I think it was more disappointment in ourselves," Josh Manson said, "because we really felt like we had them on the ropes."

So did everyone else, and that meant the collapse fueled the already present narrative: Could this über-talented team get past Round 2?

"You see the memes and all that shit, of people chirping us from the basement of their mom's house," MacKinnon said later. "The second-round demons are all you'd hear about."

Avalanche players downplayed any frustration, but stress was palpable around Denver. Questions about the team's toughness grew louder. *Denver Post* columnist Mark Kiszla wrote after the game that the Avalanche were "soft as butterscotch pudding."

"The curse is not yet over," NHL insider Elliotte Friedman said during Sportsnet's broadcast of Game 5.

And if the Avalanche were to lose Game 6, shifting the series back to Denver for a decisive Game 7, Ball Arena would be on edge—full to the brim with nervous energy.

Colorado did its best to dispel any doubt early in Game 6, creating early looks against Husso, but the Blues goalie held firm. The score stood at 0–0 when Faulk skated into the slot with a minute left in the first period and zipped a shot toward the top corner of the net. No one blocked Kuemper's sightline. He had struggled throughout the series, his vision still not 100 percent after his injury in Nashville. He wasn't able to nab the puck. The Blues took the lead.

A year earlier, the Avalanche won only one playoff game after trailing—Game 4 of an all-but-over first-round series against the Blues. But during the 2021–22 season, they had grown comfortable playing from behind, ranking near the top of the league in comeback wins. And in Game 6, the players' focus didn't stray after Faulk's goal. They embodied the words Cogliano told reporters before the game: "Feeling sorry for yourself in playoffs is death." Early in the second period, the Avalanche tied the score when Husso surrendered a rebound on a Manson shot. Standing in front of the net, J.T. Compher smacked the puck in for the equalizing tally.

The tie didn't last. Midway through the period, Jack Johnson, in for the injured Samuel Girard, couldn't corral a puck at the blueline. Trying to keep it from leaving the defensive zone, he accidentally nudged it right into the path of a charging Brayden Schenn. Kyrou jumped into the rush with his teammate, creating a two-on-one. As the Blues duo approached the net, Manson bit toward Schenn. The veteran forward fed Kyrou, who one-timed a shot over the goal line.

St. Louis had only nine shots, less than half as many as the Avalanche, but two had found the back of the net.

Kyrou had a chance to extend the Blues lead at the end of the period, but Manson made a play that showed why Sakic traded so much to get him. With St. Louis on the power play, Kyrou got the puck all alone in the offensive zone faceoff circle. Anticipating an immediate shot, Kuemper slid across the crease. But Kyrou hesitated, and Kuemper fell, leaving the net vacant.

"I had a feeling he was going to hold onto that thing," Manson said. With Kuemper out of the picture, the Blues forward moved toward the slot, fearing Cogliano would block his attempt if he shot sooner. Finally, directly in front of the net, he went to his backhand and sent the puck flying toward the goal. But instead of crossing the line, it struck Manson's chest. The defenseman had shifted into the middle of the crease and did his best goaltender impersonation to prevent a score. Kuemper approved and, at the next stoppage, thanked Manson by patting him on the chest.

Ahead of the game, Manson heard from his dad, whose Oilers eliminated Calgary the night before. An Avalanche victory would mean a father-son reunion in the Western Conference Finals. "Go win this game so I can come see my granddaughter," Dave told his son.

With the block on Kyrou's shot, Manson had done his part, but Colorado still needed to find a way to re-tie the score. Down a goal, the Avalanche created scoring chances to start the third and, midway through the period, earned a power play when Colton Parayko flipped a puck over the glass—a delay of game. MacKinnon, Makar, and the top power play unit couldn't get much going with a man-advantage, so Bednar sent his second grouping to the ice. As Parayko geared up to exit the penalty box, Byram hit Compher with a pass as the forward entered the offensive zone. Compher put the puck on net, and his shot got past Husso.

The night before the game, Compher had spoken on the phone with his mother, Valerie Compher, who was debating whether or not to drive to St. Louis from their family's home in the Chicago area. She was leaning toward not coming, and J.T. assured her that it was okay. She could watch from Illinois.

"But we always bring you such good luck!" she replied.

"Just knowing you were going to come is good enough," he told her.

Now he had come through with his second goal of the night. The third-line forward—a quality depth player, not a star—grinned as Byram and André Burakovsky mobbed him. Everyone was contributing.

Compher wasn't the last unlikely contributor to emerge that night. With 13 seconds left in the third and the game still knotted 2–2, Erik Johnson received a pass from Makar. He realized he had a step on Kyrou and burst forward along the boards. The Blues forward nearly poked the puck away, but Johnson managed to keep possession. As he neared the offensive zone, he backhanded the puck to O'Connor. The forward wasn't sure how much time was left. All he knew was there wasn't much.

O'Connor wanted to get the puck to Helm across the ice, but Kyrou's positioning made it so he couldn't pass it directly to his teammate; he had to throw it to a general area and hope Helm could get there. He sent the puck across the ice, and it bounced off the boards. Helm—one of only two Avalanche players who knew the feeling of winning a Stanley Cup—charged forward.

• • •

Back in the 2007–08 season, with the Red Wings seeking their fourth Stanley Cup win in 12 years, Detroit captain Nicklas Lidström heard about a kid impressing coaches with his speed in the minor leagues. The Wings wanted to give him a chance and were looking for an opportunity.

Detroit had selected Darren Helm in the fifth round of the 2005 draft—a surprise to the forward, who didn't think he'd get picked—and he turned pro for the 2007–08 season, playing for Detroit's American Hockey League affiliate in Grand Rapids. Late in the season, Red Wings general manager Ken Holland watched the minor league team play, and Helm stood out. Holland told coach Mike Babcock of the speedy Manitoban's progression, and with a month to go before playoffs, the team promoted him to the big-league club.

Helm felt scared walking into a dressing room with legends like Lidström, Dominik Hašek, Chris Chelios, and Pavel Datsyuk but quickly found the group welcoming. He grew comfortable on the ice, unafraid to make mistakes.

But Helm never imagined the Red Wings would count on him as a contributor during their 2008 playoff run. He had played only seven regular season games, failing to log a point. But Babcock, appreciating the 21-year-old's speed, tenaciousness, and ability to forecheck, put him in the lineup midway through Detroit's first-round series with Nashville. The Red Wings were skilled, Lidström recalled, but they weren't always fast. Helm added that element.

"I was too naïve to think anything else and just went as hard as I could and was able to sustain a spot," Helm said.

He played in 18 games that postseason, helping the Red Wings knock off Sidney Crosby and the Penguins in the Stanley Cup Final. They swept Joe Sakic and the Avalanche along the way, and Helm scored his first career NHL goal in the conference finals against Dallas. He didn't miss a single game in the Cup Final.

In Datsyuk's eyes, he's the type of player you don't win championships without.

The next year, Helm made two of the defining plays of his Red Wings career, both in a close-out Game 5 of the Western Conference Finals against Chicago. With the Blackhawks on the power play in a 0-0 contest, Helm—whom legendary broadcaster Doc Emrick described on air as the fastest guy on the team—seized the puck and skated through the neutral zone. He played keep-away with his Chicago opponents for nearly 30 seconds, putting a shot on net and earning a standing ovation from the Detroit crowd. It's a play that jumped to Lidström's mind when thinking about his time with Helm, who finished that Blackhawks game with 12 hits, more than twice as many as any other player.

"Just that tenacity of chasing down the puck all the time was hard to play against, that symbolizes the way he always played," Lidström said.

The game ultimately went to overtime and, early in the extra period, Helm batted in a rebound, sending his team to the Stanley Cup Final. Mitch Albom wrote in the *Detroit Free Press* the next day that, if the Red Wings were to win their second Cup in as many years, Helm should have his name engraved in capital letters. (Crosby and the Penguins beat Detroit in seven games to win the championship.)

Though he played with inner-circle Hall of Famers in Detroit, Helm said he learned most from the grinders on the team. He watched Kris Draper, once a Selke Trophy winner for best defensive forward, and saw his attention to detail and how hard he worked, not just in games but at practice, too. Darren McCarty, known best in Denver for punching Avalanche forward Claude Lemieux in the infamous 1997 Detroit-Colorado brawl, kept things in perspective for Helm, the forward remembered, and he was always ready to compete.

Over the course of more than a decade in Detroit, Helm became one of the veterans from whom younger players learned. Dylan Larkin, named Red Wings captain in 2021, recalled wishing him happy birthday in 2016.

"How old are you?" Larkin asked. "Thirty-three? Thirty-two?"

Helm laughed and told his rookie teammate he was only 29. His maturity and experience added a few years to the effect of his presence.

Off the ice, Helm welcomed all three of his kids in Detroit, and his second daughter's birth was quite a tale. In March 2015, his now-wife, Devon, woke up in the middle of the night. She felt the baby coming. The two hopped in Helm's Audi with Devon in the backseat. As they flew down Interstate 96, Devon started having the baby. Darren offered to pull over and help but, even in her state, she wisely told him to keep driving. "She knew there was probably nothing I could do to help," said Helm, who managed to get to the hospital five minutes after baby Rylee was born.

He might have been speedy on the ice, but it was nothing compared to how fast he drove that night.

After qualifying for the playoffs in each of the previous 25 seasons, the Red Wings finished with a losing record in 2016–17. It marked the beginning of a stretch of futile days, and when Helm's contract expired after the 2020–21 season, he wanted to play for a contending team. Colorado was his No. 1 choice, and he was excited to learn the team was interested in bringing him on board. His time in Detroit was interrupted by injuries, but he still left with his name on the storied franchise's top 20 list in career short-handed points (21, 10th) and games played (744, 17th).

"When you have players like [Henrik] Zetterberg, Datsyuk, those types of players, you have to find your niche on the team," Lidström said. "He did that."

Coming to the Avalanche at age 34, Helm quickly gained the respect of his new teammates. O'Connor said he was like Benjamin Button—a fictional character who ages in reverse—during preseason conditioning tests, and at one point during the regular season he showed Tyson Jost a one-on-one drill he used to do with Datsyuk. On a team with a young core, Helm's experience was valuable.

The veteran entered the season believing it could be his last. Helm's presence on the Avalanche even had the hated McCarty rooting for Colorado.

"He fit into that Red Wing culture and will always be a Red Wing in my mind, and I hope he goes out there and wins a Cup as a Colorado Avalanche," McCarty said during the season. "I honestly do."

Bednar described Helm's regular season as solid. In the playoffs, though, he found another gear.

• • •

Thirteen years to the day after his legendary Game 5 and overtime winner against Chicago, Helm tracked O'Connor's pass into the offensive zone faceoff circle. Bednar muttered to himself on the bench. "Shoot it," he said. "Just shoot it."

Helm thought the same thing. With the time dipping under seven seconds, his stick cut through the Enterprise Center air, unloading on the puck. His shot sailed past Niko Mikkola's stick, then over Husso's left pad and into the net. Only 5.6 seconds remained in the game, and Colorado had the lead.

"What a turn of events," said Jack Johnson, Helm's dinner date during road trips, calling his buddy's goal "essentially an OT winner."

Helm punched the air as he saw the puck go in. O'Connor, who later joked that Helm had left too much time on the clock, mobbed his linemate, and they were quickly joined by Landeskog and Erik Johnson. Cogliano, stuck in between the two celebrating masses on the bench, jumped up and down by himself.

Perhaps this was the way the second-round questions needed to be answered: a moment so sudden it took everyone by surprise. A goal that left no time for doubt, no time for catastrophe. There might have been a few ticks on the clock left, but everyone in the Enterprise Center knew the game was finished. A stunned hush overtook the crowd. Husso glanced at the jumbotron, as if he couldn't comprehend what just happened. Helm, normally reserved, let himself grin on the bench.

Bednar sent MacKinnon, Landeskog, Lehkonen, Toews, and Makar onto the ice to kill the remaining time on the clock. Thomas won the faceoff for St. Louis and got the puck to Faulk, who put a shot on Kuemper from around center ice. The Colorado netminder made the save easily and, rather than holding the puck until the official called a stoppage, wisely flipped it to his left, letting the final seconds evaporate. MacKinnon leapt into his goalie's arms. Both were heading to their first conference finals.

O'Connor felt relief, and he sensed it in his teammates too. The Avalanche were the more complete team, Jack Johnson said, but you never know what can happen in overtime or, had Colorado dropped this contest, in a Game 7.

Entering Game 6, Colorado's bottom two lines had scored only one goal in the series against the Blues. In the clincher, all three came from Avalanche depth forwards.

"Plenty of times this year in the playoffs our top lines have gotten the job done," Compher said. "I think it felt good for the third and fourth line to help with the win tonight."

As the Avalanche prepared to leave the building, multiple Blues stopped by to catch up with buddies now that the series was done. Schenn chatted with MacKinnon, one of his friends, as the Avalanche center cooled off on a workout bike. Leddy, who had played with Toews on the Islanders, caught up with his fellow defenseman, and Brandon Saad greeted former Colorado teammates.

All three defeated St. Louis players had won Stanley Cups, Schenn with the Blues and Leddy and Saad in Chicago. They knew how it felt to go through a hard playoff series and come out on the right side.

Now the Avalanche did, too.

"FRAN-KIE! FRAN-KIE!"

ST. LOUIS LIKELY had a more complete team than Edmonton, but in terms of a matchup between star players, the NHL couldn't have asked for much better than Oilers-Avalanche in the Western Conference Finals.

With a roster highlighted by past MVPs Connor McDavid and Leon Draisaitl, Edmonton got off to a hot start to the season, going 16–5–0. But the Oilers tailed off quickly and dramatically, going through a 2–11–2 tailspin starting in early December. By mid-February, they were on the outside-looking-in of the playoff picture. General manager Ken Holland, formerly with Detroit, had seen enough. He fired coach Dave Tippett.

The change worked. Edmonton rattled off five consecutive wins under interim coach Jay Woodcroft, who finished the year with a 26–9–3 record behind the bench.

Though the Oilers' defense was leaky at points during the regular season, they plugged the gaps later in the year and allowed the sixth-fewest goals per game in the league after Woodcroft took over. Their improvement was in part thanks to assistant coach Dave Manson, Josh's dad, who worked with the team's defensemen and penalty-kill unit. He paired defensemen Cody Ceci and Darnell Nurse with each other and relied on them against other teams' top forwards. Ceci credited the assistant with getting the team to play harder around its own net.

Nathan MacKinnon praised the Oilers ahead of the series, saying they were deeper than many people realized. They were more than just McDavid, Draisaitl, and Evander Kane, who finished with

22 goals on the year in 43 games played. Nine players on the team averaged more than 0.5 points per game, including Zach Hyman, who finished with a career-high 27 goals in the regular season, and former Avalanche defenseman Tyson Barrie, a power play specialist. But depth and defensive improvement don't drive headlines. Most NHL fans were interested in the showdown of stars: McDavid and Draisaitl against MacKinnon and Cale Makar. Rightfully so. Dom Luszczyszyn's Game Score Value Added statistical model ranked McDavid vs. MacKinnon the best playoff forward matchup since 2010, as far back as Luszczyszyn's model goes. To make things more enticing, the postseason was bringing out the best in both of their games. MacKinnon created the highlight of the playoffs with his coast-to-coast goal against St. Louis, and the Oilers captain averaged more than two points a game in the team's first two rounds.

"This is a big moment for the NHL: the best player in the world going up against the next best forward in his conference," Luszczyszyn wrote in The Athletic in reference to McDavid and MacKinnon, respectively.

MacKinnon heard about the hype around the matchup, and though he enjoys going against top-level talent, he didn't particularly care for the storyline. He sang McDavid's praises going into the series, calling him the best player in the world, but had nothing to add about the personal showdown.

"Hopefully it gets more viewers and lowers escrow," he said, referencing the amount of money players were losing in the wake of pandemic financial losses. "Other than that I don't care."

He cared who won, not how it happened or who looked better.

• • •

Just as they did in five of the six games against St. Louis, the Avalanche allowed the first goal of the Western Conference Finals. Five minutes into the game, Josh Manson lost track of Evander Kane on defensive coverage. It was the start of a brutal night for the Colorado defenseman, who finished the game with a minus-four rating, the worst of any player on either team. Edmonton's Ryan Nugent-Hopkins—one of four former No. 1 overall picks in the game—passed to his team-mate, creating a breakaway. Kane wristed a shot past Darcy Kuemper to put his team up.

Fortunately for Colorado, Dave Manson's Oilers defensemen had rough nights, too, and the Oilers lead didn't last long. Less than a minute after Kane's goal, André Burakovsky passed to Alex Newhook as the Avalanche broke the puck out of their defensive zone. That jump-started a two-on-one for Newhook, a skilled rookie, and J.T. Compher.

Newhook darted up ice. When aging defenseman Duncan Keith, once one of the league's top defensemen, shifted toward him, the 21-year-old passed to Compher, who buried a shot and uppercut the air in celebration. In a series billing some of the games' biggest stars, the Avalanche's first goal of Game 1 came compliments of their depth.

MacKinnon came through with their second later in the period. Devon Toews hit him with a forceful pass through the neutral zone. The center exploded with the puck past Nurse. Barreling toward the net, he poked a shot through Smith's legs, giving Colorado the lead.

The goal ignited what became a barn-burner. Zach Hyman and Makar traded goals before the period's end, Makar's coming on a play the Oilers challenged as offside. Edmonton seemed to have a good case, as it appeared Makar touched the puck in the offensive zone before Valeri Nichushkin could exit it. After video review, the officials determined Colorado's defenseman pushed the puck into the zone but didn't have control of or touch the puck until Nichushkin made it back over the line.

That made the play onside. The goal stood.

"Two video coaches texted [me] to say they think this was the right call," Sportsnet insider Elliotte Friedman said on air. "I'm betting there's not 100 percent agreement online."

There was not. Oilers fans were furious, and Woodcroft said after the game he felt Makar had control of the puck. He still disagreed with the outcome of the review, which was costly beyond that particular goal. A failed challenge results in a delay-of-game penalty, so the Avalanche got a power play. Nazem Kadri took advantage with a goal shortly after the second period began.

The Oilers answered back when Ryan McLeod knocked home a rebound allowed by Darcy Kuemper. It was a shaky sign from the Colorado goalie, whose .892 save percentage in the Blues series hadn't been up to his usual standard.

Across the ice, Edmonton's Mike Smith was also struggling. He allowed a goal to Mikko Rantanen—the Finn's first non-empty netter of the playoffs—then another on a Compher tip-in. Woodcroft had seen enough. He pulled the 40-year-old Smith, subbing in backup Mikko Koskinen.

Woodcroft wasn't the only coach to make a goalie change that game. Bednar followed shortly after Smith left the game, though not by choice. Earlier in the second period, the struggling Kuemper had skated to the Avalanche bench during a TV timeout. His vision wasn't right. He still wasn't tracking the puck well after the injury he sustained in the first round. He told the coaching staff he could stay in the game for a few shifts so Francouz could stretch before entering. But suddenly his status for the series was in question.

Less than a minute after Compher's goal, with Francouz now loose, Kuemper skated off the ice. Jack Johnson thought he was dealing with an equipment issue, as he had earlier in the year, but word trickled back to the Avalanche bench as the period went on. Kuemper was done for the night.

The net belonged to Francouz.

• • •

Kuemper and Francouz had forged a strong relationship throughout the season, a key at a position where only one can be on the ice at a time. Tandems can get toxic when goalies are too competitive with each other, but that didn't happen within Colorado's duo.

"I felt like when I played, he was on my side, and he was cheering for me," said Francouz, who appreciated Kuemper's positivity. "I did the same thing for him."

The two goalies frequently bounced ideas off each other and developed a friendship off the ice. Though Kuemper said publicly his eye was fine in the St. Louis series, he told Francouz he was still struggling. The starter was frustrated when he allowed a savable overtime goal to Tyler Bozak in Game 5, and Francouz talked to him as they traveled to St. Louis.

"I've got your back," he said. "If you can't play, I think I can do it and you can recover."

Kuemper made it through Game 6, but as he struggled with his vision against the Oilers, he took Francouz up on the offer.

No. 2 goalies have to be prepared to enter at any time. They're always one collision, one ankle twist, one accidental stick to the face away from entering the game. Fortunately for the Avalanche, Francouz had been a steady presence since returning from an ankle injury in December. He won 15 of the 21 games in which he played and finished the year with a respectable .916 save percentage.

If anyone in the NHL has a sense of Francouz's reliability, it's Andrej Šustr, who spent the 2021–22 season as a defenseman with the Lightning and Ducks. Šustr and Francouz grew up together in Pilsen, Czechia, and at times sat at the same two-person desk when at the same school from first to seventh grade.

"You knew you could count on him as a friend, whether it was with homework or showing up for street hockey," Šustr said.

Francouz started playing hockey around age seven, trying defense first. He frequently found himself around his own net while learning the position. His instinct wasn't to try and score. It was to keep opponents from doing it.

Within a couple months, he had switched to goaltender. Like many kids around the country, he idolized Hockey Hall of Famer Dominik Hašek, the goaltender who carried the Czech National Team to a gold medal at the 1998 Olympics at around the time Francouz started playing hockey. The youngster hung posters of Hašek in his room; he wanted to be just like the star goalie. When he made his NHL debut in 2018, Francouz chose jersey No. 39—Hašek's number.

Šustr remembers that Francouz was one of the first kids their age to have a decorated goalie helmet. Šustr still has a photo back in Czechia of his former classmate wearing a red mask with orange flames running down the bottom. In the picture, Francouz holds the helmet up to show his face. He looks pensively at the camera, a medal draped around his neck.

The NHL never felt like a possibility to Francouz growing up. He went undrafted and never played for a non-Czech team until leaving for Russia's top league, the KHL, when he was 25. After he signed his contract, Francouz remembers someone asking him about the NHL.

"There's no chance," he responded.

But there was. He led the Czech national team to the Bronze Medal Game at the 2018 Olympics. And, playing for Traktor Chelyabinsk, he won the KHL's goaltender of the year award in 2017–18. Heading into the 2018–19 season, NHL teams started taking notice of his development.

"His path wasn't as easy as maybe others, guys who are drafted and whose path is kind of set," Šustr said. "He always had to find his own way to be successful."

Francouz had an opportunity to sign with Nashville on a two-way deal, he said, which meant the size of his salary depended on whether he played in the NHL or AHL. Though still weighing quality offers from KHL clubs, he was close to accepting the Predators deal and making the leap to North American hockey.

Then the Avalanche swooped in. Their European scouts had watched Francouz, and they wanted him on a one-way deal, meaning he would get an NHL salary no matter if he was playing with the Avalanche or in the minors with the Colorado Eagles. The goalie signed right away.

Francouz made strong first impressions in Colorado, even if he spent most of his first year in the minors. He had a strong season for the AHL club, winning 27 games, but one of Eagles coach Greg Cronin's strongest memories of his goalie came after a rare contest in which he'd struggled. After the game, which the Eagles won in overtime after blowing a multi-goal lead, Francouz walked into the dressing room and apologized to his teammates. He didn't mean to cause so much stress, he said. It wouldn't happen again.

Cronin had rarely seen a player do something like that. But Francouz is both prideful and honest with himself.

"That kind of crystallizes what he's all about," the coach said.

Francouz played solely with the Avalanche the next season, posting a strong .923 save percentage as Philipp Grubauer's backup. But when the Avalanche traveled to the Edmonton playoff bubble after the 2020 COVID-19 shutdown, Francouz was dealing with hip issues. He ended up needing double hip surgery, sidelining him for the entire 2020–21 season.

Missing a full season with injury wasn't as tough mentally as one would expect, Francouz said, because he could put all his energy into returning for 2021–22. He recovered on schedule, but his luck took another negative turn when preseason games began. On the ice against Vegas, he suffered a high ankle sprain while moving to track the puck.

The injury put him in an even lower place than the season-ending injury the year before had, he said. He always knew he'd be back from hip surgery, but this unexpected setback felt like a slap in the face. To make matters worse, ankle sprains are a nightmare for goalies, who rely heavily on the joint to shift around the crease.

Francouz was hurting. He clung to a hope that his luck would balance out.

"I just kept believing that if it's this low, it has to go super high," he said.

Now, eight months after spraining his ankle, Francouz skated onto the ice with 12:41 left in the second period of Game 1 against the Oilers. He had a chance to reach the highs he craved when times were toughest. All he had to do was come through.

• • •

During the regular season, Francouz always felt the Avalanche skated the same way no matter if he or Kuemper were in net. They didn't make any tactical changes or subconsciously switch their mental approach. Their style and structure remained sound.

That looked to be the case after Francouz entered Game 1. Late in the second period, Logan O'Connor snatched the puck in the defensive zone and burst up ice, creating a two-on-one rush alongside Andrew Cogliano. As he neared the net, O'Connor waited until Edmonton's Evan Bouchard shifted toward him to defend. Then he moved the puck across the slot to Cogliano. The veteran, drafted by Edmonton 17 years earlier, had a partially vacated net at which to shoot, and he made the most of it. He launched the puck past Koskinen.

As the goal horn rang through the arena, Cogliano pointed at O'Connor, the creator of the play. Colorado's depth was shining, and the fourth line of Cogliano, Darren Helm, and O'Connor was a big reason why. MacKinnon said that, at points during the playoffs, the trio was Colorado's best line.

"We can't be getting outplayed by the fourth line," he joked. "I love those guys, but damn."

With a 7–3 lead, Colorado seemed to have the game under control. But that's never a safe assumption against a team led by Draisaitl and McDavid. Draisaitl found his captain for a goal late in the second period. Early in the third, seven-year veteran Derek Ryan scored his first goal of the playoffs. The tally was extra costly for Colorado. André Burakovsky blocked a Bouchard slapshot with his leg moments before the goal, and the puck broke his ankle.

The Avalanche had already lost Kuemper, and now the outlook for a key forward's series was hazy, too.

Edmonton pulled to within one goal after a Nugent-Hopkins score with seven minutes left. The Avalanche had stressed the need to learn from letting a three-goal lead slip away in Game 5 against St. Louis, but now they were on the brink of blowing a four-goal advantage.

Did this team have a problem with taking its foot off the gas? Or were the Oilers back in the game because of two all-world players and bounces starting to go their way?

Finally, Landeskog intercepted a pass from Barrie in the game's final minute. He skated up ice and shot into the empty Edmonton net. The Avalanche won 8–6.

Playing in 14-goal games against Edmonton's offense wasn't a recipe for sustained success, but it worked in Colorado's Game 1 escape. And as Bednar said multiple times during the season, he far prefers learning lessons in wins than in losses.

Francouz wasn't at fault for the near-Oilers comeback, considering the three goals he allowed all came from dangerous scoring areas. Still, he looked sharper two nights later in Game 2.

So did the Colorado teammates playing in front of him.

• • •

The Ball Arena music stopped before the Canadian and U.S. national anthems, leaving only the buzz of a full crowd. From that buzz came a chant, one in support of Francouz, the backup thrust into the spotlight.

"Fran-kie! Fran-kie! Fran-kie!" rang through the building.

The goaltender, who celebrated his 32nd birthday the day after Game 2, said the crowd support left him with a special feeling, though he sheepishly added he'd have preferred to hear the typical pro-Avalanche cheers rather than a personalized one. Instead of standing for the anthems in the goalie crease, he joined his teammates along the blue line, shuffling his weight between his right and left legs to stay loose. And after the final notes he got his wish, as the crowd burst into, "Let's go, Avs!" chants. As the building hummed, Devon Toews created an early scoring chance, bursting around Nugent-Hopkins and putting a shot on Smith within the first 40 seconds.

Makar jumped on for his first shift of the game around the same time, and the Oilers challenged him quickly in what became one of the lasting visuals of the series—a head-to-head play featuring two of the world's smoothest skaters.

McDavid grabbed a loose puck in Colorado's offensive zone, then charged past every Avalanche player except Makar, the last line of defense. Colorado's star glided backward as McDavid approached, working to cut off his angle to the net. Then, when he saw an opening, he jabbed his stick toward the puck. It bounced away from McDavid, out of harm's way.

The play showed both Makar's elite skating and his defensive abilities. Not many players—let alone ones as offensively dynamic as Makar—can separate McDavid from a puck on a breakaway, and the Avalanche defenseman made it look easy. Long gone were the days in Brooks when Oliver Chau ribbed him for his poor gap control.

Meanwhile, Francouz started steady, smothering a Kailer Yamamoto slap shot early in the first and a Kane backhand midway through the period. Across the ice, the Oilers' Smith held serve, just managing to get a piece of shots from Lehkonen and MacKinnon. Colorado missed a chance to capitalize on a five-on-three power play after a pair of Edmonton penalties, and the Oilers failed to make the most of first-rate opportunities, too. Jesse Puljujärvi, once a teammate of Rantanen for Finland at World Junior Championships, skated to a bouncing puck directly in front of Francouz but failed to put it on net, sending a shot wide.

Then, with a minute left in the first, Francouz got over-eager trying to play a puck, skating two dozen feet out of his crease. Edmonton's Cody Ceci intercepted Francouz's pass in the neutral zone and put the puck on net, but the goaltender recovered well enough to save the shot from the faceoff circle. He made it to the end of the period without allowing a score.

After combining for 14 goals in Game 1, neither the Oilers nor the Avalanche found a way to get a puck over the goal line in the first 20 minutes of Game 2.

Artturi Lehkonen and a flying second line made sure that didn't last. Four minutes into the second period, the Finnish winger pressured Darnell Nurse, who rushed a pass, leading to a turnover in Colorado's offensive zone. Rantanen tracked the loose puck off the boards. He backhanded a pass to Kadri, who put a shot on net. Standing in the faceoff circle, Lehkonen got just enough of his stick on the puck to change its direction. His deflection fooled Smith, and the Avalanche had the lead.

Lehkonen punched the air with vigor, and Kadri did the same, almost in unison. The Avalanche had finally broken through a wall, and they kept on going as soon as play resumed. The puck found Kadri once again in the offensive zone. He moved it to Manson. The defenseman's showing in Game 1 had been lackluster, but this was a new night. He settled the puck, then unleashed a slapshot that beat Smith again. The shot tucked under his glove and found the back of the net.

Manson raised his arms and screamed. Colorado had scored twice in 15 seconds.

After slapping hands with his teammates, Manson stared down the Oilers bench. He declined to say who he was looking at—"That's top-secret information," he half-joked—but noted that players were trying to get under each other's skin in an emotional game. Keith, for example, tripped MacKinnon after a whistle in the first period, and Kane was chirping at Colorado players from the start.

Manson wanted to send the Oilers a message that he wouldn't get rattled, even after his performance in Game 1. That poor showing was simply motivation to play better.

After the two quick goals, Woodcroft called a timeout, wanting to regain some semblance of control. "Take a deep breath! A deep fucking breath!" he shouted over the arena noise to his players, as captured on ESPN's *Quest for the Stanley Cup* series.

But the pause didn't have the desired effect. Less than two minutes after Manson's score, Kadri and Rantanen sprung into the rush for a two-on-one. Kadri slid the puck past Nurse and toward his wing. Rantanen buried it. In a span of just over two minutes, Kadri had three assists.

That was more than enough for the Avalanche, who seemed to have learned both from their blown lead in Game 5 of the Blues series and from Edmonton's near-comeback in Game 1. Bednar's club remained aggressive, not showing any signs of timidity or caution.

When the Oilers had chances, Francouz did his job. He kept the lead at three late in the second period, making arguably his best save of the night by using his stick to poke the puck away from Nurse on a breakaway.

Edmonton's composure had dissipated by the third. Midway through the period, a Josh Archibald hit along the boards left Bowen Byram half over the wall in front of the Oilers' bench. A sitting Zack Kassian yanked off the Colorado defenseman's helmet. Then, with five minutes left, Kane hit Makar along the boards, earning a roughing penalty.

Heading into Game 2, the Edmonton forward talked about the importance of limiting Makar's time and space, saying the Oilers needed to increase their physicality. But there's a difference between physicality and a penalty that puts a dangerous power play unit on the ice. Sure enough, Colorado made the Oilers pay. MacKinnon netted a goal with Kane watching from the penalty box.

"We want the Cup!" chants emerged shortly after the goal.

It was arguably Colorado's most complete game of the playoffs thus far. Though the Avalanche's second line was the only trio to collect an even-strength goal, the whole team came to play. A collective defensive effort snapped nine-game point streaks for both McDavid and Draisaitl, and the Cogliano, Helm, and O'Connor line didn't allow a single scoring chance while on the ice together.

So Colorado headed to Game 3 at the Oilers sparkling arena. Rogers Place was the site of the 2020 Edmonton Bubble where Francouz suffered his hip injury, as well as a 2022 regular season game in which he was hit by a flying puck as he sat on the bench.

"I don't really have good memories from that building," he told Colorado's trainers as the team hit the road. "It's time to change that."

"GOOD STICK, LEHKY"

WAS NAZEM KADRI'S career year going to end like this? With a push into the end boards? With a trainer rushing onto the Edmonton ice? With Kadri lying face down, writhing in pain?

That's how it appeared early in Game 3 of the Western Conference Finals. Connor McDavid had scored 38 seconds into the game, sending the Rogers Place crowd into a frenzy, but that energy changed less than 30 seconds later. As Kadri chased a Rantanen pass toward the boards, Evander Kane put his stick hard into the Colorado center's back and pushed. Kadri flew into the wall. The Avalanche were livid.

"You're taught from a young age that you don't do that," Gabriel Landeskog said.

Added Jared Bednar: "It's the most dangerous play in hockey."

Fortunately for Kadri, his head avoided direct contact with the boards or the ice. His right thumb didn't. He pulled off his glove within seconds of the hit, cradling his hand and wincing. He instantly knew something was wrong. Sure enough, the hit had broken his thumb in multiple places. He wouldn't play again against the Oilers, and there was no guarantee he'd be back for potential Stanley Cup Final games.

The officials sent Kane, who plays with an edge and entered the game with four career suspensions for on-ice actions, to the box with a five-minute major penalty but did not eject him from the game. The on-ice punishment didn't appease Kadri's agent, Darren Ferris, who by the end of the night was publicly calling for the league to further discipline the Oilers forward. The next day, the Department of Player Safety suspended Kane for Game 4.

But during Game 3, the night went from bad to worse for the Avalanche when they couldn't take advantage of their five-minute power play. Oilers goalie Mike Smith halted a MacKinnon tip attempt off a Landeskog pass. Edmonton also got help from the right goal post, which robbed MacKinnon. The 40-year-old Smith has a long reputation of high-ceiling but inconsistent play, and he started Game 3 playing at his best. He shut out Colorado on another power play attempt later in the period.

But Smith can't always sustain that level of play, especially when he catches bad breaks. That's what happened with 3:50 left in the first period when Valeri Nichushkin fired a centering pass intended for Bowen Byram. The puck bounced off the stick of Oilers defenseman Darnell Nurse and, with Smith unable to close off the post, somehow ricocheted into the net. For a moment, no one knew where Nichushkin's feed had gone. Then both the winger and the nearest official caught sight of it. Nichushkin pointed at the back of the net, and the official extended his arm to signify a goal.

The game's first two scores perfectly summarized the randomness of hockey. The first goal, McDavid's early shot past Francouz, came from the stick of the world's top forward playing at the peak of his powers. Nichushkin's goal came essentially by accident.

Nichushkin's second goal of the night was more purposeful. Early in the second period, Toews fired a shot from the point, but the puck bounced off McDavid's skate, right to Nichushkin in the slot. Going into the game, the Avalanche had talked about Smith not moving well, Nichushkin said, so he tried to get a shot off as quickly as possible. The puck flew past Smith's blocker side and in.

In one of the biggest games of his career, Nichushkin had scored twice. His breakout 25-goal regular season was carrying over into the playoffs. His tenacity and ability to forecheck, as well as his 6'4" height and chiseled frame, earned him the nickname "Choo Choo Train." And with the series now in Edmonton, he was making sure the Avalanche were on track. Landeskog called him a force.

"He keeps himself in top condition," Bednar said. "All the things you want to see as a pro, he has those habits every day."

Francouz, who had been so steady both in Game 2 and early in Game 3, faltered midway through the third when Ryan McLeod burst through the neutral zone and put a shot on net. The puck flew past Francouz's outstretched glove. The Avalanche lead was gone.

Francouz should have made a save on McLeod's goal. But, Bednar said, his goalie more than made up for the miscue. Midway through the third period—a crucial point in the game—J.T. Compher tripped Leon Draisaitl and headed to the penalty box, barking at the officials. It was a potentially costly play by one of only five Colorado players who had endured the team's last-place 2016–17 campaign. Now, after an off-season focused on self-improvement, all he could do was watch.

Fortunately for Compher, Francouz bailed him out. A minute into the power play, Tyson Barrie fired a puck on net that bounced off Erik Johnson's skate and right to McDavid, the last player Francouz wanted to see with the puck. The superstar unleashed a shot from the faceoff circle. But Francouz adjusted just in time, shifting across his crease and stopping the puck with his glove. He smothered the rebound.

After allowing the weak McLeod goal, the McDavid save represented an impressive and important mental reset for Francouz. He didn't let one bad play derail his night. Now he had made his most clutch save of the postseason.

The Oilers had one last chance on the power play when hard-shooting defenseman Evan Bouchard unleashed a puck that got past Francouz. Fortunately for Colorado, it bounced off the post and right to Andrew Cogliano. The Avalanche forward, whose NHL career started with Edmonton, flung the puck off the boards and up the ice and out of danger.

At the same time, Compher flew out of the penalty box, ready to make a key play in the midst of a bounce-back season.

The 27-year-old had struggled in 2020–21 and saw both his point production and playing time go down. That off-season, he said, "There were a lot of tough conversations I needed to have with myself." He needed to handle ups and downs better, he determined, and become more resilient. He created a strong game plan with Chicago-based trainer Ian Mack. The two aimed to increase his speed through exercises focused on increasing power and explosiveness, such as multi-directional running and jumping.

As he raced with Bouchard to the puck, which was still sliding up the ice, Compher showed off the speed he had worked to improve with Mack. He collided with the Oilers defenseman as the puck trickled into the Colorado offensive zone.

Bouchard tumbled to the ice, but Compher kept his balance and seized possession. He put a shot on net that slithered through Smith's pads. Not realizing it had gone in, the Colorado forward skated hard to the crease in hopes of a rebound. He saw the puck in the net just in time to fling his hands up and catch a celebrating Byram, who leapt into his arms.

The game could've been entirely different had Bouchard's shot gone in, or even if it had hit off the post at a different angle and avoided Cogliano. But that isn't what happened. Compher's roller coaster of emotions that started in the penalty box ended with elation.

Francouz and the Avalanche kept the Oilers off the board the rest of the way, including a Rantanen dive to get a puck out of the defensive zone in the final minute of play. And as Edmonton tried to gear up for another scoring chance, Rantanen intercepted a Draisaitl pass, darted up ice and scored into a vacated Oilers net.

The win brought Colorado's road record to 6–0 in the postseason. MacKinnon attributed the Avalanche success in hostile environments to a willingness to play "boring and gross." They weren't playing to please anybody or put on a show. They were playing to win hockey games, doing the little things right and playing stout defense.

But nonetheless, their skill and speed made their brand of "boring and gross" still plenty entertaining. Now they had Edmonton on the brink of elimination. And, one win from the Stanley Cup Final, they didn't want to give the Oilers life.

• • •

While breaking down the Avalanche-Oilers series with the TNT TV crew, Wayne Gretzky referred to Cale Makar as "the best player on the ice in all games."

High praise, considering the source and the fact that the Oilers-Avalanche matchup also featured McDavid, Draisaitl, and MacKinnon, who combined had 10 top-five MVP finishes.

Gretzky had a point. Makar, who had a goal and a trio of assists through the first three games of the series, didn't slow down in Game 4. Three minutes into the contest, the top power play unit took the ice after a Zack Kassian slashing penalty on Jack Johnson. Midway through the Avalanche's two minutes with an extra man, Artturi Lehkonen—a strong puck retriever on the top power play unit because of Kadri's injury—snatched possession from Zach Hyman and got it to Makar just in front of the blueline. The defenseman flung a long wrist shot on net, and it found its way past Smith. Makar raised both his arms in celebration.

The lead lasted only for a period. The Oilers scored three goals in the second period, two of which were assisted by Draisaitl. The German star was playing with a high ankle sprain and winced in pain seemingly every time he skated to the bench. His efforts had the Rogers Place crowd reengaged with the game, suddenly hopeful the Oilers season could survive to another night.

MacKinnon, meanwhile, didn't sense much confidence from his own team as the Colorado players marched into the dressing room for the second intermission. Their heads were down as they sat at their lockers.

"Fuck," MacKinnon thought to himself. "We're playing like shit." After a few moments, the center started talking to Landeskog. If any team knew how hard it was to hold a third-period lead, it was the Avalanche, who had gone into the final frame leading 3–1 in their Game 5 loss to St. Louis. The pressure to close an opponent out, especially when at home, is intense. So, MacKinnon thought, if the Avalanche could score once, it would inject some doubt into the minds of the Oilers. Then maybe they would get tight. He and Landeskog started throwing out encouragement.

33333333333333

"Screw this."

"We're not gonna just roll over."

"Let's go put them on their heels."

It worked. It also sent the game off the rails, as both teams' stars played like stars, and both teams' goaltenders did not. Toews and Hyman traded goals early in the period, and, later, Colorado pulled within one when Landeskog punched a rebound in from the crease.

"That was Gabe's best period of the playoffs," MacKinnon said, calling the captain the team's most effective player that night. "Gabe was so freakin' good."

With the Avalanche trailing 4–3, MacKinnon tripped Hyman and went to the penalty box, setting up a consequential two-minute stretch for both teams. Early in the Oilers' power play, Barrie whipped a puck toward the net that went directly off Cogliano's glove. Wincing in pain and holding his hand, the veteran stayed on the ice, not wanting to leave as the Oilers pressed.

Ryan Nugent-Hopkins found Draisaitl with a quick cross-ice pass and, as Francouz shifted over, the star forward had a half-vacated net at which to shoot. He brought his hands forward, dropping to a knee and sending the puck flying toward the net. Surely, considering Draisaitl's scoring prowess and 55-goal regular season, this shot was headed over the line. Maybe it would ice the game and send the series back to Denver.

But in perhaps a game-saving break for Colorado, the puck pinged off the post. Toews grabbed it and flung it down the ice, finally giving Cogliano a chance to skate to the bench. The veteran was done for the game, but the Avalanche were still within one.

Shortly after the Avalanche killed the rest of the penalty, Makar grabbed the puck behind Colorado's net and moved it up the boards to Lehkonen, who tapped a pass to a zooming MacKinnon entering the offensive zone. The Avalanche center burst ahead of Darnell Nurse and Hyman, leaving only Cody Ceci between him and the net. MacKinnon got a step on the Oilers defenseman, who tried diving to block the angle between MacKinnon and the net. He had no luck. MacKinnon's shot from the offensive zone faceoff circle beat Smith gloveside.

The Avalanche had erased a pair of two-goal deficits, and they weren't done. Less than a minute after MacKinnon's goal, Oilers forward Derek Ryan went to the penalty box for holding Rantanen, and the Avalanche power play took advantage. Makar fed Rantanen in the faceoff circle, and the Finnish forward buried his shot, notching his fourth goal in as many games in the series. He extended both his fists and pulled them back and forth. His team was now just five minutes from a Stanley Cup Final berth.

But, as Colorado knew well from the St. Louis series, teams are hard to finish off in the playoffs, especially teams with as many game-breakers as Edmonton. With 3:30 remaining, Edmonton forced a turnover and pushed the pace up the ice. McDavid found Draisaitl in the outer slot, and the German didn't hit the post this time. When the puck got through Francouz's legs, Kassian batted it in from the goal line, tying the game 5–5. The score stood until overtime.

Despite Edmonton's late goal, Erik Johnson remembers the mindset in Colorado's locker room bearing no resemblance to the gloom that hung over the players early in the second intermission. "We would sign up for this at the start of the third," he said. "This is a great comeback. All the pressure is on them."

Meanwhile, the injured Cogliano had an X-ray taken of his injured hand. After the team left the dressing room and returned to the ice for overtime, a doctor came into the room and told the fourth-liner that the puck had broken his middle finger.

His availability for the rest of the playoffs now in question, Cogliano started to cry.

"I could see how badly he hurt in that situation," said Peter Aragon, an Avalanche video producer who watched the exchange.

Above the ice, Sakic remained unperturbed by Edmonton's late goal. He chatted in the press box with Oilers general manager Ken Holland, then wandered through the hallway, back to his seat, to watch overtime begin.

• • •

About 20 years earlier, a six-year-old Artturi Lehkonen smiled as he sat on a stone wall. He wore black socks nearly up to his knees and a T-shirt from Lukko, the hockey team his dad coached. On his head sat an Avalanche cap brought to him by Colorado center Riku Hahl, who was back in his native Finland after his team fell in Game 7 of the 2002 Western Conference Finals.

Hahl had played for Arturri's dad, Ismo, in the late 1990s and paid his former coach a visit. He posed for a picture with Artturi, his muscular arm around the blonde-haired boy's shoulders, and spent hours playing street hockey with the youngster.

In late March 2022, when Sakic acquired Lehkonen from Montreal, Hahl reached out to Ismo, reminding him of the 2002 Colorado club that came a game short of reaching the Stanley Cup Final.

"Now Artturi has to finish the job," he told Ismo.

In Game 4 against Edmonton, the Avalanche couldn't completely finish the job—they were on a mission to win the Stanley Cup, not just make it to the Final—but when Lehkonen took the ice in overtime, he was one goal away from getting farther than Hahl did in the NHL playoffs.

A little over a minute into the extra period, Erik Johnson fired a shot that ricocheted off Ryan McLeod and into the netting behind Edmonton's goal, stopping play. Bednar opted to change lines, and with Cogliano out, the coach sent Lehkonen onto the ice with Logan O'Connor and Darren Helm, the injured forward's usual linemates. Edmonton's Brad Malone took the faceoff with Helm, and the puck bounced to Lehkonen, who tapped it back to Helm. The veteran forward passed to Makar in front of the blue line, and the defenseman put a shot on net.

Lehkonen, who sent Montreal to the Stanley Cup Final with an overtime winner the year before, cut to the goalie's crease as his teammate's shot flew through the air, and he tipped the puck into Mike Smith's right pad. The puck bounced right back to Lehkonen in front of the net. Smith sprawled, trying to recover in time to block the open net, but Lehkonen moved to his left. He had room to shoot.

Makar felt like the puck was on Lehkonen's stick for a full minute, and MacKinnon joked he thought he was going to have a heart attack while waiting for his teammate to shoot. They had no need to worry; eventually, Lehkonen wristed a shot over the goal line.

Game over. Avalanche 6, Oilers 5.

"The guy just scores big goals," Jack Johnson said.

Lehkonen skipped toward the Avalanche players spilling onto the ice, leaping into Toews's arms. The team gathered in a clump along the glass, jumping and hugging and smiling and celebrating. Cogliano, who watched from the locker room, jumped to his feet and ran to the ice, wanting to be with his teammates.

Then everyone froze, realizing that officials were reviewing the play across the ice. The issue: was Lehkonen's stick too high when he tipped Makar's shot off Smith's pads? There are important distinctions when it comes to high-sticking rules. If a player touches a puck that's higher than the crossbar and it goes into the net, the goal is waved off. But if a player touches a puck that doesn't go directly into the net, he can touch it as high as his shoulders.

"You get that rush of dopamine going crazy and then you go, 'Oh, no it could be coming back,'" MacKinnon said.

After more than a minute of deliberation, the crew made its decision. Referee Chris Rooney skated away from the review station, his arm held straight ahead. The puck had touched Lehkonen's stick before his shoulder. It was a good goal.

A gleeful Toews grabbed Makar, who ended the night with five points in the game and nine for the series. Lehkonen roared, and a joyous MacKinnon hugged him so enthusiastically that they both fell to the ice.

"That's why you trade for guys like that at the deadline," MacKinnon said after the game. "I'd trade 10 first rounders for him right now."

After the Avalanche shook hands with the Oilers, deputy commissioner Bill Daly walked onto the ice to present the Clarence S.

Artturi Lehkonen (whose jersey is partially visible at lower left) is mobbed by teammates after netting the game-winner in overtime in Game 4 of the 2022 Western Conference Finals vs. the Edmonton Oilers, completing the sweep and sending Colorado to the Stanley Cup Final.

Campbell Bowl given to the Western Conference champions. Some NHLers view touching the trophy as bad luck ahead of the Final, so the Avalanche players deliberated until Sakic joined them on the ice. The general manager had put both hands on the trophy as a player, and it didn't stop him from winning two Stanley Cups.

"Touch it," he told the group crowded around him.

So Landeskog did, placing his right hand on the handle. MacKinnon, standing to his captain's right, followed suit. None of the players tempted fate too much, though. No one picked it up.

MacKinnon walked off the ice smiling, the chinstrap of his helmet undone. "Fuckin' right!" Bowen Byram yelled before whooping and throwing his arms around skills coach Shawn Allard, who waited by the dressing room door. Assistant general manager Chris MacFarland, dressed in a dark suit and lavender shirt, fist-bumped Lehkonen, then slapped the night's hero on the butt.

Makar enjoyed a celebratory dinner with his family after the game, and Nichushkin tagged along. The Russian winger deals with a language barrier, sometimes limiting his English conversation ability, but he was comfortable and happy that night. He chatted with Gary, Cale's dad, about the eight-game series in 1972 between the Canadian and USSR national teams, then gave every Makar family member a bear hug before leaving.

Back in Finland, Ismo Lehkonen didn't let the magnitude of the game change his routine. He recorded it, perfectly comfortable waiting until morning to watch, just as he'd done in the playoffs the year before. But the father of Canadiens forward Jesperi Kotkaniemi had played spoiler then, calling Ismo after Artturi's overtime winner clinched Montreal's berth in the Cup Final.

A year later, Ismo had learned his lesson. He kept his phone far away and put it on silent. So when he saw Artturi score, it was as surprising as if he and his wife, Riitta, had not been watching a recording. When the puck went in, Ismo took a couple deep breaths, letting the moment register.

"Okay," he told himself. "Now they have a chance to win the title."

LATE NIGHTS IN THE MIDDLE OF JUNE

THE REMINDERS WERE everywhere as the Avalanche trickled into a Ball Arena lobby for a pre-series media day. Each table was embroidered with STANLEY CUP FINAL, and players had new sweatshirts and hats signifying they had made the sport's biggest stage. Photos hung from black curtains, showing past champions lifting the hallowed trophy.

But nothing was more striking than the silver, shiny, 34.5-pound mounted bowl near a new NHL Network set. Neither the Avalanche nor their opponent, the Tampa Bay Lightning, had won a game yet, but the Cup was in the building with Game 1 scheduled for the next night.

The five bands of the Stanley Cup are engraved with the names of past players to have won the trophy. Every 13 years, when the base runs out of room for more names, a band is removed and displayed in the Hockey Hall of Fame. The trophy constantly evolves. It has a near-mythical aura; players speak about it with reverence.

"I would definitely not touch it," Pavel Francouz said when asked if he had any pre-series superstitions involving the trophy. "But I think I can look at it and say nice things about it."

Perhaps intentionally, perhaps by chance, the Cup was visible from almost every player's table at media day. Gabriel Landeskog, Nathan MacKinnon, and the Avalanche were this close to their goal. They were on the brink of playing the biggest games of their lives. On the brink of broken hearts or unlocked dreams.

• • •

Colorado's inexperience was notable leading into the series. André Burakovsky and Darren Helm had won the Stanley Cup previously, but that was it. Andrew Cogliano and Artturi Lehkonen were the only other players to even make it to the Final. The Lightning were the opposite. They had won the Stanley Cup the previous two seasons, upending Cogliano's Dallas Stars in 2020 and Lehkonen's Montreal Canadiens in 2021. Almost all of their 2021–22 players were on at least one of the two previous Cup-winning teams, and one who wasn't—former MVP Corey Perry—won with Anaheim in 2007. This was a potent group that had experience and yet managed to keep its hunger. If Tampa Bay was to win its third championship in a row, it would become the first team since the early 1980s Islanders to three-peat.

The Lightning were led by 54-year-old coach Jon Cooper, who started his career coaching high school hockey after graduating from Cooley Law School in Lansing, Michigan. He never played hockey beyond the collegiate club level but worked his way up the coaching ranks, gaining experience at the junior hockey level and moving to the AHL in 2010. The Lightning hired him as head coach in 2013, and they made the Stanley Cup Final in his second full season, losing to Chicago in six games.

Though the Lightning had been contenders from their first Cup berth on, their road to back-to-back titles didn't come without heartbreak. In 2018–19, they tied the record for most wins in a regular season, going 62–16–4. Forward Nikita Kucherov won the Hart Trophy as league MVP, and goalie Andrei Vasilevskiy won the Vezina Trophy for best goalie. Add those two to Victor Hedman, one of the top defensemen in the game, and elite goal-scorer Steven Stamkos, and Tampa Bay seemed primed for postseason success.

But in a shocking turn of events, the Lightning lost in the first round to Columbus, a team that won 15 fewer games in the regular season. Not only did Tampa Bay lose, but it became the first team in NHL history to be swept in the first round after finishing the regular season with the most wins in the league. The loss was so unprecedented, so baffling, that the team put out an apology on Twitter.

"We don't have any words and we know you don't want to hear them," it read. "We understand your anger, your frustration, your sadness. Everything you're feeling—we get it. This isn't the ending we imagined, and certainly not the one we wanted. Thank you for being there the entire way."

But the Lightning stayed the course. They didn't overreact to the loss by firing Cooper or trading away members of the team's core. They made it through the jokes that come with losing in upset fashion, then won the next two Stanley Cups. In many ways they were a blueprint for Joe Sakic and the Avalanche organization, which remained patient with Jared Bednar and his star players after they lost four in a row to Vegas in 2021. Bednar even turned to Cooper after his team fell to the Golden Knights, looking for advice about how to get over the hump.

Tampa Bay had learned that the devastation of gut-wrenching losses makes championship victory sweeter—if you can get there. Now the Avalanche wanted to have their moment too, and players repeated an old cliché when talking about their opponent: to be the best, they'd have to beat the best.

The Lightning leaned heavily on their experience in their first-round matchup against Auston Matthews and Toronto. Down 3–2 in the series and trailing in the third period of Game 6, Kucherov scored a power play goal to tie the game, and Brayden Point won the game in overtime by batting in a rebound. Tampa Bay won Game 7 on the road to advance.

Cooper's group swept the Florida Panthers, who had the league's best regular season record, in the second round, then came back from a 2–0 series deficit against the New York Rangers to win the Eastern Conference Finals in six. The Lightning were ready for any situation and perfectly comfortable at the doorstep of elimination.

Even when playing a team like the Avalanche, with its deeper group of skaters, the Lightning had a trump card: Vasilevskiy. Picked in the first round of the 2012 draft, the 6'3" goalie had the size, athleticism, and technique of an NHL star, and that's exactly what he became. He finished in the top five of Vezina voting every season from 2017–18 to 2021–22. To make matters worse for opponents, he's always risen to the moment in the playoffs. He had a staggering .932 save percentage in Tampa Bay's two Stanley Cup runs and won the Conn Smythe Trophy for playoff MVP in 2021. He entered the Stanley Cup Final on a four-game winning streak in which he had a .955 save percentage, having allowed only five goals.

"Intensity, work ethic, he's top of the list," Cooper said earlier in the playoffs. "Our team, they take losses personal, but the goalie really takes it personal."

Daunting as Vasilevskiy's past performance was, it didn't make him unstoppable. During their eight-day break between the Edmonton series and the Stanley Cup Final, the Avalanche broke down everything they possibly could in regards to both the Lightning and their goalie. They studied how, in the first three rounds, he was better at stopping shots with his glove side than he was with his blocker. That could be an area where they could gain an edge.

"We felt like we could put enough pressure on him and them that eventually one is going to go in, or a couple," Jack Johnson said. "If we can get three or four, we [were] going to win the game."

MacKinnon said the Avalanche also noticed some of Tampa Bay's previous playoff opponents making the mistake of giving the puck away when in the low in the Lightning's defensive zone. Every one of the Tampa Bay defensemen was 6′1″ or taller, so they could smother opponents with their size in tight areas. The Avalanche believed they could use the high ice to drag the Lightning defensemen out to the top of the offensive zone, where they would have a tougher time stifling Colorado chances and getting the puck out of the zone.

Then there was patience. The Avalanche had, save for a couple lapses in the St. Louis series, kept focus on their game plan and process throughout the postseason. If they stuck to the style of play that brought them success all year, players believed they'd eventually break through in tight games. The Game 4 comeback against Edmonton showed that, as did Colorado's overtime wins against hot goalies Jordan Binnington and Connor Ingram.

That same mindset would be critical against Tampa Bay's stout defense and strong goaltending. This was the final, toughest task of the season. It was the one with the most pressure, too.

· · ·

Jack Johnson's media day table was positioned with the trophy right in his sight line. Johnson, who had never made it past the first round of the playoffs until 2022, couldn't look up without seeing the Stanley Cup. The gravity of the moment hit him.

"Okay," he thought to himself, "this is real."

The NHL doesn't host a media day event for any series but the Stanley Cup Final, so the event was a first for most Colorado players. So it was Mikko Rantanen's "I'm here" moment, too. He was struck by the number of reporters from countries all over the world, including Czechia and Germany. There were a contingent of Finnish journalists, too, including Artturi Lehkonen's dad, Ismo, who was covering the series for the Finnish Broadcasting Company. As Rantanen answered a question, Ismo, wearing a black top hat, approached him and slid a chocolate bar in blue wrapping across his table. It was Karl Fazer Milk Chocolate, a popular Finnish brand and a taste of home. Rantanen smiled as Ismo walked away.

MacKinnon sat wearing an Avalanche hat and a gray sweatshirt featuring a silhouette of the Stanley Cup. His playoff beard had a tint of red, and he rested his hands on the table in front of him. He wasn't in a lighthearted mood. Sakic had said earlier in the day that no one wanted the Cup more than MacKinnon, and the center said he could feel the nervous energy and was ready to get going. He exuded focus as he answered questions, including one about his, "I haven't won shit," comment in the aftermath of the Vegas loss a year earlier. He didn't crack a smile.

To MacKinnon's left, reporters swarmed Makar, some holding cell phones over their heads to snap photos. Large prints from both Colorado's and Tampa Bay's most recent Stanley Cup wins hung next to him. The Avalanche photo showed Hall of Fame defenseman

Ray Bourque hoisting the trophy in 2001; the Lightning's picture was from 2021, when Stamkos lifted the Cup for a second time.

"Obviously, they're a team that's looking to become a dynasty, and we're a team that's looking to start a legacy," the young defenseman said.

You couldn't write it any better, he added. This moment had been their focus for the whole season, just as their victory song, "Heat Waves," reminded them after every win: "Sometimes all I think about is you...."

Now they were here. Four wins away. The late nights in the middle of June had arrived.

BURAKOVSKY'S MOMENT

AS HE SKATED with the Avalanche in the week leading up to the Stanley Cup Final, André Burakovsky's injured ankle didn't keep him from his role as a humorous and fun-to-be-around teammate. Five days ahead of Game 1, Gabriel Landeskog, Burakovsky's fellow Swede, jokingly tackled him to the ice after practice. The captain lay on a laughing Burakovsky's back as Nathan MacKinnon, Rantanen, and Nicolas Aubé-Kubel pretended to break up the mock fight.

Roughhousing with Burakovsky wasn't abnormal with Avalanche players. Following a skate earlier in the year, he lay still on the ice so MacKinnon could use his stick to move him as if doing a sled push workout.

"[Burakovsky] has those dummy moments when we laugh at him in a good way," Rantanen said. "He is a goofball. Always joking around."

"He can dish it out, and he can take it just as well," said Landeskog, who frequently bickered with Burakovsky on team flights, telling him to shut his window.

As much as he enjoys being a source of humor, Burakovsky takes work seriously. He snapped his stick on the boards during a midseason practice, frustrated with his performance on a power play drill. And back when he played with Washington, he struggled with perspective, dwelling on mistakes and worrying about what coaches thought. He worked with a sports psychologist before coming to Colorado in 2019–20, trying to get in a healthier, more productive frame of mind.

"He's a bit of a deeper book," said former Washington teammate Tom Wilson, one of Burakovsky's closest friends on the Capitals. "He might come across like, 'I'm just laughing and goofing around,' but when it's go time, he's a guy you want in your corner."

Burakovsky was one of only four players on the Avalanche who had played Stanley Cup games—he won with the Capitals in 2018—but he had pre-series jitters nonetheless. The night before Game 1, he struggled sleeping and woke up at 6:00 AM. He couldn't wait to play.

"Just wait until you have kids," Landeskog joked with him. "You'll be up at 6:00 AM every day."

The 27-year-old Burakovsky, wrapping up his third year in Colorado, was set to hit free agency after the Cup Final. He had enjoyed a solid, albeit streaky, regular season. He'd set career highs in goals (22), points (61), and average time on ice (16:16). He'd registered his first NHL hat trick in December with the thrilling trio of goals against the Panthers, and he spent most of the season on one of Colorado's top two lines.

His postseason, though, hadn't gone smoothly. Moved to the third line at the start of the Nashville series, he tallied points in only one of the team's first seven playoff games. Jared Bednar benched him twice in the St. Louis series, but Burakovsky worked his way back into the lineup for the clincher against the Blues, notching an assist. He also helped set up Colorado's first goal in the Edmonton series. Then came the Evan Bouchard slapshot that broke his ankle and kept him out of the next two games.

Burakovsky battled through what his dad, Robert, described as a significant amount of pain following the blocked Bouchard shot, and the forward received injections in his foot to ease the discomfort. That, plus an individualized rehab schedule, made it possible for him to return to the Avalanche lineup for Game 4 against Edmonton and, subsequently, the Stanley Cup Final. His biggest moment as an Avalanche player was ahead of him.

• • •

Not many people in the NHL can skate with Connor McDavid. The superstar's legs propel him faster than just about anyone in the world, and yet they somehow can cut and shift his positioning without slowing down. Even fewer could keep up with him at the junior hockey level, when he played with the Erie Otters in the Ontario League.

André Burakovsky could. At 18, he had the makings not only of an NHL player, but of a high-impact one.

Burakovsky grew up in a hockey family. His dad, Robert, was known in Europe for his strong shot, and he won a Swedish championship with Malmö in 1992. Shortly before André's birth, Robert appeared in 23 NHL games with the 1993–94 Ottawa Senators. Though the brief NHL stint was the highest level at which the elder Burakovsky played, it was far from the end of his hockey career. Nearly three decades later, as a 54-year-old during the 2021–22 season, he got the itch to play and appeared in six games for a fifth-tier Swedish club.

At some point, André said, he wants his dad to give up the sport. But even when Robert assures him he's done, his son remains skeptical. He knows how much love his father has for the game.

Though he primarily grew up in Sweden and represents the country in international hockey, André was born in Austria, where Robert was playing at the time. He also lived in Germany and Switzerland during his dad's hockey career.

Robert's scoring ability turned out to be hereditary, as André inherited his dad's propensity for putting pucks in the net. Growing up, André talked not just of playing professionally in Sweden but of getting all the way to the NHL. His talent was apparent from a young age.

The father saw it as his goal to make sure his son reached his potential, partially because he felt he didn't make the most of his talents. When he was a high-level player, Robert relaxed during summers rather than working as hard as possible.

"I was a little bit lazy," he said. "I didn't want him to make the same mistake I did."

So, when it came to hockey, André remembers his dad being "extremely, extremely hard" on him, especially when he didn't think he was putting in enough work. Once, Robert didn't like André's effort level in a game. He took his son's sticks into the yard and broke them all.

He was five at the time.

"He would lose his mind if I would go out in practice and just not try and have fun and fool around," André said.

Burakovsky believes his dad's forcefulness helped him emerge as an NHL prospect in his teenage years. Heading into his draft summer, 2013, he played more than 40 games in the second-highest Swedish pro league. The Capitals saw enough to pick him 23rd overall.

Before going to Washington, Burakovsky played a year of junior hockey for Erie in the Ontario League, which, according to Robert, the Capitals believed would help his English and show him how to live like a professional. André joined multiple future NHLers in Erie, including McDavid, Connor Brown, Dylan Strome, Brendan Gaunce, and Adam Pelech. General manager Sherry Bassin started the hype about his new player even before he arrived. Strome remembers him saying, "He's got the best shot you've ever seen."

Bassin wasn't exaggerating, or at least not too much. Gaunce still raves about Burakovsky's release on wrist shots, and he wasn't the only one impressed. When McDavid, already viewed as hockey's next big thing, took the ice with his new Swedish teammate, he immediately noticed. He could really skate, and his shot wasn't one you saw very often at the junior level. McDavid described taking the ice with Burakovsky as eye-opening.

Burakovsky's Erie teammates introduced him to North American culture. He fell in love with chicken burritos from Chipotle, and enjoyed going to the mall. He signed autographs for hordes of fans when the Otters held a poster night for him early in the season, and Gaunce described him as a great teammate and a happy-go-lucky guy.

"He was just kind of like a lost puppy," forward Dane Fox said. "Just walking around, always smiling, the best moods, always joking around."

On the ice, Burakovsky played on a star-studded top power play group. Future NHLers McDavid, Pelech, and Brown were also in the five-man group, as was Fox, who led the team with 64 goals. In 57 regular season games, Burakovsky finished with 41 goals, a record for Swedish players in the OHL. McDavid's agent, Jeff Jackson, frequently traveled to watch the Otters that season, and he could tell Burakovsky had all the elements of a good pro.

Sure enough, Burakovsky made the Capitals roster the next year, and his reputation as a lovable teammate continued. Washington captain Alexander Ovechkin paused when asked to reflect on Burakovsky's time with the Capitals, then started laughing. His former teammate was fun, he said, and always willing to take jokes. Ovechkin, for example, would bite his arm as part of a pregame superstition.

Once, while the Capitals were on the road during a 2016 playoff series with the Flyers, Burakovsky kept poking Wilson while getting changed after their pregame nap. Annoyed, Wilson shoved his buddy away. Burakovsky responded by smacking him with his belt, prompting Wilson to body check him. They went flying into the wall.

For a moment, both were mad. Then they burst into laughter. These relationships, this camaraderie are what Wilson believes make hanging out with teammates and coming to the rink fun every day.

On the ice, Burakovsky exceled during Washington's Stanley Cup run in 2018. He scored a pair of goals against Lightning goalie Andrei Vasilevskiy in Game 7 of the Eastern Conference Finals, and he assisted Lars Eller's winning goal in the Capitals' Stanley Cup Final–clinching Game 5 win. He's still in the championship pictures hanging in the bowels of Washington's arena—forever part of the city's first Stanley Cup–winning team.

Despite his playoff heroics, Burakovsky struggled to establish a consistent role with the Capitals. His playing time—as well as his confidence—dipped the season after the Cup win. He went from averaging nearly 14 minutes of ice time per game to barely 11 in 2018–19. Ahead of the February trade deadline, he requested a move. He was stewing over bad games. He wasn't sleeping. The winger wanted a fresh start. Burakovsky was no longer the happy guy at the rink, and he started working with a sports psychologist that off-season.

In June, Joe Sakic pounced, acquiring the winger for a second-round pick, a third-round pick, and a minor leaguer. The Avalanche saw Burakovsky's skill and believed his speed would fit well. Sakic signed the then 24-year-old to a three-year contract. He would enter his prime with the Avalanche.

Burakovsky was golfing in his hometown of Malmö, Sweden, when his agent called to inform him of the trade. Just as he'd wanted, he had a new beginning.

• • •

Ahead of Game 1, Bednar hit his players with a number of phrases they'd no doubt heard plenty of times before. But they're over-used for a reason. They're meant to get players into the mindset to find success. Embrace the challenge, he told them, as captured on ESPN's *Quest for the Stanley Cup* series. Focus on your process. Leave the rink with no regrets. Play to your identity. Enjoy every minute.

Without Nazem Kadri and despite the long layoff, the Avalanche didn't show any rust at the start of the game. Rantanen created the team's first scoring chance less than two minutes into the game, grabbing a loose puck in the neutral zone and zooming up ice. He had a step on Nick Paul, one of Tampa Bay's main deadline acquisitions. When Ryan McDonagh shifted to guard Compher joining the rush, he gave Rantanen a path to the net. The forward moved his body slightly toward Compher as if he was about to pass but instead unleashed a backhand on net.

Vasilevskiy was there to stop it, gobbling up the puck without allowing a rebound. That came as a surprise to absolutely no one in attendance. The 27-year-old goalie is widely considered one of the best in the world. Avalanche goalie Darcy Kuemper referred to him as such during the series. Wisely, Kuemper said he couldn't afford to worry about outplaying his counterpart. He needed to focus on his own game.

Across the ice from Kuemper, the Avalanche kept peppering Vasilevskiy with shots, including one from Nichushkin that rang off the post. Eight minutes into the game, Colorado broke through. Byram, who had turned 21 just two days earlier, carried the puck through the neutral zone on a breakout, nudging a pass to Rantanen as he entered the offensive zone. Rantanen glided toward the offensive zone faceoff circle, waiting for room to shoot. Finally, with Erik Černák and McDonagh creating a sliver of space for a shooting lane, he unleashed a wrister on net.

The puck trickled through Vasilevskiy's arm and, with a whack from Landeskog crashing the net, crossed the goal line. The captain nearly missed the puck with his stick, but he didn't. Because of that, Colorado had its first lead of the series.

The Avalanche didn't let up. With a strong forecheck from Nichushkin, Makar disrupted a Victor Hedman pass up the boards intended for Paul. MacKinnon skated to the puck before it escaped the zone, then flung it to Nichushkin in the slot. The Russian winger, who has known Vasilevskiy since they were teenagers, bounced a shot through the Tampa Bay stalwart's legs.

Suddenly, the all-world goalie looked human.

Three minutes after a Paul goal cut the lead to one, MacKinnon drew a tripping penalty, sending Colorado to the power play. Shortly after, Makar drew another trip, this time on Anthony Cirelli. The Lightning forward emphatically argued the call, saying Makar fell. Tampa Bay was livid, but the official stood firm and awarded Colorado a five-on-three power play. With 23 seconds left on the two-man advantage, Rantanen found Lehkonen with a perfectly placed backdoor pass. The Finnish connection came through.

But Tampa Bay was the two-time defending Stanley Cup champion for a reason. Jon Cooper's bunch didn't panic. Ondřej

Palát scored after a highlight-reel assist from Nikita Kucherov, who danced around Toews before finding his linemate in front of the net. Then Mikhail Sergachev sneaked a wrist shot past Kuemper to tie the score. Most concerning for Colorado, Vasilevskiy seemed to find his groove. He stymied a dangerous MacKinnon chance in the slot midway through the third period, then robbed Landeskog during a power play in the final minutes of the game. Kuemper, on the other hand, was so-so in his return from injury. He probably could have played the Paul goal more aggressively, and the long-range Sergachev goal wasn't ideal, either.

All that added up to a deadlock, despite the fact that Colorado had controlled play for most of the night.

"Obviously, we'd like to stay on the gas, but at the same time, they're the Tampa Bay Lightning," Landeskog said. "They're going to find ways to score goals. [It's] just about managing it and getting back on it."

During the regular season, Bednar stressed that he considers how well his team plays to be as important as whether it wins or loses. Did they work harder than their opponent? Did they generate more chances? Were they in control of the game?

But this wasn't the regular season. In the playoffs—especially in the Stanley Cup Final—all that matters is the result.

Just over a minute into overtime, Nichushkin put together his usual forechecking wizardry, breaking up a Victor Hedman feed out of the defensive zone and then pressuring Sergachev, forcing him to rush a pass. Compher intercepted the puck near center ice, then flew into the offensive zone flanked by Nichushkin and Burakovsky. Compher put a shot on net from the crease, but Hedman sprawled to block it. The puck flew off the defenseman's body to Nichushkin, who moved it seamlessly to Burakovsky in the faceoff circle. The winger brought his hands forward as the pass reached him, sending the puck flying off his blade, toward the net, past Vasilevskiy's left skate and into Avalanche history.

After scoring the game-winner in overtime in Game 1, Colorado left winger André Burakovsky scores against Tampa Bay goaltender Andrei Vasilevskiy in Game 2 of the Stanley Cup Final at Ball Arena, a 7–0 Avs rout.

Burakovsky dropped to a knee after the goal, letting his momentum carry him toward the Avalanche bench. He punched the air once, twice, three times before rising as teammates mobbed him along the glass.

In that moment, he didn't have many thoughts. Just elation.

"It was kind of a crazy feeling," he said.

Minutes later, Burakovsky was sitting on the bench for a postgame interview with ESPN's Emily Kaplan. As he answered a question, the public address announcer called out his name as one of the stars of the game. He looked up, his chin strap undone. The winger waved to the roaring fans, a grin spreading across his still-sweaty face.

Eventually, he headed home with his girlfriend and dad, who was staying with them. They had a glass of wine and relaxed, everyone still smiling. It was, in Robert's words, a beautiful evening.

SERIES SHIFTER

LESS THAN THREE years before assisting Burakovsky's overtime winner, Valeri Nichushkin was coming off a season of hell—one that would lead him to NHL purgatory. The winger played 57 games in 2018–19 with Dallas and scored a grand total of zero goals. The coaching staff stopped relying on him, playing him for an average of only 11:55 a game. The front office did, too. General manager Jim Nill bought out the final year of his contract. It was an unceremonious end to what once looked like a promising future for Nichushkin with the Stars, who drafted him 10th overall in 2013.

Nichushkin tallied 34 points as an 18-year-old in 2013–14, finishing 12th in rookie of the year voting. But injury limited him to only eight games the next year, and he didn't produce well in his third season. So he returned to the KHL in Russia, hoping to find his game. He came back to Dallas after two productive seasons with CSKA Moscow, only to have the disastrous, goalless season. He grew disillusioned with coach Jim Montgomery. His love for the game slipped away.

"He hit bottom a little bit," Nill said.

The buyout left Nichushkin up for grabs. Anyone could give him a fresh start. But by mid-August, nearly two months after his Stars tenure ended, he remained unsigned. He was in no-man's land.

But the Avalanche were interested. His 6′4″ frame, distinct skillset, and underlying numbers suggested he was better than his performance indicated. This was someone once seen as one of the best players in his draft year, assistant general manager Chris MacFarland thought at the time. What was the downside of giving him a shot? Colorado wouldn't need to pay him much and, worst-case scenario, he just wouldn't make the team. To the front office, signing Nichushkin felt like a worthy gamble.

Joe Sakic called Nill. He wanted to know if there was anything he should know.

"Joe," the Dallas general manager replied. "This is somebody you should take a chance on."

So the Avalanche did, signing him to a one-year, $850,000 contract—a low-risk flier. It paid off for both the team and player. He had 13 goals and 27 points in 65 games. He flourished defensively, finishing eighth in voting for the Selke Trophy, which is given to the league's best defensive forward. Ultimately, he signed on for two more years with Colorado.

During his first season in Denver, Nichushkin saw Nill at an Avalanche-Stars game. He thanked his old general manager and offered an apology.

"I wasn't who I should have been with you guys," he said, referring to his 2018–19 season.

But with a change of scenery, he was starting to reach his potential. In 2021–22, he broke out. Now that Brandon Saad and Joonas Donskoi had left in free agency and the expansion draft, respectively, the Russian winger seized a role on the team's second line, averaging 19 minutes of ice time a game, up from his previous career high of 14:58. Jared Bednar credited him with improving his finishing abilities, and that development showed on the stat sheet. By season's end, he had 25 goals and 27 assists—both career highs—in 62 games.

Nichushkin said he didn't emphasize finishing in the off-season; he simply felt confident in 2021–22. That stemmed from increased ice time, he believes. He sensed that Bednar and his teammates trusted him.

Other than Mikhail Maltsev, who appeared in only 18 NHL games on the year, Nichushkin was the only Russian player on the Avalanche. He can speak some English, but there is still, to some extent, a language barrier with other players. Though that prevented him from being a particularly vocal presence in the dressing room, teammates found him approachable. Jack Johnson often chatted with him at hotel pools on road trips or in the sauna at the rink.

"He's a big sauna guy," Johnson said. "If you go into a sauna and you start talking to him, sometimes you've got to cut him off because you've got to get out of there. You're overheating."

On the ice, Nichushkin let his play do the talking. To an extent, his growth surprised Bednar. How could it not, considering how his tenure ended in Dallas? But in other ways, Bednar believed it made sense that Nichushkin found a groove, considering how the wing impressed the team with his work ethic. Some nights after games, Bednar cuts video at the rink to try and lighten his load for the next morning. Players and coaches are normally gone by the time he's done. All except for one.

"I'll be walking out of the room and I'll see Val," Bednar said. "He's just getting done lifting."

Nichushkin took on even more responsibility in the playoffs. He entered the Stanley Cup Final averaging more than 20 minutes of ice time a game, often playing with Nathan MacKinnon on the team's top line. This wasn't just a player who could contribute strong defensive minutes and maybe log a point here and there. This was a player who had the skill to match up with top-end talent without losing the grinding nature of a fourth-liner. This was the player Dallas saw when they picked him 10th overall.

Cale Makar called him a train. Andrew Cogliano called him a horse. Bednar called him an X factor.

Said the coach: "He's built for this time of year."

• • •

Tampa Bay had plenty of reason to be confident that Andrei Vasilevskiy would bounce back from a so-so performance in Game 1. Up to that point in the postseason, he had gone 11–3 with a .939 save percentage in Games 2–7 of series. Plus there was his distaste for losing consecutive games. Before falling twice in a row in the Rangers series, he had a 17-game win streak coming off playoff losses. If you don't lose twice in a row, you're hard to beat in a playoff series.

"I expect us to be way the heck better," Lightning coach Jon Cooper said heading into Game 2.

They weren't, and their mistakes started early. A minute into the game, the Lightning did the last thing they wanted. Tampa Bay defenseman Ryan McDonagh slammed fellow American J.T. Compher into the boards after the Colorado forward had passed the puck, earning himself a roughing penalty.

"Good penalty, Ryan," Compher chirped at McDonagh.

In a sport in which fast starts are so important, one of the Lightning's most-respected leaders handed the Avalanche a golden chance to get off to one. Colorado's power play unit, which had scored in Game 1, took the ice. Sensing an opportunity, the buzzing crowd was ready to burst with noise.

After watching his top unit fail to generate any high-quality chances during the first half of the power play, Bednar subbed in his second grouping. With 10 seconds left, Nichushkin came through. He gained a step on Lightning forward Nick Paul and burst toward the net. Burakovsky, the Game 1 hero, zipped him a perfect pass, and Nichushkin redirected it past Vasilevskiy. He screamed in celebration.

The play was a nod to the Avalanche's skill up and down the lineup. Their top power play unit, which featured star players like MacKinnon, Makar, Rantanen, and Gabriel Landeskog, was off the ice. Nazem Kadri was still recovering from thumb surgery. And yet the team still had the depth to put Nichushkin and Burakovsky—established top-six forwards—on the ice to headline the second power play unit.

Nicushkin's goal put Tampa Bay on its heels. The fast start Cooper wanted and expected came not from the Lightning, but from the Avalanche. They didn't let up. They forechecked hard, forcing turnovers, and their speed advantage made the Lightning look like tortoises trying to keep up with hares. Mikko Rantanen nearly scored on a backhand shortly after Nichushkin's goal, while the Lightning needed more than six minutes just to generate a single shot attempt.

Eight minutes into the game, Josh Manson scored on a two-on-one, wristing a shot past Vasilevskiy's blocker—the small hole in the goalie's game that Colorado had studied pre-series. Cogliano, back in the lineup after breaking his finger in Game 4 of Western Conference Finals, assisted the goal. The score was created by two of Joe Sakic's midseason acquisitions, more evidence of the wisdom in his deadline approach. Artturi Lehkonen sent the Avalanche to the Cup with his overtime winner against Edmonton, and Nico Sturm, who came in and out of the lineup the first three rounds, assisted an overtime goal in the Nashville series. They, too, joined the team at the deadline.

Sakic might not have made headway in trade discussions involving star forward Claude Giroux, but the players he brought in fit like a comfortable T-shirt. "Joe completed the puzzle," former Avalanche coach Bob Hartley told The Athletic's Michael Russo.

The big pieces of that puzzle, the ones already in place before the deadline, were showing up, too. MacKinnon nearly created a goal that could have been his playoff highlight if not for his masterpiece against St. Louis. As he zoomed up ice with the puck, he made a 360-degree spin around Victor Hedman in the offensive zone faceoff circle and backhanded a pass to Landeskog, who couldn't quite finish the tap-in at the net.

The highlight-reel goal didn't happen, but the Avalanche didn't have to wait long to get their third tally. When Rantanen fired a shot off Vasilevskiy's right pad, the Lightning failed to box out Burakovsky, who crashed toward the net. He whacked the rebound directly into the Tampa Bay goal.

At that point, Colorado had more goals (3) than the Lightning had shots (2). Tampa Bay looked slow and disjointed. Cooper's top line of Ondřej Palát, Steven Stamkos, and Nikita Kucherov combined for zero shot attempts in the first period. It was a bludgeoning.

"I don't think I've ever seen a team play with that much pace, with that much skill, and such a tight-knit, together group of players playing a team system that's putting so much pressure on Tampa Bay," Hall of Famer Mark Messier said on ESPN during intermission. "They had no answer for it in the first period."

The Lightning didn't in the second period, either. Five minutes in, Rantanen intercepted a Palát pass behind the net and quickly fed Nichushkin in the slot. The big Russian zipped the puck through Vasilevskiy's legs. The winger who went a full season in Dallas without a goal now had two in a Stanley Cup Final game, and he nearly notched his first-career hat trick with a backhand later in the period. But Vasilevskiy made a remarkable save to snag the shot and freeze play. Even with the Lightning looking overmatched, it was a reminder that their goalie could make saves few others in the world could.

But Vasilevskiy couldn't stop every high-danger chance Tampa Bay's skaters allowed. Toward the end of the second, Darren Helm caught the Lightning in the middle of a line change. He zipped up ice and beat the goalie, scoring his first Stanley Cup goal since 2009.

With Helm's tally, players from all four Avalanche lines had points in the game. But somehow, through the first nine Avalanche goals of the Stanley Cup Final, Makar had not logged a point. That changed during a third-period Lightning power play. On the ice for the penalty kill, the defenseman seized a loose puck in the defensive zone and sprinted forward. Andrew Cogliano jumped into the rush with him, creating a two-on-one. But Makar wasn't passing. He unleashed a perfect shot that once again beat Vasilevskiy's blocker side.

The Colorado star wasn't done. A frustrated Palát cross-checked him to the ice later in the period, and the officials sent him to the box. During the ensuing power play, Rantanen placed a cross-ice pass on Makar's stick. The defenseman beat Vasilevskiy once again, this time shooting toward his glove side.

When the third period expired, clinching a 7–0 Colorado win, Avalanche players skated toward Kuemper, congratulating him on his first shutout of the playoffs. He'd done his job, stopping all 16 shots that came his way. At one point, the crowd started a "Kuemper! Kuem-per!" chant.

But this was a game of defensive wizardry as much as Kuemper playing well. Since 1955–56, the first year NHL Stats has data, only one goalie—Patrick Roy in 1986—made fewer saves in a Stanley

Cup Final shutout. Colorado's forechecking and speed all but eliminated Tampa Bay's opportunities. The Lightning had only one scoring chance that the site Natural Stat Trick qualified as high danger, in part because they rarely had possession. Defense isn't always about stopping the opponent. Sometimes it's simply not allowing the other team to get the puck. A Logan O'Connor play, one that didn't lead to a goal, encapsulated that early in the second period. He seized a loose puck in the neutral zone, then fought off Hedman and Jan Rutta to keep possession. That allowed Manson to jump into play for a quality scoring chance, and Helm's forechecking kept the puck in the offensive zone even longer.

The Avalanche made plays like that all night. It's why all aspects of the game—from the game's underlying metrics to the score itself—were so lopsided.

"Everything was perfect that night," MacKinnon said. "It didn't even really feel like a playoff game."

But it didn't come without sacrifice. At the start of the second period, immediately before O'Connor's hustle play, Burakovsky got low to the ice to break up a Hedman pass. The puck hit his hand, shattering his right thumb. He pulled his glove off before even reaching the bench, wincing in pain. Already playing with a broken ankle, this injury would be too much to overcome. His series, after two games of the best hockey he'd played all season, was done.

Landeskog was upset for his teammate when he learned of the injury, but he also saw a parallel. Back in 2018, when Burakovsky won the Stanley Cup with Washington, he missed postseason games with a broken thumb.

"Burky," Landeskog said to him. "I hate that you're hurt and I don't ever want to see you hurt. But the last time you broke something in the playoffs, you guys ended up winning the Cup."

Burakovsky had the same thought. And thanks to his contributions, the Avalanche were two wins away from following the Capitals' path.

. . .

The Lightning weren't used to losing like they did in Game 2. In fact, it had never happened, not at this stage. It was the most lopsided playoff loss in franchise history.

"Does it suck losing a game like that? For sure," Cooper said. "But is it going to happen at times? Yeah, it is. You're just hoping it doesn't happen in the Stanley Cup Final."

This wasn't time to count them out, though. Teams don't win back-to-back championships without resilience. As Victor Hedman said, they had lost a game, not the series. In front of their home crowd, they found their footing in Game 3.

A successful Cooper challenge helped with that. Five minutes into the game, MacKinnon fed Nichushkin in the offensive zone, and the winger floated a shot past Vasilevskiy. Almost immediately after the puck entered the net, Lightning players raised their arms, calling for Cooper to look at the video. Before MacKinnon got the puck, Bowen Byram had fielded it along the blue line. From some angles, it looked like the puck had crossed the line, which would have made the Avalanche offside. Byram was concerned that was the case as he skated to the bench.

"Is it good?" he asked his teammates.

For a moment, it appeared like the goal would count as the officials prepared to drop the puck. Avalanche players thought they were in the clear.

Then Cooper called for them to halt. He was still considering whether to challenge for offside. The coach deliberated on the bench, with referee Gord Dwyer asking for a decision. Eventually, Cooper nodded at Dwyer. He wanted the play reviewed. It was a risky challenge. If the Lightning won, the score would go back to 0–0. But if Cooper miscalculated, Colorado would have the lead and go to the power play with Tampa Bay charged for delay of game.

After a lengthy review, the NHL's situation room overturned the call. A potentially game-altering decision went in Tampa Bay's favor. Though he didn't express any disagreement with the situation room's final decision, Bednar was frustrated at how long officials gave Cooper to decide to challenge. He thought they should have dropped the puck.

"It was long," he said. "It was three times the length we normally get."

Added MacKinnon: "I think the ref has got to drop it. I don't know what they're waiting for. They had their chance [to challenge]."

Despite the erased tally, Colorado still managed to score first. While on a power play midway through the period, Rantanen put a shot on Vasilevskiy. The puck bounced off Landeskog and toward the net, and the Avalanche captain did what he does best. Unafraid of contact, he charged toward the loose puck and poked it in. It was 1–0. For real this time.

But, as the Avalanche had learned throughout the playoffs, games change quickly. Usually, with their high-powered offense, they benefited from the swings, but not in Game 3.

Colorado was at the tail end of a penalty kill midway through the first period when Toews skated the puck up ice and blasted a shot at Vasilevskiy. The goaltender made the save and allowed a rebound. Anthony Cirelli grabbed the puck in his defensive zone, then darted up ice. He played pitch-and-catch with Patrick Maroon, skating past Makar before receiving the pass back from his teammate. He charged to the net. As he tried to move the puck from his forehand to his backhand, he lost control. But chaos in front of the net can lead to goals, and that's exactly what happened. The puck went through Kuemper's legs.

Instead of a 2–0 game in the Avalanche's favor, which it would have been had Toews' shot found a way past Vasilevskiy, the score was tied. Then, with five minutes left in the first period, Toews seemed to mishit a cross-ice pass—Bednar later blamed it on the ice quality—intended for Makar, instead putting the puck right on Palát's skate. The Tampa Bay winger moved it into the offensive zone, handed possession off to Stamkos, then skated to an open area of ice. His captain found him all alone with a pass, and Palát beat Kuemper for a goal.

The Avalanche wouldn't lead again. Tampa Bay accounted for four of the five goals scored in the second period, putting the game out of reach. Bednar pulled Kuemper for Francouz midway through the second, giving his No. 2 a taste of Stanley Cup Final action and raising questions about whether he'd be the better option for Game 4. Bednar said postgame that Kuemper didn't have a good night. But neither, he added, did the entire team.

The Lightning, meanwhile, looked like the dominant team the league had grown to expect. They did it all without standout center Brayden Point, who had torn his quad in the first round of the playoffs. He tried to play through the injury the first two games of the Avalanche series but wasn't his normal self. He didn't appear in Game 3 and, though Cooper didn't rule him out, wouldn't play again in the series.

With two minutes left in the game, Cogliano and Pat Maroon started scuffling, and shoving matches broke out between Avalanche and Lightning players. Logan O'Connor and Ross Colton took it a step further. The two threw off their gloves and started to whale on each other, both landing multiple punches. O'Connor brought his opponent to the ice before officials separated them.

The Avalanche winger hadn't been happy with his game. He wanted to send a message to anyone who thought his team was only skilled with no physicality.

"I think people underestimate that with us," O'Connor said. "We're not going to just roll over."

Colorado players weren't as downcast as might be expected after the loss. Rantanen was pleased to hear immediate chatter in the postgame locker room. They were still confident. The Finn thought his team created good scoring chances in the third, which the underlying metrics backed up. That was something to build off of going into Game 4.

"We were not expecting a sweep," MacKinnon said, adding the Lightning were too proud to simply go away. "Good or bad, we're not going to trade our spot with anyone in the world. We've waited a long time for this."

• • •

During the evening between Games 3 and 4, Makar sat between his dad, Gary, and Sakic at Armature Works, a Tampa restaurant with event spaces. Though his teammates were convinced throughout the year that he should win the Norris Trophy as the league's top defenseman, Makar had shrugged off questions about the award. But now it was time to find out if he'd won it.

Longtime *Saturday Night Live* cast member Kenan Thompson hosted the ceremony, cracking a joke about Will Smith slapping Chris Rock at the Academy Awards, reminding the audience that— though hockey players were present—no fighting was allowed.

"This is the NHL Awards," he said, "not the Oscars."

He called Auston Matthews "the only dude who scores more in Toronto than Drake" and made note of the Lightning, saying they had already won two Stanley Cups during the pandemic and now were going for their "Booster Cup." Makar got a nod, too, with Thompson saying he should be sponsored by cocoa butter because of how smoothly he skates.

Wearing a gray suit, Makar laughed at the right times and sipped a glass of water, not a cocktail from the open bar. Unlike everyone in the room but Hedman, a fellow Norris finalist, he had a game the next day.

Makar's cheeks carried their normal rosiness, and he sported a faint mustache and stubble. The 23-year-old's youth was apparent, especially next to his fellow Norris finalists. Roman Josi, who had finished with an astounding 96 points on the year, looked—as always—like a Swiss model. He wore a high-buttoned sport coat and had combed his hair to appear both neat and natural. Then there was the towering, 6'6" Hedman, whose beard looked as thick as the hair atop Makar's head.

Both Josi and Hedman are in their thirties, with more than 10 years of NHL experience. Each already had a Norris Trophy on his résumé, Josi winning in 2020 and Hedman in 2018.

The Avalanche, meanwhile, had never had a Norris winner, though Hall of Famer Ray Bourque finished second in his only full year with the club. Bourque knows what it takes to bring home the award, having won it five times with the Boston Bruins, and he liked Makar's chances—and not only for 2021–22. "Once he wins it once," Bourque said, "he's going to be holding onto that thing for a little while."

Calgary Flames assistant general manager Chris Snow, who had been diagnosed with ALS three years earlier, walked onto the stage with his family to present the 2022 trophy. Earlier in the evening, Makar chatted with Snow's two children, Willa and Cohen. He crouched so he could be on their eye level. "Just three Calgary kids," Snow's wife, Kelsie, tweeted with a picture.

"And the winner of the Norris Trophy is ..." Snow started, before letting his son finish the announcement. "Cale Makar!" Cohen said.

Makar hugged his parents, then walked to the stage, giving both Willa and Cohen fistbumps. When he reached the microphone to accept the trophy, the young defenseman acknowledged Josi and Hedman, then thanked his parents, friends, Colorado's front office, and Avalanche owners Stan and Josh Kroenke, both of whom attended the event. He finished his speech with a salute to his Colorado teammates, never letting the focus stray from a crucial Game 4.

"The boys," he said, "we've got some important things to do tomorrow."

THUMBS UP

WHEN EVANDER KANE sent Nazem Kadri flying into the boards in Game 3 of the Western Conference Finals, the injured forward thought his season was finished. With his status as a pending free agent—Colorado likely wouldn't have cap space to re-sign him—that would have meant his Avalanche career was probably done, as well.

Kadri's father, Sam, was in Edmonton when Nazem got hurt against the Oilers, and he could instantly tell how upset he was when he saw him afterward. Nazem had been feeling good on the ice that postseason, which his numbers—14 points in the Avalanche's first 12 playoff games—reflected. To go from that to potentially out for the season was devastating. Plus he was 31 and had already been in the league for well over a decade. Who knew if he'd ever get this close to a championship again?

As Kadri's teammates prepared for what would end up being a clinching Game 4 on June 6 in Edmonton, the center was back in Denver undergoing thumb surgery. Doctors initially told him he would miss four to six weeks, which would have meant no postseason return. Sam took a more optimistic approach.

"You do not know how you're going to feel the next day," he told his son. "Day by day you're going to get better and better and feel better and better, and you may come back."

Kadri started to have hope. When he saw TSN post a report on Instagram that he was likely out for the postseason, he decided to give fans some, too. Never lacking confidence, the center left a short comment: "Ya we'll see…"

Mikko Rantanen, one of Kadri's closest friends on the team, didn't think the center would be able to return. Devon Toews, on the other hand, didn't rule it out. Unable to hold a stick comfortably, Kadri skated without anything in his hands after the surgery. Skills coach Shawn Allard worked with him on the ice to keep him in shape. A trainer had to help Kadri tie his skates. He couldn't do it with his injured thumb.

Kadri reincorporated a stick into his skating routine 10 days after his surgery. That's when his father started to feel like he might actually make a return. Kadri looked tentative at points, clearly limited by the injury, but continued progressing. The day before Game 4, he took the ice for an optional practice—his first time back with the group.

"We turned a six-week [recovery] timeline into two weeks," he said.

If he were to play, he would not only have to deal with the pain of the initial breaks, but also with the pins from surgery popping through his skin. So before putting Kadri in the lineup, Bednar wanted assurance. Obviously, Kadri wouldn't be 100 percent, and the coach didn't want him playing if he was too limited to contribute.

The center felt good, though, all things considered. He went to bed the night before Game 4 with a sense he'd play. Still, there was no certainty. When he talked to his dad that evening, he said he didn't know his status. Sam ultimately ended up canceling his flight to Tampa, unsure his son would be in the game.

But Nazem went through the team's skate the next morning, and there were no hiccups. He and Bednar finalized the decision. Nicolas Aubé-Kubel was out of the lineup. Kadri was in.

Years earlier, as a young Montreal Canadiens fan growing up in London, Ontario, Kadri visited the Hockey Hall of Fame during a trip to Toronto. He saw the Stanley Cup at the museum and posed for a picture, his right hand on the trophy's base and left arm extended around its back. He smiled wide, his dark hair running halfway down his forehead.

Now, all grown up, he had a chance to play for the famed trophy. Wearing his white No. 91 jersey, Kadri stood near the back of the line of Avalanche players before pregame warmups. He was one of the last to take the ice but tried out a shot on net almost immediately. Nothing, he knew, was going to come easily that night. Shooting and passing hurt. He'd have to strategize, given the lack of velocity he could get on his shot, and hope for deflections and rebounds to put pucks on net. But he was playing. Injury might have delayed his Stanley Cup Final debut, but a broken thumb wasn't going to stop him from making his mark.

• • •

Heading into Game 4, Nathan MacKinnon had an idea. With Kadri set to play, MacKinnon thought Jared Bednar should make a lineup tweak. The Colorado star had been playing on the top line with Gabriel Landeskog and Valeri Nichushkin, so it seemed likely Kadri would slot in as second-line center between Mikko Rantanen and Artturi Lehkonen.

But that isn't what MacKinnon wanted. He suggested Bednar move Lehkonen and Rantanen up to the top line so the top-six forward group looked like this:

1. Lehkonen–MacKinnon–Rantanen
2. Landeskog–Kadri–Nichushkin

The lineup made sense, MacKinnon thought, because the game was in Tampa, and home ice comes with a tangible, tactical edge in the NHL rulebook. At the start of every period and after every stoppage, the coach of the home team—in this case Jon Cooper—gets to watch what players the visiting coach sends onto the ice and can adjust accordingly.

So with the series in Tampa, Cooper could dictate matchups throughout the game. In Game 3, the coach avoided putting his top offensive line—Ondřej Palát, Steven Stamkos, and Nikita Kucherov—on the ice against MacKinnon's line, presumably so they wouldn't have to play defense against Colorado's best offensive forward. The Stamkos-led trio primarily played against the Avalanche's second line.

MacKinnon knew that would likely happen again in Game 4, and he thought it made sense to move Nichushkin and Landeskog, both high-end defensive players, to the line centered by Kadri. That way, when Palát, Stamkos, and Kucherov took the ice, Colorado would have three of its strongest defensive forwards going against them. Cooper would still prefer that matchup to his biggest offensive threats going against MacKinnon, but a strong defensive second line for Colorado could limit their effectiveness.

Bednar agreed. Ahead of the game, he wrote out the top-six forward group just as MacKinnon suggested.

• • •

Ahead of the game, the Amalie Arena lights dimmed. The jumbotron flashed a series of videos to pump up the crowd, and local hip-hop artist Vo Williams performed a Lightning-themed song. The lyrics reminded everyone in the building that Tampa Bay had won before, that its players already had their names engraved on the Stanley Cup. That they were coming back for more.

Stadium workers gave fans noise-makers designed to sound like thunder. Unlike in the crowd toward the end of Colorado's series against Edmonton, the stands were full of belief. These fans had seen the Lightning come through again and again in their run to back-to-back Cups. Now they had a chance to even the series.

Darcy Kuemper was under siege less than a minute after the game began. Brandon Hagel nearly knocked a loose puck into the Avalanche net, but the goalie made a strong save with his left pad. Unfortunately for him, the Lightning kept possession. The puck kicked out to Erik Černák, who unleashed a shot so hard that it knocked off the goaltender's mask.

With nothing protecting his face, Kuemper tried to regain his position. He was too late. Anthony Cirelli put the rebound past him. MacKinnon raised his right hand, confused as to why the play hadn't been blown dead as soon as Kuemper's mask came off. But the officials handled the situation correctly. If there is an immediate scoring chance after a goalie's mask comes off, the play is allowed to continue. Back in the fall, Kuemper had multiple equipment issues with his skates. Now he caught another bad break with his gear at the worst possible time. After a dicey performance in Game 3, it was hardly the start he wanted.

The Lightning continued to make life difficult on Colorado, blocking shots and keeping Andrei Vasilevskiy's workload light early in the game. The Avalanche managed only one shot through the first 10 minutes. They had chances for more but couldn't capitalize. Kadri missed the net after seizing a Landeskog shot attempt that bounced off the end boards. Alex Newhook almost connected with Logan O'Connor right in front of the net. At the last second, though, Palát got his stick on the puck to break up the connection.

Tampa Bay's scoring opportunities, meanwhile, were both better and more plentiful in the opening period. The Avalanche needed Kuemper, battling with his eyesight and inconsistency throughout the playoffs, to step up. The goalie came through. He halted a Cirelli shot through traffic and, after MacKinnon turned a puck over midway through the period, stymied a Nick Paul breakaway. With just under five minutes left, he made a brilliant glove save to snatch a Stamkos shot out of the air. Then, at the end of the period, the goalie helped kill off a Lightning power play.

He kept Colorado in the game. And the Avalanche had shown over and over during the season that when they stayed in a game long enough, they usually found a way to do damage.

Early in the second period, Rantanen set up MacKinnon in front of the net, and the center nearly beat Vasilevskiy for his first goal of the series. Lehkonen created a chance on a partial breakaway moments later. The Avalanche looked like themselves again. When Nico Sturm drew an interference penalty in front of the net with four minutes remaining, Victor Hedman skated to the box.

If Černák's shot knocking off Kuemper's helmet was a bad break for Colorado, the team's first goal came on a good one. Midway through the power play, MacKinnon found Rantanen with a well-placed cross-ice pass. The Finn put a shot on net from the faceoff circle. Vasilevskiy made the initial save, but a rebound bounced off his pad, right into the path of MacKinnon's feet as the center moved toward the net. The puck deflected off MacKinnon's skate and in. Landeskog pointed to the star center after the play, making sure he knew it was his goal.

For the first time in the Stanley Cup Final, MacKinnon had scored. Pressure had been mounting after he didn't put a puck in the net the first three games. Sportsnet's Ken Wiebe, for example, wrote that his lack of goals was "impossible to ignore," even if he was creating chances for others. ESPN's Kristen Shilton wrote about the topic, too, calling it "a mini-scoring drought."

But with a puck off his skate, that narrative was now behind him. And, more importantly for the Avalanche, the game was tied.

MacKinnon's power play goal highlighted a growing difference between the two teams in the series. Colorado's special-teams units were thriving. Tampa Bay's were floundering. The Avalanche had six power play goals in four games after MacKinnon's score, and their penalty kill had been equally as effective. Aside from a Corey Perry goal on Pavel Francouz after Game 3 was already out of hand, the Lightning hadn't scored on the power play all series. That continued in the second period when Colorado killed off a Bowen Byram hooking penalty.

Nonetheless Tampa Bay regained the lead with a Victor Hedman backhand goal that fluttered past Kuemper. It was a shot Kuemper should have saved. It was also the last one he missed all night.

Even though they trailed, the Avalanche had tilted the game back in their favor by the start of the third period. But, with Vasilevskiy playing as well as he had all series, they needed someone to step up.

• • •

Two things were true about Nico Sturm. He was one of the least-likely candidates on the Avalanche to be a hero at a key time, as well as the exact type of player winning teams have emerge in pivotal moments. Everyone has stars in the playoffs. Depth often is the separator.

Sturm had been in and out of the lineup throughout the postseason, and he'd averaged fewer than nine minutes of ice time in the games he had played. He hadn't notched a point since assisting Makar's Round 1 overtime winner. And since coming to the Avalanche at the trade deadline, he had yet to score a goal.

On days earlier in the playoffs in which Bednar opted to scratch him from the lineup, Sturm stayed on the ice late after morning skates to work with Shawn Allard, the team's skills coach, known for his lively on-ice presence. And as Sturm skated, readying himself for an opportunity that might not come, Allard repeated a frequent message.

"You're going to do something this playoff run," he would say. "I know it."

Sturm's moment came in Game 4. With the third period underway and Colorado's fourth line on the ice, Darren Helm put a long shot on net. Sturm deflected the puck as it headed toward Vasilevskiy, and the star goalie allowed a rebound. It bounced right back to Sturm.

The trade-deadline acquisition, who dreaded going to the rink earlier that season because of how poorly he was playing for Minnesota, used his backhand to flick a shot at Vasilevskiy. It bounced off Andrew Cogliano's leg and somehow sneaked into the net. The game was tied at 2–2.

Because of the deflection, Sturm got credit for an assist, not a goal. But he had created the play Allard promised him was coming. He dropped to a knee as he skated behind the net, fist-jabbing the air with excitement.

Cogliano, meanwhile, had managed to score without having to use his broken finger to shoot. A win-win.

Tampa Bay hadn't allowed a non-power play goal on home ice since Game 6 of their first-round series with Toronto, and goals from fourth lines are never frequent. In such a big moment, this one might have felt like a stroke of luck. But it wasn't. It's what happens on teams with depth. Big contributions come from all over. If Sakic needed validation for trading for Sturm and Cogliano and signing Helm in the off-season, this goal gave it.

"If you just have one guy or two guys that always have to come up big for you," Sturm said, "you're never going to win a Cup."

With the fourth line flourishing, the second line that came together at MacKinnon's suggestion had a strong night, too. While Landeskog, Kadri, and Nichushkin were on the ice together, Colorado generated 10 scoring chances and allowed only four, according to Natural Stat Trick.

Colorado didn't score again in regulation, but Kuemper's play kept the game tied. He halted a long Hedman shot in the final minute of the period, then moved across his crease to stop Paul from scoring on a rebound. He eventually was able to freeze the puck when he covered a Ryan McDonagh shot 20 seconds later. Even though he'd allowed a savable score to Hedman, the goalie put together a performance worthy of the haul Sakic gave up for him.

That's what it took just to get to overtime.

• • •

Going into the sudden-death period, the Avalanche wanted to limit the Lightning's chances to change lines. They harped on hanging onto the puck, which would force the Lightning to expend energy. If they did regain possession, they might have to dump it back into the Avalanche zone to change lines and get fresh legs on the ice.

That seemed to work from the jump. Colorado dominated possession, generating scoring chance after scoring chance. The Lightning needed their star goaltender to bail them out. And for a while, Vasilevskiy did. He had to jab his leg out to ensure a Nichushkin shot didn't get past him and had to use his glove to stop a Logan O'Connor breakaway.

Across the ice, Kuemper stopped the most dangerous chance he faced as a Paul shot zinged off his helmet. Tampa Bay managed only three shots; the Colorado goalie stopped them all.

Meanwhile, when the Avalanche got pucks past Vasilevskiy, they had posts to contend with. Devon Toews hit the post with a shot, and Byram knocked a one-timer off the crossbar midway through the extra period. Sakic punched the air in celebration after Byram's near-goal, thinking it had gone in. Upon realizing it hadn't, the general manager then threw his head back in exasperation.

Chances don't matter in overtime. Only goals do. So Colorado continued to push. The team knew it might have to be patient, O'Connor said, especially against such a sound defense and a goaltender of Vasilevskiy's caliber. But the Avalanche knew they'd eventually get rewarded if they didn't deviate from their game plan.

"There's no way we can lose," Rantanen thought to himself. "We are so unlucky if we lose this game."

A little more than halfway through the first overtime period, the Lehkonen-MacKinnon-Rantanen line put together a strong shift. As the Avalanche had envisioned, the Lightning were wearing down. Some Tampa Bay skaters headed to the bench for a line change when Brandon Hagel cleared the puck and it trickled down the ice toward Kuemper, who met it in the faceoff circle to the left of his net. The goalie sensed he could catch the Lightning in a change, so he immediately passed to Lehkonen, who zipped the puck through the neutral zone. It reached Kadri, who had just hopped onto the ice, as he entered the offensive zone.

The center avoided Ryan McDonagh's stick, then shifted the puck from his backhand to his forehand. That allowed him to move in front of an exhausted Mikhail Sergachev, who hadn't been able to get off the ice for a line change. On the bench, Jack Johnson rose to his feet to watch the play develop.

"I think he's got a step on this tired defenseman," he thought to himself.

He was right. Nothing stood between Kadri and the net. He forehanded toward Vasilevskiy's blocker side. It sailed under the goalie's arm and toward the net.

"It's in!" Sportsnet announcer Chris Cuthburt yelled. "Or is it?"

Still nursing a broken thumb, Avalanche center Nazem Kadri manages to shoot the puck past Lightning goalie Andrei Vasilevskiy for a 3–2 overtime victory in Game 4 of the Stanley Cup Final in Tampa, Florida.

Kadri didn't seem to think so. He didn't celebrate as he looked toward the net. He bent over, as if wondering how he hadn't scored.

No one on the ice seemed to know where the puck was. No one, that is, except Bowen Byram. Standing in the neutral zone, the young defenseman had seen the twine flex from the impact of the shot. He sprinted toward the net excitedly, gesturing to the referee. The puck had stuck in the upper part of the net, lodged between the back bar and the twine. Stamkos saw it then, too. He knocked it from the top of the net and skated off the ice.

On the bench, some players saw the puck go in. Jack Johnson saw the net move and knew it was a goal. Toews, on the other hand, wasn't quite sure, but he heard commotion on the forward's end of the bench. Newhook, Compher, O'Connor, and Helm all jumped in glee, but then froze when they didn't notice anyone on the ice celebrating. Rantanen, standing to Helm's left, initially thought Vasilevskiy had swallowed the puck. But then he saw a dejected Stamkos look toward the rafters.

The Avalanche spilled onto the ice. Compher, O'Connor, and Landeskog reached Kadri first, mobbing him along the glass across from the bench.

"Are we sure?" Sturm repeated as he and his teammate celebrated. "Are we sure? Are we sure?"

Soon, everyone was, indeed, sure. The goal was good. Kadri, broken thumb and all, had scored the overtime winner.

"This is what I've been waiting for my whole life," he said.

Back in London, Ontario, his close friend Jason McNeil jumped up and down so aggressively he joked he nearly went through his living room floor when he realized the puck was in. In his state of elation, he booked a flight to Denver.

The Avalanche were headed home, the Stanley Cup on the line.

• • •

As movie-like as Kadri's overtime winner was, the drama didn't end when the puck hit the net. Jon Cooper walked into the Lightning interview room, dressed in a dark blue suit with a pocket square. He started to answer the first question of the press conference, then paused, looking into the distance for five seconds. He let out a short breath. There was something he wanted to get off his chest.

"You know, I love this league…" he started. He called the NHL the best league in the world. He talked about how hard his team worked to get to a third-consecutive Stanley Cup. Then, with his eyes closed, he dropped a sentence, a disjointed thought that nonetheless managed to get a point across.

"This one is going to sting much more than others, just because I think it was taken, it was potentially…I don't know."

Translation: he was mad at the officiating. He continued, saying it would be hard for him to speak that evening, that he would talk to reporters the next day.

"You're going to see what I mean when you see the winning goal," he said. He paused for four more seconds. He appeared to be holding back tears. "And my heart breaks for the players. Because we probably should still be playing."

The coach stood, took the steps down from the raised table, and left. Media members packed into seats looked at each other. Confusion hung over the room. In the minutes after, though, word started trickling out. Tampa Bay thought Colorado had too many men on the ice at the time of the goal.

Kadri had hopped on the ice for Nathan MacKinnon, who was not involved in the play. But MacKinnon was still more than the permissible five feet from the bench when Kadri made his move to replace him. It was certainly an aggressive—and perhaps illegal—change. Kadri was on the ice for four seconds and had received the puck by the time MacKinnon, who didn't sprint to the bench, reached the wall.

Scouting the Refs, a website that analyzes officials, rules, and Department of Player Safety rulings, broke down the play.

"Replays showed six skaters on the ice for the Avalanche, along with seven for the Lightning," the article said. "Either the officials outright missed it, or they granted some additional leeway to the changing players. We're going with the latter."

The league released a statement after the game saying all four officials met with Hockey Operations, as is normal protocol. All four said they did not see too many men on the ice. The Athletic's Michael Russo also reached out to two former referees who commented on the play anonymously. Both said a penalty shouldn't have been called. A former linesman contacted by Russo said the exchange was close, but loose line changes happen frequently, and few officials would have blown a play like that dead in overtime. The former linesman added the Lightning had seven players on the ice, including two who—like MacKinnon—were standing at the bench.

Bednar watched the replay of the goal multiple times after the game to see what Cooper was talking about, and he also said he counted seven Lightning players on the ice. Plus, he said, line changes like that happen "every second shift."

"I don't see it as a break, a non-break," he said. "I think it's actually nothing."

The play was essentially the reverse of the Too Many Men controversy that cost Colorado back in January, when the Predators had won in overtime after the Avalanche were called for a questionable bench minor. This time, the officials' eyes worked in Colorado's favor.

The lack of penalties called in the game also played a role. As is often the case in tight playoff games, the officials seemed hesitant to penalize players as the night went on. Clear penalties committed by both teams weren't whistled.

Cooper's monologue became the game's main storyline. Was it an act of gamesmanship by a trained lawyer, a statement he hoped would lodge in officials' subconscious ahead of Game 5? Was he genuinely at a loss for words, devastated for his players? Was it a mix of the two?

No matter what Cooper's motivation was, and no matter if the play was correctly handled by officials or not, the game was done. The Avalanche won, moving them one victory from the Stanley Cup. They felt it in their dressing room. The celebration justifiably was bigger than normal. Byram, the team's youngest player, approached Erik Johnson and threw his arms around him. Fired up, Johnson hugged him back. But he offered a reminder, too.

"One more," he told Byram. "One more."

LETDOWN

LOGAN O'CONNOR TRIED to swat the thought away as if it were a fly. He knew it would do him no good to dwell on what Game 5 could mean. But pushing dreams out of your mind isn't easy. As the game approached, O'Connor was struggling not to get ahead of himself.

The stage was set for Colorado to finish off the Lightning at home and win the Stanley Cup. Family members and friends were flying in from all over the globe, and anticipation surged through the team. Everyone's childhood dream was painfully close. Tonight could be the night, the pesky voice in O'Connor's head said. He could lift the Cup in front of his home crowd, surrounded by loved ones.

The same visions were running through Nico Sturm's head.

"Holy fuck," he thought going into the game. "We could do it today."

Longtime veteran Andrew Cogliano was caught up in the moment, too. The whole team was. It was human nature. Aside from Helm and Burakovsky, no one on the roster had been in this situation. Sure, Colorado had finished off three playoff series during its run to the Final. But this was different. This was the last stop on the train's route. The Stanley Cup was in the building.

"We kind of wanted it to be over," Josh Manson said.

They were looking too far ahead.

As puck drop approached, the crowd was ready for a coronation. When Nathan MacKinnon skated off the ice at the end of pregame warmups, fans roared, one banging the bottoms of two aluminum cups together to add more noise to the buzzing building. "We want the Cup!" chants rained onto the ice.

Tampa Bay had no intention of letting that happen. A 3–1 hole might have been new to the Lightning, but they were comfortable playing while down in series. Just ask the Rangers and Leafs, who had watched their leads slip away earlier in the postseason. In his pregame speech, Jon Cooper told his players that the Avalanche were already planning their parade. The building would be on edge, the coach added. Tampa Bay could use that to its advantage.

"Great challenge for us," Lightning forward Pat Maroon told his teammates. "I fucking like this."

Colorado's players, meanwhile, didn't seem to like it quite as much. They were indeed on edge, thinking about the moments that would follow a victory, not what it would take to get there. It felt like everyone in the building expected them to win, and players felt that pressure. Sturm struggled to sleep the night before. Mikko Rantanen called it one of the more difficult game preparations of his career. MacKinnon said everyone felt like they might puke.

All of that showed. The Avalanche didn't play poorly, but they weren't at their best, either. They lacked the juice that had carried them through their first 15 playoff wins. Bednar didn't like Colorado's start. He didn't sense them jumping to the attack.

"They're playing nervous, boys," Cooper told his bench during the game. "Take advantage of it."

J.T. Compher and Nazem Kadri both committed penalties within the first seven minutes of the game—a quick way to zap offensive rhythm and, perhaps, a sign of nervous play. But Colorado's penalty kill came through, allowing only two total shots on the pair of Lightning first-period power plays. MacKinnon drew a penalty shortly after the Lightning's second power play ended, and Kadri nearly beat Andrei Vasilevskiy before Tampa Bay touched the puck. But Colorado couldn't get much going once its time on the man-advantage began. The unit that had thrived against Tampa Bay was lacking its crispness.

Darcy Kuemper did what he needed to early. He stopped shots by Ross Colton and Corey Perry while the Avalanche were penalty-killing, then grabbed a difficult attempt from Brandon Hagel. But he ended up being the first goalie to blink, making a costly blunder with the period nearing a close. Defenseman Jan Rutta, who had scored only four combined goals over the previous three regular seasons, skated the puck along the boards and into the offensive zone. He wound up as he neared the offensive zone faceoff circle, then blasted a slapshot under Kuemper's arm and in. No one blocked Kuemper's vision. He should have made the save and he threw his head back after missing it. Bednar specifically mentioned the goal postgame as one he wished Kuemper had grabbed.

Colorado had chances to tie the game toward the end of the period. Artturi Lehkonen nearly scored in a scramble in front of the net. Shortly after, Devon Toews sprung Nathan MacKinnon on a breakaway, and the center managed to work a shot between Vasilevskiy's legs. Unfortunately for Colorado, the shot was from an odd angle. It buzzed through the crease and out of danger. Landeskog had a chance in the slot moments later, but Vasilevskiy recovered to make the save. The Avalanche weren't playing poorly, necessarily, but they were missing the last bit of needed execution.

The Avalanche had to wait until after intermission to get on the board. Five minutes into the second period, when Makar put a shot on net, Vasilevskiy allowed an uncharacteristic rebound off his glove. Valeri Nichushkin charged toward the puck and knocked it in, tying the game.

That gave the Avalanche the momentum, and they looked as if they might use it to their advantage moments later when Compher drew a holding penalty on Alex Killorn. Colorado kept possession of the puck as an official raised his arm, so the action continued, leading to one of the more consequential plays of the game. Kuemper went to the bench for an extra attacker since play would be blown dead for the penalty if Tampa Bay gained possession. But at the same time, J.T. Compher held Killorn's stick. The officials called him on it.

Instead of an Avalanche power play, both Compher and Killorn were assessed two-minute minor penalties. A heated Compher argued with the official after being escorted to the box. The teams were set to play four-on-four hockey for two minutes.

Avalanche forward Valeri Nichushkin celebrates after tying Game 5 of the Stanley Cup Final 1–1 in the second period. It was one of the few bright spots in the 3–2 loss to the Lightning, who forced a Game 6 in Florida.

That changed quickly. Makar was called for tripping as his stick got caught in Ondřej Palát's legs. Jared Bednar disagreed, pointing out that Makar wasn't trying to defend Palát. Rather, the Colorado coach insisted after the game that his defenseman was turning and Palát's legs got caught on his stick. But the play was done, and Makar joined Compher in the box.

That handed Tampa Bay a four-on-three power play, which is harder to defend than a normal five-on-four. With fewer bodies in the way, the attacking team has more space to maneuver, allowing it to get the defending players in less-favorable positions. Sensing an opportunity, Cooper sent four forwards onto the ice rather than mix in a defenseman such as Victor Hedman, who is on Lightning's normal power play unit. A "Ref, you suck!" chant came from the crowd as the official prepared to drop the puck.

Kuemper made a save on a Steven Stamkos shot almost immediately at the start of the four-on-three, and Manson blocked a pair of shots. But the Avalanche weren't able to gain possession of the puck to clear it. With 17 seconds left before Compher and Killorn were to exit the box, Stamkos passed to Nikita Kucherov. The 2019 MVP, still considered one of the league's most dangerous wingers, fired a puck toward the net from the high slot. It hit off the post and ricocheted in, giving the Lightning the lead again.

Helm slammed his stick to the ice in frustration. It was only the Lightning's second power play goal of the series, but it was one the Avalanche believed they shouldn't have had the chance to score.

And that wasn't the end of Colorado's disagreements with the officiating. On a power play toward the end of the second period, Makar used his world-class speed to dart through Killorn and Mikhail Sergachev, straight to the net. Vasilevskiy poked the puck away, but Makar thought one of the Lightning defenders should have been called for hooking or a slash. In an uncharacteristic outburst, the young defenseman screamed at the officials, pulling his mouthguard out to make sure they could hear him clearly.

"You're a fucking joke!" he yelled.

Makar regained his composure in time to score a third-period goal, though he had a bit of help from traffic in front of the net. Vasilevskiy allowed a rebound, and the puck hit off Tampa Bay's Erik Černák's skate. It bounced back toward the net, right through the goalie's legs and in. Makar pointed at Nichushkin, thinking his teammate had scored. The winger, who was battling with Černák in front of the net, seemed to think the same thing, letting out an adrenaline-filled scream.

It was, in fact, Makar's goal, since no Colorado player touched it after his initial shot. But credit didn't matter. All that counted was the score, which was now tied. "We've got them on the ropes," Sturm thought on the bench. "This is it."

The sense of inevitability returned. So did the crowd's "We want the Cup!" chants.

But they didn't get it, at least not in Game 5. With under seven minutes to go, Hedman found Palát in the slot, and the winger shot. The puck trickled through Kuemper's legs, giving the Lightning a lead they didn't relinquish.

Back in Palát's native Czechia, a group of 150 people were locked in on the action in the middle of the night. Palát's parents organized a watch party in their local rink, and guests munched on baked goods and goulash as they saw their hometown hero score a season-sustaining goal for the Lightning. It was Palát's 11th goal of the playoffs, tying him for the team lead. He is the type of player that made Cooper's club click. He isn't a star himself but is capable of playing with them, bringing a blue-collar edge to whatever line he's on.

Makar blamed himself for the play, telling reporters he lost an assignment and the puck wound up in the net. "Can't happen," he said.

Then, in an ironic twist late in the third period, the refs called MacKinnon for jumping onto the ice early, giving the Lightning a power play. Tampa Bay didn't get the call in Game 4, but did two nights later. The only difference between the plays, ESPN's Ray Ferraro said on the broadcast, was that Tampa Bay didn't also have seven players on the ice when MacKinnon left the bench early in Game 5.

Colorado killed the penalty, but by the time it ended, the Avalanche had less than a minute of time to pull Kuemper and try for an equalizer. The game ended before they could score. None of their mistakes during the game were egregious, but they had never seemed to find the extra gear that had carried them to this point. They'd have to wait two days before they could regroup and try again.

"That's how we battle, boys!" Maroon yelled to his teammates as they skated toward Vasilevskiy to celebrate the win. "That's how we battle!"

The Lightning had life.

"You look at this series. Was it meant to go six or seven? Damn right it was," Cooper said after the game. "There's two damn good hockey teams here."

The Avalanche still held a 3–2 lead in the Stanley Cup Final. Game 5 was only one loss. But in that moment—with the anticipation and the pressure and the family members packed in seats—it felt like more. This was their most devastating loss of the playoffs. The mood Pavel Francouz sensed in the postgame locker room was as if the team had lost the series. Multiple players felt like crying. Instead of celebrating on the ice with the trophy he dreamed about, MacKinnon pedaled on a workout bike. He was miserable.

And there was a cost to the loss beyond the delay in the Stanley Cup handoff. Nichushkin, a dominant force all series, left the arena limping, his foot broken from a seemingly innocuous play in the third period. His status for the rest of the series was now up in the air. Upset at both the loss and his injury, he tore up the interior of his car to the point that it needed to be repaired. His wife drove him home because he was unable to use his foot to operate the pedals.

All year, Colorado had rebounded well after losses. But bouncing back is harder against a team with a championship pedigree and a resolute unwillingness to go away. Now the Lightning had their mojo back. The Avalanche, facing a team craving a dynasty, were going back on the road.

THE MEETING

WEARING A DARK BLUE suit with a white pocket square, Gabriel Landeskog drove to carpool buddy Nathan MacKinnon's house the morning after Game 5. The frustration from the night before hadn't faded. Landeskog knew that, if his team had taken care of business, the players would be celebrating at this moment, bathing in adulation from fans around the city.

Instead, the captain was spending a half hour in his car for a drive he didn't want to make, all to get on a plane he didn't want to board.

He and MacKinnon tried to take the right approach as they headed toward the Denver airport. They talked about the 2016 Penguins, who lost Game 5 of the Stanley Cup Final at home against the Sharks, then won the series in San Jose in Game 6. The Blues missed a chance to win the Cup in St. Louis in 2019, they remembered, then won Game 7 in Boston. If those teams could do it, surely the Avalanche could, too.

But, even though Colorado was 8–1 in playoff road games, Landeskog wasn't in a great spot mentally as he walked across the tarmac to the team's 10:00 AM flight. By dredging up those past winners and the challenges they overcame, he and MacKinnon were trying to talk themselves into believing.

Fortunately for the captain, Andrew Cogliano, the most experienced player on the team had an idea. He approached Landeskog and MacKinnon on the plane. The veteran thought the team could use a reset. He suggested a meeting. Nothing formal, but a chance for everyone to share how they were feeling.

"I had a few things I wanted to say," Cogliano said.

Landeskog hadn't called a players-only meeting all year, but he agreed with Cogliano that this felt like the right time. He put a message in the team group text, telling players to be in the meal room at 6:30 PM.

• • •

Tampa's JW Marriott is less than a block from Amalie Arena and a two-minute walk from the water where the Lightning held championship boat parades the previous two years. The 26-story building features spacious bedrooms and a downstairs bar—a perfect spot for Avalanche executives, owners, and players' family members to sip drinks on off nights during the Stanley Cup Final.

In MacKinnon's mind, the building came with good omens, or at least his room assignment ahead of Game 6 did. He was delighted when he learned he'd been given room No. 1787 because Sidney Crosby, his idol and friend, wears No. 87 for Pittsburgh. He immediately told Cogliano, who is also buddies with Crosby. The two laughed.

"We both felt it was fate," MacKinnon said on ESPN the next night. "We both love Sid, and we knew we were going to win when I got that room number."

Perhaps connecting the room number to the fate of the team was a stretch. But as Cogliano said later, hockey players always look for a mental edge in the playoffs. And why wouldn't they? In a game based on the unpredictable bounces of a six-ounce rubber disc, why not cling to anything that helps you believe?

Crosby played a role in a much more direct sense than the room number. As one of the few people who could relate to MacKinnon's situation, he reached out to his friend, knowing he was probably hurting.

"Sometimes you need a reminder that it's a series," Crosby said. "Regardless of what's on the line, you've got to remember it's not easy to win it."

The night the Avalanche arrived in Tampa, their dinner was chicken, salmon, and steak in their meal area, a ballroom on the second floor. Players sat at a half-dozen tables, and some had already finished by 6:30. Those who were still eating stopped as Landeskog, sitting at his table, started the meeting. He opened with a general statement, opening the floor for anyone to speak.

The 5'10" Cogliano rose from his seat and walked to the front of the tables so he could face his teammates. Pavel Francouz didn't quite know what was going on. Cogliano looked like a coach. Then he started to speak.

"It was like a movie," Francouz said.

Cogliano talked about how much difficulty he'd had staying in the present leading up to and during the Avalanche's Game 5 loss. It was understandable, and he guessed other players had felt the same way. The Stanley Cup had been in the building, ready to be hoisted. But preoccupation doesn't help with production, and even if the Avalanche hadn't played terribly that night, they hadn't played well enough to finish off the back-to-back Cup winners. They hadn't played like champions.

The good news, though, was that the team still had two chances to win one game. There was no reason for players to be down on themselves, Cogliano said. It was okay that the Avalanche hadn't played their best in Game 5—they didn't lose because of a lack of care—but they had to learn from it. Players had to push through the temptation to anticipate too much. If they played their style of hockey, they were going to have success.

For the players, hearing that Cogliano felt the same way they did was key. Francouz said, "He was talking for me, too," when the forward mentioned the stress of Game 5. Landeskog noticed heads nodding around the room. Logan O'Connor, one of less experienced forwards on the team, said he had felt guilty about getting ahead of himself during the game the night before. The speech showed him he wasn't alone.

"It was just like so much raw emotion," O'Connor said. "He just had the whole room in awe almost because everything he said, everyone else was thinking."

As he listened to Cogliano's speech, Mikko Rantanen was struck by how long the veteran had been in the league. This was a guy who had played 1,140 regular season games and 115 more in the playoffs. He'd put his body through 15 full seasons and, at 35 years old, this was the closest he'd come to a Stanley Cup. Rantanen wanted to win for himself, but he wanted to win for players like Cogliano, Jack Johnson, and Erik Johnson, too—veterans who had played so long but hadn't won yet.

By the end of his speech, Cogliano, who had been on the team for only three months and was playing through a broken finger, had the Avalanche in awe by the end of his speech. Some players were in tears, Erik Johnson said.

"You never expect your fourth-line left winger to lead and inspire the group the way he did," MacKinnon said.

MacKinnon spoke, too, saying he also struggled with the weight of the moment during Game 5. It felt like a heavy day. Darren Helm, one of the team's oldest players, added his perspective as well. Earlier in the evening, he'd told Landeskog about his experience with the 2008 Red Wings. Detroit suffered an overtime loss at home in Game 5, then won the next game and the championship in Pittsburgh.

If anyone knew the Avalanche could rebound in a Game 6, it was him.

The meeting only took 15 or 20 minutes. Cogliano didn't need much time to captivate the room, to give the players exactly what they needed. The frustration and disappointment Landeskog felt in the morning was gone.

"Can we play now?" the captain said as he walked with team-mates to his room.

The captain felt at ease as he drifted off to sleep. The Avalanche didn't have to win the Stanley Cup the next night. They just had to win one game. That was simple enough.

THE FINALE

THE MORNING OF the game, Cogliano was again front and center, this time in the Amalie Arena press conference room. He and Mikko Rantanen, the same two players who had spoken to reporters ahead of Colorado's Game 4 win, walked in together, and Cogliano switched the NHL nametags so he could sit on Rantanen's left—just as he had the morning of the previous victory. Once again, he was looking for a mental edge, the same way he and Nathan MacKinnon were the night before when they discussed the Sidney Crosby–related room number. If this press conference seating arrangement had worked ahead of a Game 4 win, why change it for Game 6?

By this point in the postseason, both teams were battling injuries. Hockey is a physical sport played at blazing speed, and that's reflected nowhere more clearly than on a playoff injury report. Colorado was down two regular contributors in Samuel Girard (broken sternum) and André Burakovsky (broken foot and broken thumb), and a multitude of others were playing through injuries. Andrew Cogliano and Nazem Kadri had broken fingers, Nico Sturm a torn UCL and Darren Helm an abdominal tear. Darcy Kuemper was coming off his eye injury, and Gabriel Landeskog was less than four months removed from knee surgery. Though Landeskog never said anything publicly about the pain, MacKinnon said his captain's knee was "killing him all freaking playoffs."

Landeskog hadn't gone through morning skates at all during the postseason, instead taking maintenance days to rest his knee. The day of Game 6 was no different, but he had a pair of new Warrior brand gloves he needed to break in. Walking around the dressing room that morning, he noticed Jayson Megna, a reserve forward who hadn't played all postseason, wore the same-sized gloves. The captain approached his journeyman teammate.

"Do you mind wearing my gloves in morning skate?" he asked.

Megna viewed his job as helping out in whatever way needed, so he obliged without hesitation. Throughout the playoffs, Jared Bednar said that, if the Avalanche were going to win, they would need everyone to step up. Megna's chance to step up didn't come in a playoff game, but contributions, big or tiny, come in different forms.

The Lightning had a similarly lengthy list of ailments, including Nikita Kucherov (MCL sprain) and Anthony Cirelli (AC joint sprain and dislocated shoulder), both of whom were playing hurt. Brayden Point was still out after his quad tear.

But the main question hanging over Game 6 was Nichushkin. He limped into Amalie Arena ahead of the game wearing a flip-flop on his swollen foot and a dress shoe on the other. Bednar was worried. The first two pain-killer shots Nichushkin had taken that morning hadn't worked, and he sat in frustration, thinking his season was over. Then he realized the doctor had put the shot in the wrong spot. He pointed out where it hurt the most, and the doctor tried another injection. This time the pain eased.

Nichushkin told his godfather he didn't think he would be able to play if the series reached a Game 7. But he felt good enough to go for Game 6. He was in.

• • •

Bednar walked into the dressing room and stressed a fast start, telling his players that scoring first would force the Lightning out of their defensive structure. Colorado had outplayed them the entire series, Bednar said, reminding his team it still had a series lead.

"We've got to beat them one time," Bednar told his players, holding up his left index finger. "Let's get the fucking job done."

MacKinnon wasn't nearly as nervous in the game's lead-up as he was two nights earlier. The team felt like everyone in Denver expected them to win Game 5. Now, in enemy territory, that pressure was gone. The players could just go out and play hockey.

When the game began, that looseness looked as if it would lead the Avalanche to the start they wanted. Ten seconds into the first period, Rantanen snatched a puck behind the net and fed MacKinnon in the slot. Vasilevskiy used his pads to halt MacKinnon's shot, then snuffed out a rebound attempt with his body. MacKinnon threw his head back in exasperation, but the early opportunity was a positive side.

Looseness didn't preclude mistakes or disagreements with officials, and Colorado's frustration grew moments after MacKinnon's near-goal. Makar shoved Brandon Hagel before a Lightning pass reached him, and the referee blew the play dead. He sent the defenseman to the box for interference. "That's a tough standard," Bednar called to the officials.

The Avalanche's penalty kill came through again, as it did throughout the series. (Colorado killed penalties at an 89.5 percent success rate in the six Stanley Cup Final games.) But this particular penalty zapped the team's momentum and handed it right to Tampa Bay. Less than four minutes into the period, Makar lost track of the puck deep in the Colorado zone, and it bounced to Steven Stamkos off Ondřej Palát's skate. The Lightning captain settled the puck mere feet from Kuemper, then fired it through the sprawling goalie's pads.

MacKinnon skated to the bench, his mouthguard hanging from his lip. The Avalanche had allowed their opponent to score first for the third game in a row. Though the building erupted, Devon Toews said he didn't sense panic on the Avalanche bench. If anything, Stamkos's goal calmed the Avalanche down. They believed they simply had to stick to their style of play and the game would turn, just as it had in the team's nine-previous comeback wins during the postseason.

From the outside, though, the Avalanche looked as if they might be in trouble. They had lost an emotional Game 5, and now they were down to a proven champion that seemed to be getting stronger as the series went on. Tampa Bay, now with the lead, could rely on its smothering defense. And if the Lightning were to hang onto the lead, the Avalanche would have to head back home for a Game 7, more pressure on their shoulders than they'd faced all season.

The Stamkos goal came off a high-danger chance, a shot Kuemper would have a hard time stopping under any circumstances. But in this case, he looked scrambled on the play, leaving his legs wide open. It was a less-than-encouraging sign from a player the Avalanche needed to perform well.

Vasilevskiy, meanwhile, looked like, well, the best goaltender in the world. When Erik Johnson found Kadri with a centering pass in front of the net, the Tampa Bay goalie slid to his right, using his large frame to halt the puck. Two minutes after Kadri's near-goal, Rantanen found Lehkonen with a backdoor pass, but Vasilevskiy repositioned himself quickly, and Lehkonen's tip-in attempt went off the post. It felt like a missed opportunity for the Avalanche, but on the bench Bednar was encouraged, praising Rantanen for getting the puck into a dangerous scoring area close to the net.

Colorado, just as it had throughout the playoffs, continued to push. Early in the second period, Hagel knocked Manson down in Colorado's offensive zone, leading to a penalty call. The Avalanche kept possession immediately after the contact, so play continued. Kuemper raced to the bench, knowing Colorado could bring on an extra attacker since play would stop as soon as the Lightning got the puck. Landeskog—wearing the gloves broken in by Megna that morning—cycled the puck to Byram at the blue line. The young defenseman whipped a pass to MacKinnon low in the offensive zone faceoff circle. The star center wound up as the puck approached.

Back in October, when Colorado was in Tampa for a regular season game, MacKinnon said he wanted to make his one-timer from the faceoff circle more of a threat. It's a shot he worked on frequently after practices, and the extra effort paid dividends here, at the biggest of moments. MacKinnon unloaded on the puck as Byram's pass reached him. The shot flew toward the net and grazed off Vasilevskiy's blocker—the world-class goalie's one area of slight weakness—and in. Tie game.

A furious Stamkos argued with the officials, saying the play should've been blown dead when Nick Paul tried to chase the puck out of the zone in the moments after Hagel's penalty. But the officials called the play correctly, as Paul didn't touch the puck until after the referee's hand went up. The Lightning never officially had possession, so play was allowed to continue.

Amalie Arena, which rocked with noise after Stamkos's early goal, now filled with a nervous buzz. The Lightning, the behemoth of the league the past two seasons, were no longer in control. Four minutes later, Manson nearly beat Vasilevskiy when a three-on-two rush left him alone in front of the net. And the defenseman wasn't done getting involved offensively. After Kuemper stopped Corey Perry with a nifty pad save and the post robbed Byram of a goal, Manson received a stretch pass in the neutral zone from Rantanen and led a three-on-two with Lehkonen and MacKinnon, who slapped the ice with his stick, demanding the puck.

Manson complied, moving the puck to his center as the Avalanche entered the offensive zone. Tampa Bay knew the danger MacKinnon posed, so Ryan McDonagh cut toward him, leaving Manson wide open. MacKinnon tried to backhand the puck to the defenseman, but it instead bounced off McDonagh's skate. The Avalanche center swiped at it, this time nudging it to his left. To Lehkonen.

The Finnish winger brought his wrists through the puck. The quick release fooled Vasilevskiy, and the puck zinged into the far corner of the net. In just over a year, Lehkonen had scored two overtime winners to send his team to the Stanley Cup Final, and now he'd scored the goal that had a chance to stand as the game-winner in a Cup-clinching game.

"He does what he does," Manson said. "Score big goals."

Now Colorado had the lead.

And once again the Lightning were irate. Ahead of the goal, Manson's stick got caught between Pierre Edouard-Bellemare's arm and body. When the defenseman yanked it free, he brought Bellemare to the ice, which Tampa Bay thought warranted a penalty call. Manson saw it differently.

Avs left winger Artturi Lehkonen pumps his fist after scoring against the Lightning in the second period of Game 6 in Tampa, making it 2–1 Colorado. The goal stood up as the game-winner, as the Avalanche went on to win the game and the 2022 Stanley Cup championship.

"That's what happens when you hold onto a guy's stick," he said.

Furious that there wasn't a call against the Avalanche, Patrick Maroon used his stick to whack Manson, his former teammate on the Ducks, after Lehkonen's goal. As the Colorado defenseman raised his arms looking for officials to call a slashing penalty on Maroon, the Lightning forward then skated to referee Gord Dwyer and started screaming in his face. Bellemare and McDonagh also came over to air their grievances.

None of it mattered. The goal was on the scoreboard, the tie broken.

The composure that had helped Tampa Bay to back-to-back championships started to waver. Shortly after Maroon's outburst, McDonagh was called for a boarding penalty on Darren Helm. As in Game 4, the officials appeared hesitant to award power plays, but they had no choice after McDonagh's play.

Colorado couldn't take advantage this time, and after Vasilevskiy denied a Logan O'Connor shot, the teams went to intermission. The Avalanche were 20 minutes away.

• • •

No one needed to tell the Avalanche what they were up against. The Lightning had trailed by a goal in the third period of an elimination game against Toronto earlier in the playoffs, and rebounded to win in overtime. Cooper's bunch had been in this situation. Colorado would need to play a complete period if it hoped to unseat the champs.

Seconds into the third period, MacKinnon, not known as a shot-blocker, slid in front of an Erik Černák attempt. It was a good start.

A minute later, though, the Lightning created what would be one of their best chances of the period. Bowen Byram, who had played exceptionally all series, got too deep in his offensive zone when the Avalanche had the puck, and Tampa Bay's Mikhail Sergachev capitalized when he regained possession. He passed up ice to Corey Perry, and with Byram behind the play, the Lightning had a two-on-one. As Perry carried the puck into his offensive zone, Erik Johnson shifted toward him, and the Lightning forward passed to Kucherov. Arguably Tampa Bay's most dangerous offensive player, Kucherov had a golden opportunity. He smacked the puck toward the net, but it ricocheted off the post.

Colorado had caught a break. Back on the bench, according to Erik Johnson, MacKinnon turned to Byram. The rookie had made a mistake trying to get too involved offensively, and though aggression is good, the third period of a potential clincher is not the time for recklessness.

"You can't fucking do that," MacKinnon said.

The Avalanche didn't make the same mistake twice, proceeding to play some of the best hockey of their season the rest of the way. They took a page from the Lightning's book and smothered their opponent, blocking every shot they could all while creating scoring chances on the other end of the ice. Vasilevskiy had to make a point-blank save on Nichushkin after a Lehkonen feed, and Kadri stole a Hagel pass to get a clean shooting opportunity. His shot flew wide, but he generated another chance shortly after, feeding Nichushkin in the slot. Once again, Vasilevskiy made the save. The Avalanche forechecked hard during that shift, keeping the puck in the offensive zone for more than a minute and wearing the Lightning down.

As a player, Joe Sakic rarely felt nervous when on the ice for big moments. Watching from the general manager's box, where he has no control, is a different beast. But he felt his nerves dissipate as the third period went on. The Avalanche were playing as well as Sakic had ever seen. How could he not feel confident?

Tampa Bay didn't register its first shot of the period until it was more than halfway done, and it came on a McDonagh wrister from more than halfway across the ice—an easy save for Kuemper. They were putting together a textbook defensive effort.

"Everyone knew what was at stake at the end of the line if we played the right way," Erik Johnson said.

Kuemper's second stop was much more difficult. With 6:34 left, Palát slid the puck to an open Kucherov in the Lightning's offensive zone faceoff circle. The star winger blasted a shot toward the net 30 feet away, but Kuemper read it perfectly, sliding over in time to stop the puck. It was a clutch play. In the biggest game of the Colorado season, he was stepping up.

After the stop, Byram patted Kuemper on the head as he skated by. "That's a helluva save!" Landeskog said from the bench. Kuemper's backup, Pavel Francouz, approached the starter later in the night and called the Kucherov stop "the one save you were waiting for the whole game."

Colorado didn't allow another shot until after Cooper pulled Vasilevskiy with 2:10 left on the clock. Kucherov appeared to have a good look 30 seconds later, but Landeskog sprawled across the ice and used his skate to block the attempt. The force of the puck knocked the blade off his skate, and he lost his balance when he stood up. Toews managed to clear the puck, and while the Lightning scrambled to recover it, MacKinnon started dragging Landeskog to the bench.

"Leave me!" the captain yelled as they neared the door. MacKinnon listened and darted back to play defense. Landeskog crawled the rest of the way until he was safely out of play.

Paul put a shot on Kuemper with 1:10 remaining, but Colorado's goalie blocked it with his right pad. It ended up being the last shot-on-goal of the season allowed by the Avalanche. In the final minute, with Tampa Bay's net empty and the Lightning trying everything they could to make something happen, Colorado allowed nothing.

"We went out there and we probably played one of the most perfect clinching third periods in the history of hockey," Byram said.

Exaggeration? Maybe. But maybe not.

Toews killed seven seconds fighting for a puck along the boards, and MacKinnon blocked a Kucherov shot attempt. The Lightning winger got the puck back moments later but caught a bad break, his stick snapping as he tried to shoot. MacKinnon raced for the puck along the boards, then backhanded it toward the Tampa Bay net. His attempt at an empty net rolled wide, but the linesman waved off an icing call at the last second, believing Victor Hedman could have made more effort to get to the puck. The crowd was irate.

Because the linesman waved off icing, Hedman had to spend valuable seconds bringing the puck back up the ice. He passed to Palát in the offensive zone, unknowingly setting up one final Makar special play in a season full of them. The Avalanche defenseman charged at Palát, forcing him out of the zone. The Tampa Bay forward then tried to pass the puck, but he ended up sending it down ice into the corner behind the Lightning net.

Instead of going for a change, Makar instinctively darted after the puck. Only nine seconds remained when he and Stamkos met along the boards. By hustling down and challenging Stamkos for the puck, Makar burned four of those precious seconds, all but clinching an Avalanche win. When Tampa Bay finally gained possession, Alex Killorn tried to connect with Perry on a desperation pass up ice, but Toews made sure it didn't reach his opponent cleanly. With 0.1 seconds left, the puck bounced to Nichushkin, who—broken foot and all—had played 22:50, the most of any Avalanche forward. As he whacked the puck toward Tampa Bay's end of the ice, the final horn sounded.

"Colorado has won the Stanley Cup!" Sean McDonough called on ESPN.

"The dynasty will be denied, and a new legacy begins!" Chris Cuthbert shouted on the Sportsnet broadcast. "They've reached the summit!"

"They will lift Lord Stanley a mile high!" Conor McGahey yelled for the Altitude Sports Radio audience back in Colorado.

Nichushkin raised his arms above his head. Landeskog threw his stick in the air. Rantanen, who had hopped onto the ice early in anticipation of the celebration, led the Avalanche bench toward Kuemper. The goalie, meanwhile, fought through his celebrating teammates to find Francouz. He pulled his backup in for a hug.

Away from everyone were MacKinnon and Erik Johnson, the longest- and third-longest-tenured members of the team, respectively. Those two had gone through the hard times together, from the 48-point 2016–17 season to Matt Duchene's trade request. Now here they were, Stanley Cup champions. They found each other jumping off the bench and fell to the ground in an embrace. For a moment, MacKinnon was worried Johnson hit his head as they landed on the ice. But no, everyone was fine. Great, even.

27

THE CELEBRATION

MACKINNON FOUND Jared Bednar as the coach walked onto the ice. They threw their arms around each other. After all the sacrifices he and his family made as he climbed the coaching ranks, Bednar had reached the highest of highs. So had his top forward, the one Joe Sakic said wanted to win more than anyone.

"Bedsy!" MacKinnon said. "We did it, man! We've come a long way."

But perhaps Andrei Vasilevskiy summed it up best. After the initial hugs and celebration, the Avalanche made their way to center ice for the customary handshake line. When Bednar reached Vasilevskiy, who led the Tampa Bay line, the goaltender looked the Avalanche coach in the eye.

"Your team was too good for me," he said, his mask propped atop his head and his stick still in hand.

Like Vasileskiy, the rest of the Lightning handled defeat with grace. Landeskog considers Victor Hedman, his fellow Swede, to be like a big brother. They'd put their friendship aside during the series and hadn't spoken, but when they reached each other on the ice, the 6′6″ Hedman wrapped his arms around Landeskog, patting him on the head with his right hand. That hug, Landeskog said, will always stick with him.

Steven Stamkos gave kudos to his opposing captain, too, telling him to enjoy the win. "It's the best feeling in the world," he said. Pierre-Eduoard Bellemare, who had been a member of the Avalanche the year before, embraced the former teammates whom he, at least in 2022, was unable to join as champions, and Vasilevskiy hugged

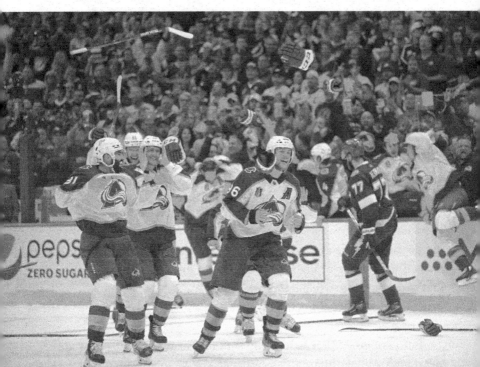

Colorado Avalanche players throw their gloves and sticks in the air in celebration of defeating the two-time-champion Tampa Bay Lightning in six games to win the 2022 Stanley Cup.

fellow Russian Valeri Nichushkin, whom he'd befriended more than 10 years earlier.

When Bednar reached Cooper, the coach who had offered him advice the previous off-season, the two hugged. Cooper had weathered heartbreak to get to the top. Now Bednar had, too. The Colorado coach reiterated to his counterpart that the Lightning, who epitomized a team that battled through hardships, had been the Avalanche's inspiration.

"Sometimes you've got to lose those tough ones to enjoy this right here," Cooper told Bednar before pulling him in for a final hug.

After saluting their home fans, the Lightning trickled off to their locker room, leaving the Avalanche alone on the ice to celebrate. Due to a positive COVID-19 test, NHL commissioner Gary Bettman was unable to lead the trophy presentation, so deputy commissioner Bill Daly filled in. First, he called for Cale Makar, announcing him as the winner of the Conn Smythe Trophy for playoff MVP. Makar skated forward after elated teammates Darcy Kuemper and Erik Johnson shoved him toward Daly. The defenseman accepted the award, smiled for a picture with the deputy commissioner, then skated directly to the bench with the trophy. He handed it to a staffer without even lifting it above his head or looking into the crowd. He had a more important trophy to hoist.

"He just wanted to get a touch on the Stanley Cup," his brother, Taylor, said.

Eighteen Professional Hockey Writers Association members voted on the Conn Smythe, and 18 listed the defenseman as their No. 1 choice. MacKinnon, who tied with Edmonton's Evander Kane for the most goals throughout the playoffs, finished second, with Mikko Rantanen and Vasilevskiy in third and fourth place, respectively.

Makar—whose mom, Laura, ate kale salad ahead of the game for luck—finished the playoffs with 29 points in 20 games. He scored an overtime winner against Nashville, and assisted Artturi Lehkonen's overtime goal against Edmonton to send Colorado to the Cup Final. It was a remarkable run, one that showed the hockey world that his speed and well-rounded game could not only translate to the postseason, but dominate there, too. And now, at age 23, he had already won a Calder Trophy, Norris Trophy, and Conn Smythe Trophy, joining Hall of Famers Brian Leetch and Bobby Orr as the only players to collect all three. And only he, Orr, and Nicklas Lidström had won the Norris and Conn Smythe in the same year. When ESPN's Emily Kaplan asked Landeskog what teams can do to follow the Avalanche's championship blueprint, he simply responded, "Find a Cale Makar somewhere."

If only it were that easy. He is a once-in-a-generation player whose career is just beginning.

Then the lights dimmed. Finally, the Stanley Cup made its way onto the ice, carried by two employees of the Hockey Hall of Fame. Daly called Landeskog forward. The captain—who had told Joe

Sakic during that miserable 2016–17 season that he didn't want to be traded, that he wanted to be part of the team's turnaround—finally touched the cool, shiny metal, his dream realized.

He raised the trophy, all 34.5 pounds of it, and tilted his head back to kiss it. "Let's go!" he called, extending the last syllable, his voice cracking due to laughter or happy sobs. Or maybe both. And, as he'd promised years earlier, Landeskog passed the Cup to Erik Johnson first. The longest-tenured player on the team had rebounded from a concussion the season before to appear in 77 regular season games, and every one in the playoffs.

The Cup handoff was underway. The trophy went from Johnson to Andrew Cogliano to Nathan MacKinnon to Jack Johnson to Nazem Kadri to André Burakovsky to Darcy Kuemper to Mikko Rantanen to Darren Helm to Devon Toews to Valeri Nichushkin to Pavel Francouz to Cale Makar to J.T. Compher to Josh Manson to Artturi Lehkonen to Nico Sturm to Samuel Girard to Logan O'Connor to Nicolas Aubé-Kubel to Ryan Murray to Kurtis MacDermid to Bowen Byram to Alex Newhook to Jacob MacDonald to Jayson Megna to Justus Annunen. The third-string goalie then carried the Cup to Jared Bednar, interrupting the coach's interview with Sportsnet. Bednar, a championship hat already on his head, lifted the trophy skyward. Like the team he coached, he had evolved during the Avalanche's rise. He'd pressed the proper buttons during the playoff run, whether it was scratching then reinserting Burakovsky, sticking with Kuemper as his starting goalie after a tough Game 3 of the Cup Final, or splitting up the team's best forwards to even out an elite top two lines.

"You could have the best coach on a bad team and it's really not going to matter," Erik Johnson said. "But when you have a really good team like we had, coaching gives you that extra push, the intangibles that an average coach wouldn't."

Sakic hoisted the trophy, too, receiving it from assistant coach Nolan Pratt, his teammate when the Avalanche won the Cup in 2001. It was just as heavy as he remembered. MacFarland got the trophy shortly after. Both executives let the excitement wash over them.

Cale Makar lifts the Stanley Cup for a spin around the ice at Amalie Arena in Tampa, Florida. Earlier, Makar received the Conn Smythe Trophy as the playoff MVP—the Colorado defenseman led the team with 29 points.

After the handoff, the Avalanche gathered for a team picture. Aubé-Kubel skated the Stanley Cup to the front of the group. As he neared his teammates, though, his skate blade hit a crack in the ice, causing him to lose his balance. The base of the Cup hit the ground, and the hard, frozen surface left a dent. MacKinnon's mouth fell open for a moment, and he wasn't alone. Assistant equipment manager Brad Lewkow's eyes bugged. Kadri brought his hands to his head.

But the Cup, aside from an indentation that could be fixed, was okay. Players started to laugh, and Aubé-Kubel tried to play it off by lifting his left index finger to make a No. 1. As Sportsnet's Chris Cuthbert said, "He may hear about that for the rest of his career."

Aubé-Kubel, who had been a healthy scratch in the final three games of the series, had now given an already historic team another record: fastest to damage the trophy. It didn't dampen anyone's mood, aside from perhaps the Hall of Fame employees tasked with keeping an eye on the Cup.

Family members soon began rushing through the Zamboni door onto the ice. MacKinnon, his face wet with sweat and tears, pulled his father in for a hug, and then his mother. Kadri—who had just said on Sportsnet that anyone who thought he was a liability in the playoffs could now "kiss my ass"—lifted the trophy with his father, Sam, the man who couldn't afford to play hockey as a Lebanese immigrant but swore his kids would. Toews's parents, Werner and Tammy, found Sakic. They thanked him for taking a chance on their son. Jack Johnson, whose smile perhaps was wider than anyone else's that night, hugged his wife. His three young children weren't in Tampa, but they had already told him they wanted to eat ice cream out of the Cup. Their dad and his teammates had made sure they'd get that chance.

Loved ones who weren't there found a way to be part of the experience, too. Burakovsky video-called his father, Robert, who was back in Denver keeping an eye on André's dog. Byram beamed as he FaceTimed with his older sister, Jamie. Shawn, their father, shouted into the phone that he'd drink Jamie's share of beer.

Sturm found both Cogliano and Helm, his fellow bottom-six forwards. There were days, Sturm said later, during which his body hurt and he felt like he couldn't practice. He looked at the two veteran forwards in those moments and saw how hard they worked. If they could practice, he could too.

"I want to be like you when I'm 34," the 27-year-old told each of them.

At one point, Landeskog, MacKinnon, Erik Johnson, Rantanen, and Compher gathered near center ice. They posed for a photo. They were the last remaining members from the 48-point team of five years earlier. Together, they'd found a way to the top.

"Who would've thought? Five years ago, dead last in the NHL," Johnson said. "Now we're Stanley Cup champions."

In the coming days, the defenseman would hear from a plethora of members in the hockey community. Hall of Famers Paul Kariya and Jarome Iginla, both of whom he played with earlier in his career, would reach out, and so would childhood teammates and friends. Matt Duchene, who requested out and became the centerpiece of Sakic's most masterful trade, would text him, too. Johnson would have a thousand messages when everything was said and done.

But that came later. The hours after Game 6 were for bathing in the immediacy of the glow. He went back to the ice, champagne in his eyes from the locker room celebration, and skated onto the empty ice, reflecting on the journey and the accomplishment.

Around 2:00 AM, after popping bottles and drinking out of the Cup in the locker room, the Avalanche players began to trickle toward the Amalie Arena exit. Lehkonen, the game-winning goal scorer, wore his suit jacket and tie with no shirt. Manson carried a wrestling-like championship belt over his shoulder. Landeskog, already drunk, left with the Cup. He lifted the trophy for the media still in the area to see.

"We're taking it back to Denver!" he yelled.

Nichushkin and MacKinnon were among the final players to leave. A stadium worker pulled the injured, but smiling, Nichushkin onto a flatbed dolly normally used for transporting beer. MacKinnon reminded his teammate to ice his foot, but Nichushkin, clearly a few drinks deep into the night, had other things on his mind. He told MacKinnon that the NHL wasn't going to allow him to take the Stanley Cup to his native country because of Russia's invasion of Ukraine. But the NHL's decision didn't ruin his mood. "Good-bye, Tampa Bay!" he called, making a peace sign with his hand.

MacKinnon followed the winger out. The Avalanche had left the building, off to the JW Marriott ballroom, the site of a private party—the first of many to come.

MacKinnon, who had said in his season-ending press conference the year before that he "hadn't won shit," had played some of the best two-way hockey of his career over the two-month playoff grind, buying into the defensive side of the game. In his eyes, he and his linemates had dominated every assignment Bednar had given them through the postseason.

Now he was a champion. Cogliano—after 15 long seasons, 1,140 games, and one key Stanley Cup Final meeting—was a champion. Nichushkin, broken foot and all, was a champion. Byram, worried that his career was in jeopardy a year earlier, was a champion. Landeskog. Makar. Rantanen. Kadri. Bednar. All of them. Champions at last.

Four days later, the city of Denver and the state of Colorado gathered for a celebratory parade. And with the crowd looking to cheer every time it could, Erik Johnson delivered a speech in front of the City and County Building and led the crowd in a rendition of "All the Small Things." Then he called MacKinnon forward. Still sporting the beard he grew for the playoffs, MacKinnon set his beer on the lectern and greeted the fans. The Stanley Cup sat on a table to his right.

"My ninth year I finally won something, I guess," he said, grinning.

They all had.

EPILOGUE

THREE DAYS AFTER leading the Avalanche through the NHL Draft, Joe Sakic finally took a step back from the day-to-day grind. Not just for a reflective few days or a summer vacation. For good. He was done as general manager, promoted to president of hockey operations after completing the job the Kroenke ownership group brought him in to do.

Sakic's new role would mean fewer phone calls and fewer meetings, more time for family and more time for golf—all while keeping a decision-making role.

The transition confirmed what league insiders had suspected throughout the season. The organization did, in fact, have a succession plan in place that centered around Chris MacFarland. Sakic and owner Josh Kroenke had spoken over the past couple of years about moving MacFarland up from assistant general manager to general manager. Why let someone they trusted so much go elsewhere to get a promotion? The 52-year-old MacFarland, in Sakic's mind, was the perfect general manager candidate. Now he had a chance at his dream job with the team he'd just helped win the Stanley Cup.

But not everyone would stay. Championship rosters are hard to preserve, especially given the league's tight salary cap. Darcy Kuemper signed with Washington. André Burakovsky went to Seattle. Calgary landed Nazem Kadri. That joyful procession through the streets of Denver on June 30 was not only a celebration. For some players, it was also a good-bye.

Summer brought the Stanley Cup tour in which every player and coach had his own day with the trophy. Freshly repaired after its post-win indentation, the Cup started in Sorel-Tracy, Quebec, the hometown of Nicolas Aubé-Kubel, the trophy-denter himself.

He celebrated with a parade through the small town, stopping to bring the Cup into a barber shop and a restaurant owned by his friend. With a crowd watching, he poured a drink—a combination of tomato juice and beer, a local favorite—into the bowl of the Cup and drank for all to see.

Over the coming weeks, the Cup traveled across both North America and Europe. In Finland, Artturi Lehkonen was fêted at a parade with Mikko Rantanen in attendance to lead the chants supporting his teammate. Gabriel Landeskog showed the Cup to his elementary school in Stockholm. Nazem Kadri—believed to be the first Muslim to win the Cup—brought it to his hometown mosque in London, Ontario. Cale Makar and J.T. Compher both used the bowl to eat pancakes. Bowen Byram feasted on French toast from the Cup.

Then there was MacKinnon, who took the Stanley Cup to his family home in Nova Scotia and carried it to the lake out back, where he had spent hours skating in the winter. Landeskog and Andrew Cogliano both made the trip to Halifax for the celebrations, riding in MacKinnon's parade in a horse-drawn carriage. They shared drinks by the harbor that night, the weather perfect for a summer celebration.

By the time the final player, Erik Johnson, had his day with the Cup in early September, preparation for the next season was well underway, with players skating and working out regularly. The Avalanche had long craved a short summer, an easy tradeoff when it meant they'd made it all the way to the Stanley Cup Final in late June. Now fall weather and training camp were close—a new beginning with a goal of reaching old heights—and the time for celebrations was nearing its end.

Perhaps, if the breaks fell in the Avalanche's favor, they could experience it again.

NOTES AND SOURCES

THIS BOOK WAS SOURCED mostly through the hundreds of interviews I conducted while covering the Colorado Avalanche for The Athletic during the 2020–21 and 2021–22 seasons, as well as press conferences I attended while on the beat. This book contains both original reporting, as well as scenes and dialogue I previously wrote about in stories for The Athletic.

In instances in which I detail scenes for which I was not present, I interviewed at least one person who was either present or had direct knowledge of the scene. Reconstructed dialogue comes from at least one person present, someone with direct knowledge of the conversation, or video. If I write that someone "thought," "believed," or "felt," something, I obtained that information from either that person or a person with direct knowledge of their feelings. Secondary sources are cited in the notes.

Most reporting in this book was fully on the record. Sometimes I cite sources on background, meaning I identify them as "a player" or "an executive."

I used data from CapFriendly and Puckpedia for salary cap figures, as well as Hockey-Reference.com and Elite Prospects for statistics and Natural Stat Trick for five-on-five analytics. They were all invaluable resources.

I also relied on other journalists' extensive reporting, including work published in The Athletic, ESPN, NHL.com, the *Denver Post*, Sportsnet, and TSN. This book would not have been possible without the great work done by other journalists, and I'm very thankful to all of them.

What follows are chapter-by-chapter notes on sourcing. I list primary sources interviewed on the record. I listed people to whom I asked direct questions in press conferences under interviews, then also made a note when I used information from questions I did not ask at press conferences.

Introduction
Information in this chapter comes from events I witnessed firsthand, as well as video from the 2001 Stanley Cup parade.

Chapter 1
Information in this chapter comes from events I witnessed firsthand, as well as interviews with Gabriel Landeskog, Pierre LeBrun, Chris MacFarland, and Joe Sakic. I also used information from press conferences and Patrick Roy's public statement after his resignation as Avalanche head coach. Also:

Elliotte Friedman, "32 Thoughts: What's Up with Every Team Heading into the NHL Draft?" *Sportsnet*, July 3, 2022.
Pierre LeBrun, "How Joe Sakic Built a Cup champion: NHL GMs Marvel at Avalanche's Patient, Methodical Rise," *The Athletic*, June 27, 2022.
Tim Wharnsby, "Joe Sakic Thriving in Role as Avalanche Exec," *CBC*, October 17, 2013.
Steve "Dangle" Glynn's Twitter.

Chapter 2
Information in this chapter comes from interviews with Gabriel Landeskog, Milan Hejduk, Greg Zanon, Paul Stastny, Erik Johnson, Blake Comeau, Peter Wallen, Nathan MacKinnon, and Joe Sakic. I also used information from press conferences. Also:

Peter Baugh, "The Evolution of Avalanche Captain Gabriel Landeskog, and What Comes Next," *The Athletic*, July 14, 2021.
Amalie Benjamin, "Avalanche Keep Matt Duchene, Gabriel Landeskog," *NHL.com*, March 1, 2017.
Craig Custance, "How You Doin'?" *ESPN the Magazine*, November 28, 2011.

Chapter 3
Information in this chapter comes from interviews with Ryan Graves, Erik Johnson, Mikko Rantanen, Chris MacFarland, Jack Johnson, Kelly Johnson, and Joe Sakic. I also used information from press conferences. Also:

Peter Baugh, "'Far and Beyond Everything I Imagined': How Jack Johnson Reached 1,000 NHL Games and What His Night Looked Like," *The Athletic*, March 2, 2022.

Peter Baugh, "Ryan Graves Q&A: 'Excited' to Help the Devils Take Next
    Step after Proving Himself with the Avalanche," The Athletic, July 16,
    2021.
Pierre LeBrun, "Which Contender That Upgraded Its Goaltending Last
    Summer Has an Edge Going into the Playoffs?" The Athletic, April 11,
    2022.

Chapter 4

Information in this chapter comes from events I witnessed firsthand, as well as interviews with Jared Bednar, Brendan McNicholas, Devon Toews, Jack Johnson, Nathan MacKinnon, Nazem Kadri, Ashley Kadri, Gary Makar, Devon Toews, Jack Johnson, André Burakovsky, Justin Barron, David Savard, and Joe Sakic. I also used information from press conferences and a public statement released by the NHL Department of Player Safety. Also:

Peter Baugh, "Nazem Kadri's High Hit on Justin Faulk Overshadows
    Nathan MacKinnon's Heroics in Avalanche's Game 2 Win," The
    Athletic, May 20, 2021.
Nazem Kadri, "I Am Who I Am," Players' Tribune, May 4, 2022.
Mark Kiszla, "Avalanche Should Cut Ties ASAP with Cheap-Shot Artist
    Nazem Kadri," Denver Post, May 21, 2021.
Dom Luszczyszyn, "By the Numbers: Grading Every Team's Contract
    Efficiency," The Athletic, July 17, 2019.
Aaron Portzline, "Blind-Sided: Blue Jackets' Jack Johnson Is Bankrupt;
    Who Led Him There Is Biggest Shocker," Columbus Dispatch,
    November 19, 2014.
Josh Yohe, "GMJR Defends Jack Johnson, Wants Him to Finish His
    Career as a Penguin," The Athletic, August 20, 2020.
Colorado Avalanche's Twitter
JFreshHockey's Twitter

Chapter 5

Information in this chapter comes from events I witnessed firsthand, as well as interviews with Jared Bednar, Gabriel Landeskog, Paula Newhook, Peter Aragon, Jayson Megna, Nathan MacKinnon, Nazem Kadri, Mikko Rantanen, Jack Johnson, Logan O'Connor, Chris MacFarland, Graysen Cameron, Marty Richardson, and Joe Sakic. Also:

Peter Baugh, "Avalanche's Jared Bednar and Cale Makar Give Humboldt Broncos Bus Crash Survivor Graysen Cameron a Memorable Day," The Athletic, June 2, 2021.

Avalanche 360, Altitude Sports.

Phil Brand, "Rays' Coach Stays the Course," *Pro Hockey News*, May 28, 2009.

Ryan S. Clark, "How an Entire Family's Love and Sacrifice Helped Jared Bednar Reach His Dream Job," The Athletic, October 16, 2019.

Ryan S. Clark, "Who Is Jared Bednar? Just Ask Those Who Know Him Best," The Athletic, August 30, 2020.

Kaleb Dahlgren, "People of YU," York University, June 28, 2021.

Nick Faris, "Kaleb Dahlgren Lives Big: How a Humboldt Crash Survivor Found Solace," *theScore*, March 16, 2021.

Gare Joyce, "Denial of Death," ESPN.

Ron Knabenbauer, "Bednar Helps Create Humboldt Broncos Memorial Golf Tournament," *NHL.com*, August 17, 2018.

Katie Strang, "Joe Sakic on Humboldt Tragedy: 'It Brings You Back,'" The Athletic, April 7, 2018.

Ken Wiebe, "Jared Bednar's Evolution into One of the Brightest Coaching Minds in Hockey," *Sportsnet*, June 14, 2022.

Chapter 6

Information in this chapter comes from events I witnessed firsthand, as well as interviews with Erik Johnson, Mikko Rantanen, Devon Toews, Rand Pecknold, Sam Anas, Bowen Byram, Joe Sakic, and Jared Bednar. I also used information from press conferences. Also:

Peter Baugh, "Avs Have 'a Perfect Fit' in New Defenseman Devon Toews," The Athletic, February 11, 2021.

Sam Anas's Twitter.

Chapter 7

Information in this chapter comes from events I witnessed firsthand, as well as interviews with Jett Alexander, Gabriel Landeskog, Jared Bednar, Erik Johnson, Rick Tocchet, Darcy Kuemper, Nathan MacKinnon, Jack Johnson, Joe Sakic, Mikko Rantanen, Ville Touru, Patrik Laine, Sebastian Aho, and Artturi Lehkonen. I also used information from press conferences. Also:

Peter Baugh, "'Kind of Surreal': How College Student Jett Alexander Became the Avalanche's Temporary Emergency Backup Goalie," The Athletic, December 2, 2021.

Peter Baugh and Adam Vingan, "'Not Fair to Players': Inside a Frustrating Night as the Avalanche and Predators Play through Their COVID-19 Outbreaks," The Athletic, December 16, 2021.

Chapter 8

Information in this chapter comes from events I witnessed firsthand, as well as interviews with Cale Makar, Gary Makar, Mike Green, Jared Bednar, Nathan MacKinnon, Ryan Papaioannou, Greg Carvel, Adam Herman, Ashley Herman, Dennis Cesana, Oliver Chau, Wade Klippenstein, Mitchell Chaffee, Richard Halgin, John Leonard, Mario Ferraro, Jake Gaudet, John Leonard, Colin Felix, and Marc Del Gaizo. I also used information from press conferences. Also:

Peter Baugh, "Avalanche Defenseman Cale Makar's Skating Has the Hockey World in Awe: The Hips, Edges, Balance... 'Just Perfect,'" The Athletic, February 7, 2022.

Peter Baugh, "Avalanche Forward Logan O'Connor's Family Business Helps Keep Calgarians—and Now His Teammates—in Style," The Athletic, April 3, 2022.

Peter Baugh, "Can the Avalanche's Cale Makar Become the NHL's First 30-Goal Defenseman Since 2009? 'The Sky Is the Limit,'" The Athletic, December 4, 2021.

Peter Baugh, "Diss Tracks, Dorm Life and a 2-Year Plan to Build an Avalanche Star and Rebuild a Sinking Program: Cale Makar at UMass," The Athletic, February 21, 2022.

Peter Baugh, "The Rise of Cale Makar: The AJHL, a Family Chicken Recipe, and a Kid Who 'Looked Like Someone's Little Brother,'" The Athletic, June 21, 2022.

Adam Kimelman, "Makar Made Avalanche Big Lottery Winners before Helping Them to Cup Final," NHL.com, June 11, 2022.

"Leaving a Good First Impression," Medicine Hat Tigers, June 2, 2014.

Cale Makar's school project.

Wade Klippenstein's emails (read over phone).

Chapter 9
Information in this chapter comes from events I witnessed firsthand, as well as interviews with Jared Bednar, Nazem Kadri, Gabriel Landeskog, and Nathan MacKinnon, I also used information from press conferences. Also:

Peter Baugh "Avalanche, Broncos DJ on Playing an Arena in 2021: Just Trying to 'Create a Little Bit of Energy,'" The Athletic, February 26, 2021.

Chapter 10
Information in this chapter comes from events I witnessed firsthand, as well as interviews with Jared Bednar, Chris MacFarland, Jack Johnson, Kelly Johnson, Gabriel Landeskog, Cam Fowler, Josh Manson, Tyson Jost, Nico Sturm, Logan O'Connor, Madeleine McCarty, J.T. Compher, Darcy Kuemper, Leon Draisaitl, Taylor Turnquist, and Joe Sakic. I also used information from press conferences. Also:

"Meet the Avs," *NHL.com*, March 1, 2021.
Michael Russo, "Trade Pickups Help Avalanche Complete Cup Puzzle, Cherish 'Being Part of Something Special,'" The Athletic, June 27, 2022.
Tyson Jost interview on *The Has-Beens* podcast, Episode 36, August 31, 2022.

Chapter 11
Information from this chapter comes from interviews with Joe Sakic, Chris MacFarland, Ismo Lehkonen, Ville Touru, Mikko Rantanen, Nathan MacKinnon, Andrew Cogliano, Jim Nill, Nico Sturm, and Josh Manson. I also used information from press conferences and a statement given to me by Phillip Danault through the Los Angeles Kings. Also:

Peter Baugh, "Artturi Lehkonen and the Avalanche Are a Match Decades in the Making, from a Hahl Jersey to a Rantanen Connection," The Athletic, April 8, 2022.
Pierre LeBrun, "How the Avalanche Finally Landed Artturi Lehkonen from the Canadiens," The Athletic, June 15, 2022.

Bob McKenzie and Jim Lang, *Everyday Hockey Heroes*. New York: Simon and Schuster, 2018.

Curtis Pashelka, "Andrew Cogliano's Value to Sharks Went Beyond Statistics: 'He's Like a Brother to Me,'" *San Jose Mercury News*, March 21, 2022.

Chapter 12

Information from this chapter comes from events I witnessed firsthand, as well as interviews with Jared Bednar, Nathan MacKinnon, Erik Johnson, Bowen Byram, Shawn Byram, Stacy Byram, Wade Klippenstein, Jordan Mackenzie, Marcin Goszczynski, Logan O'Connor, Gabriel Landeskog, Nico Sturm, Devon Toews, and Josh Manson. I also used information from press conferences. Also:

Peter Baugh, "Bowen Byram's Next Step: Avs Top Prospect Eyes NHL after World Juniors Heartbreak," The Athletic, January 12, 2021.

Peter Baugh, "Dizzy, Foggy, and Feeling 'Like I Was a Corpse': Inside Bowen Byram's Harrowing First Year with the Avalanche," The Athletic, November 17, 2021.

Peter Baugh, "How the Avalanche Landed Ben Meyers: An Easy Interview, a Personal Connection, and 'Lofty Goals,'" The Athletic, April 14, 2022.

Ryan S. Clark, "Anything Is Possible at This Point When It Comes to the Avs and Bowen Byram," The Athletic, July 15, 2020.

Corey Pronman, "Pronman's Mock Draft 2.0: How Have Trades Impacted the 2019 NHL Draft?" The Athletic, June 19, 2019.

Video feature: "How Avalanche's Byram's Time Away from Hockey Gave Him a Greater Appreciation for the Game He Loves," Sportsnet, June 24, 2022.

Chapter 13

Information from this chapter comes from events I witnessed firsthand, as well as interviews with Nathan MacKinnon, Sidney Crosby, Jon Greenwood, Jody Koch, Danny Tirone, Willy Raskob, Reid Brown, John LaFontaine, Ian McCoshen, Garrett Cecere, Sean MacTavish, Tom Ward, Tyler Vessel, Marcin Goszczynski, Gabriel Landeskog, Josh Manson, and Joe Sakic. I also used information from press conferences. Also:

Peter Baugh, "Frisbee, Figure Skating and Dancing to 'Electric Feel': The Early Years of Avalanche Star Nathan MacKinnon," The Athletic, April 19, 2021.

Peter Baugh, "'I Need Him': Meet the Behind-the-Scenes Trainer Who Has Helped Nathan MacKinnon Take Off," The Athletic, August 11, 2021.

Peter Baugh, "Inside Nathan MacKinnon's Day with the Stanley Cup: Avalanche Star Celebrates in Halifax," The Athletic, August 22, 2022.

Ryan S. Clark, "Already Elite, Nathan MacKinnon Wants More," The Athletic, March 19, 2019.

Ryan S. Clark, "Guess Who Liked the Nathan MacKinnon Memes about His Nutrition? Nathan MacKinnon," The Athletic, September 17, 2021.

Ryan S. Clark, "Keep It 100? Yeah, Nathan MacKinnon Does That and Then Some," The Athletic, January 30, 2020.

"Halifax Mooseheads Acquire Top Draft Pick MacKinnon from Baie-Comeau," NHL.com, July 13, 2011.

Gare Joyce, "Mooseheads' MacKinnon: Next Big Thing," Sportsnet, December 12, 2011.

Gare Joyce, "Nate the Kid," ESPN the Magazine, February 24, 2010.

Nathan MacKinnon interview on Spittin' Chiclets podcast, August 17, 2019.

Nathan MacKinnon interview on High Button Sports podcast, Episode 299, December 18, 2020.

John Moore, "MacKinnon Drives Drouin to Practice," YouTube, April 15, 2013.

Neate Sager, "Nathan MacKinnon Braced for Baie-Comeau Boobirds: 'I'm Sure Their Fans Are Going to Have Fun with It,'" Yahoo! Sports, April 30, 2013.

Greg Wyshynski, "How Nathan MacKinnon Molded the Colorado Avalanche into Stanley Cup Champions," ESPN.com, June 26, 2022.

ЧЕРКАС АТЛАНТ interview with Nikita Zadorov on YouTube.

Colorado Avalanche's Twitter.

Joel Klettke on Twitter.

Chapter 14

Information from this chapter comes from events I witnessed firsthand, as well as interviews with John Mitchell, Erik Johnson, Pierre LeBrun, Jared Bednar, Blake Comeau, Mikko Rantanen, Nathan MacKinnon, Nico Sturm, Devon Toews, Cale Makar, Gabriel Landeskog, Josh Manson, Gary Makar, Paul Coffey, Jack Johnson, and Joe Sakic. I also used information from press conferences. Also:

Nick Groke, "How the Matt Duchene Trade from the Avalanche Unfolded over Months—and How It All Ended for Colorado," *Denver Post*, November 6, 2017.

Pierre LeBrun, "How Joe Sakic Built a Cup Champion: NHL GMs Marvel at Avalanche's Patient, Methodical Rise," The Athletic, June 27, 2022.

Sportsnet staff, "Nathan MacKinnon on Trading Matt Duchene: 'It Did a Lot' for Avalanche Room," *Sportsnet*, January 22, 2018.

Greg Wyshynski, "Matt Duchene: Not Easy to Ask for Trade but Wanted Playoff Hockey," ESPN.com, November 6, 2017.

Stephen Whyno on Twitter.

Chapter 15

Information from this chapter comes from events I witnessed firsthand, as well as interviews with Nathan MacKinnon, Logan O'Connor, Nico Sturm, Jared Bednar, Gabriel Landeskog, Josh Manson, Devin Gannon, Lana Manson, and Mikko Rantanen. I also used information from press conferences. Also:

Emily Kaplan on ESPN broadcast of Avalanche–Golden Knights (October 26, 2021).

Chapter 16

Information from this chapter comes from events I witnessed firsthand, as well as interviews with Nazem Kadri, Ashley Kadri, Colin Martin, Sam Kadri, Josh Manson, Logan O'Connor, Brendan McNicholas, Jack Johnson and Erik Johnson. I also used information from press conferences, as well as a statement from the Colorado Avalanche. Also:

Peter Baugh, "Nazem Kadri, 'Heavy Baggage' and a League That Doesn't Forget: Can He Turn the Page with a Long Avs Run?" The Athletic, April 27, 2022.

TNT broadcast following Avalanche-Blues Game 3 (May 21, 2022).

Akim Aliu's Twitter.

Tarik El-Bashir's Twitter.

Jazzy Kadri's Instagram.

Nazem Kadri's Instagram.

Chapter 17

Information from this chapter comes from events I witnessed firsthand, as well as interviews with Nathan MacKinnon, Nazem Kadri, Sam Kadri, Gabriel Landeskog, Josh Manson, Valerie Compher, Erik Johnson, Logan O'Connor, Darren Helm, Nicklas Lidström, Ken Holland, Darren McCarty, Kevin Epp, Dylan Larkin, Jared Bednar, J.T. Compher, and Jack Johnson. I also used information from press conferences, as well as a statement from Pavel Datsyuk provided through his agent. Also:

Mitch Albom, *Detroit Free Press*, May 28, 2009.

Elliotte Fridman and Jeff Marek's "32 Thoughts," podcast on *Sportsnet*.

Mark Kiszla, "Avalanche Turns Soft as Butterscotch Pudding with Chance to Hammer St. Louis out of NHL Playoffs," *Denver Post*, May 25, 2022.

Christian Murdoch photo, *Colorado Springs Gazette*.

Tracy Myers, "Avalanche Fan Makes Signs to Support Kadri," *NHL.com*, May 26, 2022.

Sportsnet broadcast during Avalanche-Blues Game 5 (May 25, 2022).

Chapter 18

Information from this chapter comes from events I witnessed firsthand, as well as interviews with Pavel Francouz, Nathan MacKinnon, Jack Johnson, Andrej Šustr, Greg Cronin, Jared Bednar, and Josh Manson. I also used information from press conferences. Also:

Dom Luszczyszyn, "McDavid vs. MacKinnon: Where Does It Land among the Best Forward Matchups Since 2010?" The Athletic, June 2, 2022.

Daniel Nugent-Bowman, "How Dave Manson Is Making the Oilers' Blue Line Better," The Athletic, May 5, 2022.

Quest for the Stanley Cup, ESPN series.

Sportsnet broadcast during Avalanche-Oilers Game 1 (May 31, 2022).

Chapter 19

Information from this chapter comes from events I witnessed firsthand, as well as interviews with Jared Bednar, J.T. Compher, Ian Mack, Nathan MacKinnon, Peter Aragon, Erik Johnson, Ismo Lehkonen, Jack Johnson, and Gary Makar. I also used information from press conferences, as well as a statement I obtained from Nazem Kadri's agent. Also:

TNT broadcast during Avalanche-Oilers series.

Chapter 20

Information from this chapter comes from events I witnessed firsthand, as well as interviews with Jack Johnson, Nathan MacKinnon, Jared Bednar, Mikko Rantanen, and Ismo Lehkonen. I also used information from press conferences. Also:

Ryan Satkowiak, "The Road Less Traveled: Jon Cooper's Rise Up NHL Coaching Ranks," *USA Hockey Magazine.*
Dave Stubbs, "Stanley Cup Evolving Again with Removal of 12 champions," *NHL.com,* September 20, 2018.
Kristen Shilton's Twitter.
Tampa Bay Lightning's Twitter.

Chapter 21

Information from this chapter comes from events I witnessed firsthand, as well as interviews with Mikko Rantanen, Gabriel Landeskog, Tom Wilson, Robert Burakovsky, Connor McDavid, Jeff Jackson, Dane Fox, Alexander Ovechkin, and Jared Bednar. I also used information from press conferences, as well as quotes obtained by Mark Lazerus for the story we worked on together, which is cited below. Also:

Peter Baugh, "Cup Memories, Old Pals, and Avalanche Ambitions: André Burakovsky's Past and Present Collide on Trip to Washington," The Athletic, October 21, 2021.
Peter Baugh and Mark Lazerus, "McDavid, Burakovsky, MacDermid, Burritos, and 'Sting Pong': Untold Tales of the Erie Otters," The Athletic, June 6, 2022.
ErieHighlightReel on YouTube (#AskAnOtter interview and interview on his poster night).
NHLPA Staff, "Player Q&A | André Burakovsky," NHLPA website, November 6, 2018.
Quest for the Stanley Cup, ESPN series.
NHL, *Best of Mic'd Up*, video on YouTube.

Chapter 22
Information from this chapter comes from events I witnessed firsthand, as well as interviews with Mark Gandler, Jim Nill, Jack Johnson, Jared Bednar, Cale Makar, Andrew Cogliano, Nathan MacKinnon, Gabriel Landeskog, and Logan O'Connor. I also used information from press conferences. Also:

ESPN telecast of Avalanche-Lightning Game 2 (June 18, 2022).
NHL, *Best of Mic'd Up*, video on YouTube.
Quest for the Stanley Cup, ESPN series.
Michael Russo, "Avalanche's Valeri Nichushkin Is Having Himself a Playoffs—and Earning Himself a Payday," The Athletic, June 19, 2022.
Michael Russo, "Trade Pickups Help Avalanche Complete Cup Puzzle, Cherish 'Being Part of Something Special,'" The Athletic, June 27, 2022.
Kelsie Snow's Twitter.

Chapter 23
Information from this chapter comes from events I witnessed firsthand, as well as interviews with Sam Kadri, Nazem Kadri, Ashley Kadri, Jason McNeil, Nathan MacKinnon, Nico Sturm, Jack Johnson, Mikko Rantanen, Logan O'Connor, and Peter Aragon. I also used information from press conferences. Also:

Peter Baugh, "Inside Nazem Kadri's Avalanche Return and an OT Cup Final Goal for the Ages: 'Can't Make That Stuff Up,'" The Athletic, June 23, 2022.
Peter Baugh, "Nazem Kadri, 'Heavy Baggage' and a League That Doesn't Forget: Can He Turn the Page with a Long Avs Run?" The Athletic, April 27, 2022.
NHL, *Best of Mic'd Up*, video on YouTube.
Quest for the Stanley Cup, ESPN series.
Michael Russo, "Too Many Men? Stanley Cup Final Gets a Dose of Controversy with Disputed Avalanche OT Goal," The Athletic, June 23, 2022.
Kristen Shilton, "How Nathan MacKinnon Can Pull Out of a Scoring Drought," ESPN.com, June 22, 2022.
Sportsnet telecast, Avalanche-Lightning Game 4 (June 22, 2022).

"Too Many Men on Avs' OT-Winner vs. Bolts?" *Scouting the Refs*, June 23, 2022.

Ken Wiebe, "MacKinnon's Lack of Goals in Final Concerning as Avalanche Let Lightning Back In," *Sportsnet*, June 21.

TSN's Instagram.

Chapter 24

Information from this chapter comes from events I witnessed firsthand, as well as interviews with Logan O'Connor, Nico Sturm, Jack Johnson, Josh Manson, Jared Bednar, Pavel Francouz, Nathan MacKinnon, Devon Toews, and Mark Gandler. I also used information from press conferences. Also:

ESPN broadcast of Avalanche-Lightning Game 5 (June 24, 2022).

Nathan MacKinnon interview on *High Button Sports* podcast, Episode 400, July 24, 2022.

NHL, *Best of Mic'd Up*, video on YouTube.

Quest for the Stanley Cup, ESPN series.

Joe Smith, "How Ondřej Palát's Czech Republic Hometown Celebrates Their 'Hero' in Cup Final," The Athletic, June 25, 2022.

Chapter 25

Information from this chapter comes from interviews with Gabriel Landeskog, Nathan MacKinnon, Sidney Crosby, Andrew Cogliano, Pavel Francouz, Logan O'Connor, Erik Johnson, Jack Johnson, and Mikko Rantanen. Also:

Nathan MacKinnon interview on ESPN after Game 6 of Avalanche-Lightning, June 26, 2022.

Nathan MacKinnon interview on *High Button Sports* podcast, Episode 400, July 24, 2022.

Chapter 26

Information from this chapter comes from events I witnessed firsthand, as well as interviews with Andrew Cogliano, Nathan MacKinnon, Jayson Megna, Mark Gandler, Devon Toews, Josh Manson, Mikko Rantanen, Erik Johnson, Pavel Francouz, Bowen Byram, and Joe Sakic. I also used information from press conferences. Also:

Avalanche-Lightning Game 6 broadcasts from ESPN, Sportsnet, and
   Altitude Sports Radio (June 26, 2022).
NHL, *Best of Mic'd Up*, video on YouTube.
Valeri Nichushkin interview with *Sport Express* in Russia.
Quest for the Stanley Cup, ESPN series.

Chapter 27
Information from this chapter comes from events I witnessed firsthand, as
well as interviews with Gabriel Landeskog, Jared Bednar, Taylor Makar,
Laura Makar, Werner Toews, Tammy Toews, Chris MacFarland, Jack
Johnson, Robert Burakovsky, Nico Sturm, Erik Johnson, and Joe Sakic.
Also:

Chris Cuthbert on Avalanche-Lightning Game 6 broadcast for Sportsnet,
   June 26, 2022.
Nazem Kadri interview on Sportsnet after Game 6 of Avalanche-
   Lightning, June 26, 2022.
Gabriel Landeskog interview on ESPN after Game 6 of Avalanche-
   Lightning, June 26, 2022.
NHL, *Best of Mic'd Up*, video on YouTube.
Quest for the Stanley Cup, ESPN series.

Epilogue
Information in this chapter comes from events I witnessed firsthand, as
well the team's press conference with Joe Sakic and Chris MacFarland.
Also:

Colorado Avalanche's Twitter.
Dave McCarthy, "Kadri Brings Stanley Cup to Mosque in London,
   Ontario," *NHL.com*, August 27, 2022.
Philip Pritchard's Twitter.

ACKNOWLEDGMENTS

I'M INCREDIBLY GRATEFUL to Triumph Books for giving me the chance to do this project, including Noah Amstadter, Josh Williams, Michelle Bruton, and Alex Lubertozzi, my editor. Thank you for all your help. A number of people played a role in helping me get this book to the finish line during a short hockey off-season. Michael Knisley, one of my favorite professors at the University of Missouri, edited every chapter of this book before I turned in the manuscript. My friends Bennett Durando, Aaron Reiss, and Peter Schmidt also helped with editing. Charlie DiSturco, Max Baker, Roshan Fernandez, Joe Bloss, and Emily Leiker helped transcribe new interviews I conducted over the summer. I greatly appreciate all of their work.

Thank you to The Athletic for granting me permission to write this book. Thank you to Dan Uthman for hiring me as a college football writer straight out of college, and thank you to Kate Hairopoulos for being my first editor. Thank you to Grace Raynor, David Ubben, Colton Pouncy, Tori McElhaney, Justin Ferguson, Nicole Auerbach, Chris Vannini, Max Olson, Audrey Snyder, Ari Wasserman, and Lindsay Jones for both making me feel welcome when I joined the company and for convincing me to start watching *The Bachelor*. Thank you to Craig Custance and James Mirtle for taking a chance on me as a hockey writer despite my limited experience covering the NHL, and thank you to Jake Leonard for being the best editor I could have imagined. Ryan S. Clark, who left the Avalanche beat before I joined, was crucial in helping me get adjusted to the job. It was also a joy covering playoff series with Adam Vingan, Jeremy Rutherford, Daniel Nugent-Bowman, Mark Lazerus, Michael Russo, Joe Smith, and Pierre LeBrun during the Avalanche's Stanley Cup run. I appreciate all of them.

Thank you to everyone who took time to do interviews with me for this book, as well as those who helped coordinate those interviews, including Brendan McNicholas and Danielle Bernstein from the Avalanche, as well as various players' agents.

Thank you to all the people I talked to around the rink and who made the job fun, including Aarif Deen, Sasha Kandrach, George Stoia, Conor McGahey, and, of course, the great Peter McNab, who is so generous with his expansive hockey knowledge.

Thank you to everyone who spoke to me as I was trying to figure out how to start this process: Mirin Fader, Seth Wickersham, Joan Niesen, Jesse Dougherty, Zach Berman, and David Black. I also greatly appreciate Emily Kaplan for her support and for taking the time to write the foreword to this book. Thank you to my professors at the University of Missouri who helped me get to this point, including Michael Knisley, Tom Warhover, Jennifer Rowe, Julie Melnyk, Sam Cohen, and Julija Šukys. You all made me better. And thank you to the Clayton High School Globe for giving me my start in writing.

My friends' love and encouragement means the world to me. Thank you to Auggie Mense, Kelsey Hurwitz, Bennett Durando, and Teddy Hans for keeping me grounded, and also thank you to Teddy for answering my countless hockey questions. Thank you to the dear friends I made during college—both from Mizzou and elsewhere—including Tyler Kraft, Connor Lagore, Max Baker, Anne Rogers, Daniel Woodman, Mario Bravante, George Roberson, Anthony Ashley, Taylor Blatchford, Nancy Coleman, Alex Schiffer, Aaron Reiss, Sydney Freveletti, Alessandra Cutolo-Ring, Emily Giambalvo, Jack Pollard, Joon Ahn, all the ballers at the Mizzou Rec, my Grext crew (Kaleigh, Camille, Nick, Andy, Emily, Bennett, Liam, Emmalee, Christina), my baseball group text (Liam, Bennett, Max, Joe, Eli), and countless others. Thank you to Simran Singh for being my childhood best friend. Thank you to Marilyn Gund, Lindsey Anderson, Neil Docherty, Marina Henke, Gwyneth Henke, Brian Gatter, and all my friends from St. Louis. Thank you to Andrew Kowalkowski, Aisha Zamir, Alex Monier, Lauren Indovino, Hannah Hartman, Julie Flynn, Candace Weiss, and all the folks who have made Denver feel like home. I love all of you.

Finally, thank you to my family, especially my mom and dad, Richard and Elizabeth, and sister, Maggie. None of this is possible without your endless love.